Writing Poetry

Barbara Drake

SECOND EDITION

Writing Poetry

Barbara Drake

Linfield College

Harcourt Brace College Publishers

Fort Worth   Philadelphia   San Diego   New York   Orlando   Austin   San Antonio
Toronto   Montreal   London   Sydney   Tokyo

Publisher	Ted Buchholz
Acquisitions Editor	Stephen T. Jordan
Developmental Editor	Karl Yambert
Project Editor	Margaret Allyson
Production Manager	Jane Tyndall Ponceti
Book Designers	Bill Brammer, David A. Day
Permissions Editor	Sheila Shutter

Copyright acknowledgments appear on pages 363–69, which constitute a continuation of this page.

Printed in the United States of America

ISBN 0-15-500154-X

Library of Congress Number 93-77381

8 9 0 1 2   0 1 6   9 8 7

Preface

When *Writing Poetry* was originally published in 1983, I wanted it to be an all-purpose poetry writing textbook, a fount of inspiration and information on the writing process, a solid first step for beginners, and a source of ideas for writers and teachers at all levels. On the other hand, I also wanted the book to be modest—substantial but not self-important or intimidating. I wanted it to behave like a visitor in the classroom, sitting discreetly at the back, responding if called upon but letting the students and their writing receive most of the attention. Since then, students and teachers who have used the book in a variety of situations have told me that the book is, in fact, user friendly. I am delighted when someone talks about picking it up for a minute and putting it down an hour later. They tell me about giving copies as presents for friends who want to write. Some teachers like to go through the chapters in order, making assignments in a fairly uniform way. Others rearrange chapters to suit their own courses and students. Still others use the book as a backup, asking students to familiarize themselves with the contents and allowing them to use the various writing suggestions as they wish.

In revising the book, I have kept all of those readers and writers in mind. With years of experience in writing workshops, both as a student and teacher, I know the problems of seeking a balance between learning the craft by study of models and theory on one hand and focusing on the works-in-progress of student writers on the other. Beginners, in particular, need to absorb a lot of information, to familiarize themselves with published poems and ideas about poetry. They also need support and advice with their own poems. There is almost never enough time to do all one wants to do in the hours of a class. Consequently, I have tried to design a self-teaching book, one that can be used according to the situation in a class, and one that will invite the reader to turn pages whether or not there's going to be a test.

Central to this aim are the poems I've chosen as examples. I am an avid admirer of every poem in the book. These are poems I enjoy and appreciate each time I read them. I believe they are the kind of poems that fill a reader with optimism about the possibilities of creating something wonderful. They fill the mouth with language-pleasure and the mind with insight and experience. Although they are sophisticated poems by sophisticated poets, they are also accessible and engaging. I hope the selections will intrigue and challenge readers and lead them to search out whole books by the authors they particularly enjoy. Additions to this revised edition include works by Sharon Olds, Yusef Komunyakaa, Lorna Dee Cervantes, Wendell Berry, Maxine Kumin, Lucille Clifton, Seamus Heaney, and others. As always, I would like to include even more but there just isn't room. Short of publishing a book ten times this size, I am pleased and satisfied with the range of models.

Another major addition is a new first chapter addressing the question: What is poetry? Introductory poetry students are sometimes troubled by that question and even experienced teachers and writers can be hard pressed to come up with a satisfying answer. Though I can't give a narrow definition, I hope that Chapter 1 will help students feel at home with the traditions, issues, and varieties of poetry. A "poetry quiz" in that chapter is aimed at raising questions and bringing out assumptions about poetry early on in a class or workshop, questions about puzzlers such as why people write poetry in the first place and the proper approach to workshop criticism of rough drafts. I hope this quiz will be a source of both amusement and serious discussion.

I have made some small but important changes in the order of chapters. Information on publishing now appears in an appendix instead of in a chapter, so that all chapters focus on the writing itself. In response to interest in set forms expressed by teachers and students and also to give a timely opportunity to clarify some of the nuances of free verse, the expanded chapter on form and forms appears earlier in the book. I have also updated the summary of interesting developments in modern and contemporary poetry that appears in Chapter 14.

Other new features include study questions and a glossary. Study questions for almost every poem in the book direct attention to techniques and strategies of writing. A glossary of key terms, boldfaced at their first appearance in the various chapters, will help students feel confident in understanding and using the vocabulary of poetry and creative writing.

Finally, although the original book had an abundance of suggestions for writing, I have added some writing exercises to complement new examples and to provide an even broader choice. These exercises are aimed at helping the writer to loosen up and achieve that state in which imagination and language begin the toe-tapping, free-stepping dance that leads to good creative work. They are also inductive lessons in the art and craft of poetry, aimed at getting inside the writing process with interesting results.

Of course the suggestions for writing should never be used in a restrictive way, and any poems you get from them are your own. The whole point of the exercises is to use them to get started, in whatever way they work best for you.

I hope that students and teachers alike will feel at home with *Writing Poetry*. Anyone may rearrange the furniture. I sometimes use the games and exercises of Chapter 13 early on in a course, to help everyone get started. Similarly, at the beginning of a semester I sometimes refer students to the overview of modern poetry in Chapter 14. Nevertheless I've kept these chapters at the end because the techniques and strategies of the earlier chapters seem more central to the writing process.

I have used the materials in this book with very good results, and again, it is my pleasure to share them with you.

I would like to thank the following reviewers of the second edition for their valuable suggestions: Thomas Klein (Bowling Green State University), Jill Waldron (Los Angeles Pierce College), and Mindy Weinreb (Bucknell University).

I would like to express my appreciation to the capable staff at Harcourt Brace and Company: Stephen T. Jordan, acquisitions editor; Karl Yambert, developmental editor; Margaret Allyson, project editor; Bill Brammer and David A. Day, book designers; Jane Ponceti, production manager; and Sheila Shutter, permissions editor.

Barbara Drake

Contents

1

Beginning with Poetry

It shouldn't surprise anyone that the word "poetry" comes from a Greek word meaning a maker or creator and that poetry means something made up or created. Poetry is often said to be inspired, and to be inspired means to be filled with breath. Thus etymology associates poetry with the breath of life itself, the something that comes out of nothing and lives to tell about it.

Of course "something made up" is a rather broad definition. Many things besides poems can be made up or created: lies, advertising slogans, designer dresses. How do we know that the made-up thing we've just committed to paper is a poem? And who says?

Poets themselves have offered creative, if perhaps still elusive, definitions of poetry. The nineteenth-century American poet Emily Dickinson, for example, said that "If I read a book and it makes my whole body so cold no fire can warm me, I know that is poetry. If I feel physically as if the top of my head were taken off, I know that is poetry." The nineteenth-century English poet William Wordsworth called poetry "the spontaneous overflow of powerful feelings" and said that it comes from "emotion re-collected in tranquility." However poetry is described and defined, though, the main things that come up repeatedly are rhythm, language, and emotion, and the relation among them. The beat, the word, and the feeling. These are basic elements we use in writing poetry.

As Emily Dickinson implies, one of the best ways to know poetry is through experience. Following are several poems. They may or may not make you feel as if the top of your head has been taken off, but reading them will help give you experience with various kinds of poetry. As you read through these poems, consider which ones most fit your own idea of poetry. Consider which ones could help you in your own writing and which ones you would most like to have written.

1

In "Not Waving but Drowning," Stevie Smith tells a sad story in a lively, irreverent way. She uses the odd touch of letting the dead man speak briefly for himself. Stevie Smith, an Englishwoman who died in 1971, was known for her offbeat, ironic humor. **Irony** is *figurative speech* involving a double viewpoint. The speaker may say one thing and mean the opposite, as in sarcasm, or contradictory views of reality may co-exist. In this poem, it is ironic that others see a happy, friendly gesture in a man's dying cry for help.

Not Waving but Drowning

Nobody heard him, the dead man,
But still he lay moaning:
I was much further out than you thought
And not waving but drowning.

Poor chap, he always loved larking
And now he's dead
It must have been too cold for him his heart gave way,
They said.

Oh, no no no, it was too cold always
(Still the dead one lay moaning)
I was much too far out all my life
And not waving but drowning.

STEVIE SMITH

---

1.   Does this poem fit your idea of poetry? Is it the language of the poem, its subject, or something else that determines your answer?
2.   In what ways does this sound like a poem?

An English poet of the nineteenth century, Matthew Arnold, sets a very different mood in "Dover Beach." Arnold is said to have begun

"Dover Beach" on his honeymoon. The poem expresses the idea that lovers in a beautiful but sorrow-filled world find solace in one another. The **tone** of the poem is magnificent but somber. Notice the contrast between the largeness of the world and the smallness of the lovers.

Dover Beach

The sea is calm tonight.
The tide is full, the moon lies fair
Upon the straits;—on the French coast the light
Gleams and is gone; the cliffs of England stand,
Glimmering and vast, out in the tranquil bay.
Come to the window, sweet is the night-air!
Only, from the long line of spray
Where the sea meets the moon-blanched land,
Listen! you hear the grating roar
Of pebbles which the waves draw back, and fling,
At their return, up the high strand,
Begin, and cease, and then again begin,
With tremulous cadence slow, and bring
The eternal note of sadness in.

Sophocles long ago
Heard it on the Aegean, and it brought
Into his mind the turbid ebb and flow
Of human misery; we
Find also in the sound a thought,
Hearing it by this distant northern sea.

The Sea of Faith
Was once, too, at the full, and round earth's shore
Lay like the folds of a bright girdle furled.
But now I only hear
Its melancholy, long, withdrawing roar,
Retreating, to the breath
Of the night-wind, down the vast edges drear
And naked shingles of the world.

Ah, love, let us be true
To one another! for the world, which seems
To lie before us like a land of dreams,
So various, so beautiful, so new,
Hath really neither joy, nor love, nor light,
Nor certitude, nor peace, nor help for pain;
And we are here as on a darkling plain
Swept with confused alarms of struggle and flight,
Where ignorant armies clash by night.

MATTHEW ARNOLD

---

1. Does Arnold's language seem like the sort of language you would use in writing a poem? Why or why not?
2. Does "Dover Beach" seem more or less poetic than "Not Waving but Drowning"? Explain.
3. If you were choosing a model for your own poetry, which of the two poems, "Not Waving but Drowning" or "Dover Beach," would most help you get started? Both? Neither? What sort of reading helps inspire you to write poetry?

Contemporary writer Sharon Olds has written an entire book of poems about her father and his death. "His Stillness" tells about the moment when her father learns that his illness cannot be cured and reveals an insight the poet gained about her father and herself from witnessing that moment.

His Stillness

The doctor said to my father, "You asked me
to tell you when nothing more could be done.
That's what I'm telling you now." My father
sat quite still, as he always did,

especially not moving his eyes. I had thought
he would rave if he understood he would die,
wave his arms and cry out. He sat up,
thin, and clean, in his clean gown,
like a holy man. The doctor said,
"There are things we can do which might give you time,
but we cannot cure you." My father said,
"Thank you." And he sat, motionless, alone,
with the dignity of a foreign leader.
I sat beside him. This was my father.
He had known he was mortal. I had feared they would have
to tie him down. I had not remembered
he had always held still and kept silent to bear things,
the liquor a way to keep still. I had not
known him. My father had dignity. At the
end of his life his life began
to wake in me.

SHARON OLDS

1. Is this a poem? How do you know? Would it still be a poem if the words were arranged into ordinary paragraphs instead of being broken into shorter lines?

2. In what ways does "His Stillness" sound like a poem? Does it seem rhythmical? Does it feel like a poem emotionally? Are the words "poetic" in any particular way?

3. What does **dialogue** add to the poem? Compare the dialogue in this poem to that in "Not Waving but Drowning." Does dialogue make a poem seem more or less "poetic"?

All three of these poets—Smith, Arnold, and Olds—write more like one another than any one of them writes like Gertrude Stein, who experimented with language as modern artists experiment with visual imagery. Even today many readers would not know what to make of the following two selections from Stein's *Tender Buttons,* published in 1914:

A Petticoat

A light white, a disgrace, an ink spot, a rosy charm.

GERTRUDE STEIN

A Sound

Elephant beaten with candy and little pops and chews
all bolts and reckless reckless rats, this is this.

GERTRUDE STEIN

---

1. Do these seem like poems? Explain.
2. We said above that definitions of poetry usually involve rhythm, language, and emotion. In what ways are these three elements part of Stein's poetry?
3. Stein was a contemporary and associate of many modern artists including the Cubists, notably Pablo Picasso. If you know what Cubist art looks like, how might you compare it to these works by Stein? Can words be used like paint?

We can often identify poetry on the page even before we read it just because of the way it looks. The following work by Vern Rutsala doesn't necessarily look like a poem. This particular form is called a **prose poem.** As you read through it, consider how this term is appropriate.

Salt and Pepper

Monogamous as wolves they move through their lives
together, rarely separated. To honor their feeling for fidelity we
have developed the habit of asking for them together, knowing
that they keenly feel any separation, however brief. Though salt
is our favorite, a relative really, we never indicate this in order to
spare pepper's volatile but delicate feelings.

VERN RUTSALA

---

1.   In what ways is "Salt and Pepper" like prose? In what ways is it like poetry?
2.   Poetry is sometimes described as saying things that cannot be said in any
     other way. That is, to *paraphrase* a poem, to try to put its meaning in some
     other words, is to destroy it. Does Rutsala's prose poem fit that description?

A **concrete poem** represents in its appearance the thing it is about.
There is only one word in the following, a word repeated numerous times
in a variety of large and small letters. Mary Ellen Solt makes no statement
in the usual sense. Does the poem seem to be saying something, or is it
mainly a picture?

Lilac

MARY ELLEN SOLT

1. How does this representation of a lilac differ from a likeness of the flower drawn without using words or letters?
2. How might "Lilac" be defined as a poem? Would it be difficult or impossible to paraphrase it without destroying the original?
3. One of the terms we have been applying to poetry is **rhythm,** which suggests sound that includes repeated stresses or accents. Could the definition of rhythm be stretched to include the visual repetition of letters and shapes in "Lilac," apart from its sound?

Just from these few examples, we see that poetry encompasses a wide variety of writings, from the formal, nineteenth-century elegance of "Dover Beach" to the linguistic firecrackers of Gertrude Stein, from Vern Rutsala's sardonic **personification** of two common condiments to Sharon Olds's stark testimony to life's hard lessons.

Whenever people get together for a poetry-writing workshop, they are bound to bring with them varying assumptions about poetry. Because these assumptions are largely unspoken, teachers and students can go through class after class operating on very different grounds, believing that their own ideas about poetry are shared by everyone, until something happens to reveal their different views.

The following exercise is aimed at helping bring out some of these assumptions about reading and writing poetry. It's not necessary to write down your answers. Use the questions as the basis for a workshop discussion, and don't be afraid to argue your point. Maybe some of these ideas seem so obvious you'll be surprised if anyone disagrees with you. Maybe you've never thought about some of these questions before, and so you're not sure what you think, but there are no right or wrong answers. Just go with your instincts and see what happens. If you think of some other aspect of poetry that isn't covered, make up your own question and add it to the list.

The Poetry Quiz

Multiple choice—choose all that apply.

1. People write poetry because: a) they want others to love them; b) they want to be rich; c) they want to be famous; d) they're unhappy; e) they feel something that can't be expressed in any other way; f) they love words.

2. You know you have written a poem when: a) reading what you have written brings tears to your eyes; b) what you have written sounds like poems you have read in literature books; c) other people look at you with strange, guarded expressions; d) you would feel a little nervous about showing it to your relatives; e) it's published; f) it feels right.

3. Poetry is about: a) language; b) wanting to live forever; c) the world being a terrible and beautiful place; d) elevated subjects; e) everything.

4. If you want to write poetry you should: a) read a lot of poetry; b) read theories of poetry, including ancient works in dead languages; c) not read any poetry because it might change the way you write; d) fall in love; e) get a really crummy but interesting job in order to have something to write about; f) think about it constantly; g) write every day.

5. Poetry is made of: a) words; b) sounds; c) meanings; d) pauses, breaks, spaces, quiet places, and unsaid things; e) symbols; f) **rhyme** and **meter.**

6. Poetry is like: a) music; b) a cereal box—disposable after you've dealt with the contents; c) a riddle; d) therapy.

7. The best poetry: a) has a moral center and makes us better human beings; b) has no lesson to teach; c) is really strange and hard to figure out but is probably good for us; d) was written by people who are all dead now.

8. Form is to poetry what: a) a harness is to a horse; b) a straitjacket is to a mental patient; c) a flowerpot is to a geranium; d) the law is to society; e) salt is to soup; f) a smorgasbord is to a diner.

9. You can tell it's a poem by looking at it because: a) it's short and leaves a lot of white space on the paper; b) it doesn't use punctuation or capital letters; c) the different sections all have the same number of lines; d) it's long and narrow like a grocery list; e) none of the above.

10. Poets use rhyme and meter: a) to intensify poetry; b) because poets are basically conservative people; c) because rhyme and meter are

beautiful; d) because they don't know any better; e) only if they were born before the invention of **free verse;** f) occasionally.

11. Poetry is: a) elitist, written and read by only a few; b) popular, written and read by everyone sooner or later; c) a form of communication; d) a form of personal expression written mainly for the writer.

12. When you discuss a poem in a writing workshop the point is: a) to tear it to pieces; b) to be careful not to hurt the writer's feelings; c) to figure out the meaning; d) to describe what you see happening in the poem; e) to help the writer improve the poem; f) to get ideas for your own poems.

Talking about the answers to these questions would be a good place to start with the difficult question: What is poetry? The question is difficult because it involves not only matters of form and content but values as well. What makes poetry good? What makes it great? Does writing a poem for love or attention or a good grade serve a higher or lower purpose than writing a poem for self-satisfaction or love of language? Can we identify a poem simply by the way it looks on the page? We could compile a long list of contradictory statements about poetry: poetry says things no one has ever said before *or* poetry keeps saying the same things over and over in different ways; poetry reflects the time and society in which it was written *or* poetry transcends time and place; poetry is a bridge to emotion—it comes from emotion and recreates emotion *or* poetry is an artifact, an object, a thing in itself; poetry is spiritual and uplifting *or* poetry deals with sensory experience and is earthly; you need to read a poem many times and analyze it extensively before you can really appreciate it *or* it doesn't matter if you understand or study a poem—you can still enjoy it.

The list could go on and on. Poetry dates to our prehistoric ancestors and comes with a mixed bag of associations and assumptions. The advantage of this is that you have both a rich tradition to learn from and a great freedom to make of poetry what you will. The only mistake you can make in learning to write poetry is to be lukewarm about it. Passion, curiosity, love of language, willingness to give time and attention, an open mind—these are the elements that will nurture your study of reading and writing poetry.

Exercise

Go to the library, look around, and find out what kinds of poetry people are writing these days. Read new poems published in the past year or two. Spend some time reading current magazines that publish poetry and read collections of poems by contemporary authors. Don't stop looking until you find at least one poem that you truly like and that interests you. Make a copy of it. Be sure to note the author's name and where you found the poem (publication name and date). Then, from your past reading, come up with a poem you like and make a copy of that too. What makes them both poems? What made you choose them?

Bring the poems to your class or workshop and have a group reading. It's not necessary to analyze these poems—just enjoy them. Feel free to comment on things you notice or like about them. Is it the language that appeals to you? Does a poem give you a creepy but interesting feeling? Does it make you long to travel to foreign countries? Does it make you feel better about breaking up with someone you loved? Does it shock you? Notice what you and others look for in poems, what you like and what bores you, what puzzles and what intrigues you, what speaks to the heart and what seems distant and irrelevant. Your choices will tell you something about what you and others expect from poetry, both reading and writing it.

Suggestions for Writing

1. Reading poems you enjoy often has the effect of giving a sort of permission to open the imagination and start words flowing. Keep a notebook handy as you read other people's work and jot down ideas or words or anything that drifts up in your own thoughts that might become the nucleus of a poem.

2. Write a poem about writing poetry, but don't say that's what it's about. Disguise it and make the reader guess.

2

Memory

What is your earliest memory? Is it of a shadowy face looking down at you in your crib? A broken toy? An accident? A noise? Your first day of school? What kind of mental picture do you have of some early memory? When you describe it, what words do you use? However early or late, cloudy or sharp they may be, give your memories close attention—they may be the beginnings of poems.

In the following poem by Diane Wakoski, the speaker says at a crucial point, "It was the first thing I heard." We don't know whether the poem actually depicts the poet's own memories or something she has borrowed or made up, but we do know that this poem deals with memories so painful they have been hidden in images of wind, hot coals, and small, safe details. The dangerous part of the memory, which causes fear and guilt, is mentioned only briefly, but with devastating effect. It is the sound of "my father beating my mother." The speaker says, "There was nothing I could do." Notice the words that make this memory poem feel real.

Wind Secrets

I like the wind
with its puffed cheeks and closed eyes.
Nice wind.
I like its gentle sounds
and fierce bites.
When I was little
I used to sit by the black, potbellied stove and stare
at a spot on the ceiling,
while the wind breathed and blew
outside.

"Nice wind,"
I murmured to myself.

I would ask mother when she kneeled to tie my shoes
what the wind said.

Mother knew.

And the wind whistled and roared outside
while the coals opened their eyes in anger
at me.
I would hear mother crying under the wind.
"Nice wind," I said,
But my heart leapt like a darting fish.
I remember the wind better than any sound.
It was the first thing I heard
with blazing ears,
a sound that didn't murmur and coo,
and the sounds wrapped round my head
and huffed open my eyes.
It was the first thing I heard
besides my father beating my mother.
The sounds slashed at my ears like scissors.
Nice wind.

The wind blows
while the glowing coals from the stove look at me
with angry eyes.
Nice wind.
Nice wind.
Oh, close your eyes.
There was nothing I could do.

DIANE WAKOSKI

1. Does "Wind Secrets" seem to express the **voice** and *point of view* of a child or an adult? Explain.
2. Poets often compare one thing to another for dramatic effect. What are some of the comparisons the child in this poem makes? What do the comparisons tell us about the child's feelings?
3. What are some reasons for writing in the voice of a child?

Perhaps Wakoski's poem reminds you of some strong childhood fear. Were you frightened by the chirruping of tree frogs at night? By the threat of nuclear warfare? By the shadow of a coat hanging on a hook? By an abandoned house you had to pass on the way home from school? You can use the intensity of that memory to bring energy to a poem.

Perhaps your childhood memories are intensely happy. In "Fern Hill," Welsh poet Dylan Thomas recalls a childhood spent in a beautiful rural setting.

Fern Hill

Now as I was young and easy under the apple boughs
About the lilting house and happy as the grass was green,
   The night above the dingle starry,
    Time let me hail and climb
   Golden in the heydays of his eyes,
And honoured among wagons I was prince of the apple towns
And once below a time I lordly had the trees and leaves
   Trail with daisies and barley
  Down the rivers of the windfall light.

And as I was green and carefree, famous among the barns
About the happy yard and singing as the farm was home,
   In the sun that is young once only,
    Time let me play and be
   Golden in the mercy of his means,
And green and golden I was huntsman and herdsman, the calves
Sang to my horn, the foxes on the hills barked clear and cold,

And the sabbath rang slowly
In the pebbles of the holy streams.

All the sun long it was running, it was lovely, the hay
Fields high as the house, the tunes from the chimneys, it was air
     And playing, lovely and watery
          And fire green as grass.
     And nightly under the simple stars
As I rode to sleep the owls were bearing the farm away,
All the moon long I heard, blessed among stables, the night-jars
     Flying with the ricks, and the horses
          Flashing into the dark.

And then to awake, and the farm, like a wanderer white
With the dew, come back, the cock on his shoulder: it was all
     Shining, it was Adam and maiden,
          The sky gathered again
     And the sun grew round that very day.
So it must have been after the birth of the simple light
In the first, spinning place, the spellbound horses walking warm
     Out of the whinnying green stable
          On to the fields of praise.

And honoured among foxes and pheasants by the gay house
Under the new made clouds and happy as the heart was long,
     In the sun born over and over,
          I ran my heedless ways,
     My wishes raced through the house high hay
And nothing I cared, at my sky blue trades, that time allows
In all his tuneful turning so few and such morning songs
     Before the children green and golden
          Follow him out of grace,

Nothing I cared, in the lamb white days, that time would take me
Up to the swallow thronged loft by the shadow of my hand,
     In the moon that is always rising,
          Nor that riding to sleep
     I should hear him fly with the high fields

And wake to the farm forever fled from the childless land.
Oh as I was young and easy in the mercy of his means,
   Time held me green and dying
  Though I sang in my chains like the sea.

DYLAN THOMAS

---

1. Which words and phrases in "Fern Hill" give you the clearest impression of the speaker's childhood? Which do you remember after reading the poem?
2. Wakoski's "Wind Secrets" starts off as a child's playful fantasy and turns into something harsher near the end. Is there any comparable change in "Fern Hill?" What is the feeling at the end of Thomas's poem?

Sometimes a poem can confuse us the first time we read it. Only after we've read the poem and go back for a second reading can we really begin to understand it. Poets definitely expect their readers to pay close attention and to read more than once. Notice how this works in "Where to Begin," Sherod Santos's poem about an early memory he doesn't understand until many years after the event.

Where to Begin

Where to begin? My earliest
Memory is dipped in an acid
Of ammonia and sweat. An
Enamelled box with large,

Weirdly illuminated numerals;
And a sweltering room
Where the curtains billow out-
Side in on a man and woman,

Mid-embrace, who've just
Stopped dancing to stare at me
With a barely concealed
Displeasure. Leaning over,

In a friendly way, the woman
Smiles, and in a voice
Just slightly sweeter than
She is, says, "Now we play

Some hide-and-seek." A damp
Bandanna drawn from around
Her braided hair (its warm
Compress against my eyes)

Is tied in a knot at the back
Of my head. A door clicks
Shut, locks—from the
Caustic fumes I can tell

It's the cleaning closet
I'm in—and a faraway music
Washes over a second sound,
Like a "no" that's muffled repeatedly

Until it replicates a groan.
I don't dare move or say
A word. I don't dare
Trouble the spawn of light

Motes floating in the dark
Behind my lids, each one
A face I search until
The light pours over me

Prayerlike and cool. When I
Come to, the blindfold's
Off, the man is gone, and in
Yet another tone of voice—

Throaty, close-up, edged
With rum—she tells me *he*
Is hiding now, "and he
Can see you, though you can't

See him." The threat works:
From that moment on, I'm aware
Of him, his eyes on me,
Of a presence in the world

(*The world without, the world
Within*) that is sinister and
Unpitying. I'm far too scared
To tell anyone, and it's only

Years later that Mother recalls
The curtained windows (and
The Blaupunkt radio!) of our
Two-room house on the coast

Of Bermuda; and the Lancashire
Maid, discharged early for
Showing up drunk, who looked
After me when I was three.

SHEROD SANTOS

---

1. Did the person speaking understand what was happening when it was happening? Which parts seem clearer, which parts less clear? Does everything come clear at the end?
2. Sensory words, called **images,** help make the writing come alive. Images evoke smell, sight, taste, sound, temperature, touch, and muscle tension. What are some of the sensory words or images that get your attention in "Where to Begin"? What role do these words play in the poem?

In writing about memories, we are not restricted to our own. In the following poem, Maxine Kumin compares her mother's memory of riding horses as a child to her own earliest memory of riding a horse. Both memories are framed by an event involving horses in the present. As an adult, Maxine Kumin still rides and raises horses on her New England farm, so it is natural for her to look back over a lifetime of riding to see where it began.

Notice that Kumin's poem fits into the pattern of "something in the present reminds you of something in the past," a useful strategy for organizing poems and other literary works.

The Confidantes

Dorothy Harbison, *aetat* 91,
stumps into the barn on her cane and my arm,
invites the filly to nuzzle her face,
her neck and shoulders, her snowdrift hair
and would very likely be standing there
still to be nibbled, never enough
for either of them, so sternly lovestruck
except an impatient middleaged daughter
waits to carry her mother off.

In Camden, Maine the liveryman
at the end of town, a floridly grand
entrepreneur, sends for Dorothy
whenever he has a prospect at hand.
She is nine or ten. Given a knee
up she can ride any horse on the place.
If the deal goes through, a 50¢ piece
pops in her pocket, but Dorothy's pride
soars like a dirigible, its ropes untied.

It was all horses then, she says,
combing the filly's mane with her fingers,
soothing and kneading with practiced hands
from throatlatch to sensitive poll to withers.
All horses. Heavenly. You understand.

It's the year of the Crash. I'm almost four.
My father is riding a horse for hire
In the manicured parkland at Valley Green.
When he clops into sight the trees take fire,
the sun claps hands, dust motes are becalmed.

They boost me up to his shifting throne—
Whoa, Ebony!—and I put my palms
flat on the twitching satin skin
that smells like old fruit, and memory begins.

Leaving, Dorothy Harbison
speaks to the foal in a lilting croon:
I'll never wash again, I swear.
I'll keep the smell of you in my hair
and stumps out fiercely young on her cane.

MAXINE KUMIN

---

1. How do you know that "Dorothy Harbison, *aetat* [at the age of] 91" is the speaker's mother? What information do we get about the speaker's own identity and age?
2. How does Kumin use stanzas and indentation to organize the parts of the poem?
3. How does Kumin use Dorothy Harbison's own words to tell her story? What do these quotations add to the poem?
4. What do you think the title means? How would the poem be different if its title were "Horses"?

Like Sherod Santos's and Diane Wakoski's memory poems, Maxine Kumin's poem feels so natural and realistic we are convinced that it is true, whether it is or not. This quality of "likeness to the truth" is called *verisimilitude* and can be an important quality in any form of literature.

Writing from memory, however, is not limited to facts. And even realistic-seeming poems such as these may not be true in the literal sense. The poet may reshape a memory in order to interpret emotion and make a point. The poet may even fantasize and use the form of a memory to give the fantasy verisimilitude.

This next poem, by Philip Levine, appears to originate in childhood memory. The title suggests the warmth of nostalgia, but we realize, almost as soon as the poem begins, that the memories are not exactly realistic in the way they are presented.

Those Were the Days

The sun came up before breakfast,
perfectly round and yellow, and we
dressed in the soft light and shook out
our long blond curls and waited
for Maid to brush them flat and place
the part just where it belonged.
We came down the carpeted stairs
one step at a time, in single file,
gleaming in our sailor suits, two
four-year-olds with unscratched knees
and scrubbed teeth. Breakfast came
on silver dishes with silver covers
and was set in table center, and Mother
handed out the portions of eggs
and bacon, toast, and juice. We could
hear the ocean not far off, and boats
firing up their engines, and the shouts
of couples in white on the tennis courts.
I thought, Yes, this is the beginning
of another summer, and it will go on
until the sun tires of us or the moon
rises in its place on a silvered dawn
and no one wakens. My brother flung
his fork on the polished wooden floor
and cried out "My eggs are cold, cold!"
and turned his plate over. I laughed
out loud, and Mother slapped my face,
and when I cleared my eyes the table
was bare of even a simple white cloth
and the steaming plates had vanished.
My brother said, "It's time," and we
struggled into our galoshes and snapped
them up, slumped into our peacoats,
one year older now and on our way
to the top through the freezing rains

of the end of November, lunch boxes
under our arms, tight fists pocketed,
out the door and down the front stoop,
heads bent low, tacking into the wind.

PHILIP LEVINE

1. How does Levine give the poem a dreamlike feeling? For example, what feeling do you get from the words, "it will go on / until the sun tires of us or the moon / rises in its place on a silvered dawn / and no one wakens?" What could he mean when he says "the steaming plates had vanished"?
2. How would you describe the writer's attitude here? Is he serious, humorous, sarcastic? Does he exaggerate in any way?
3. Is this poem like "Wind Secrets," "Fern Hill," "Where to Begin," or "The Confidantes" in any way?

One of the literary devices used by Levine is **hyperbole,** that is, exaggeration for effect, such as when the seasons seem to change almost instantly. Ironically, the childhood he depicts as privileged, beautiful, and comfortable quickly turns into a life of hard knocks and bad weather.

No doubt one of the reasons we want to write is to share our lives with others. This may sound egotistical, but it is a good reason, involving both what is unique about ourselves and what we have in common with others. Good poetry passes along new perceptions and confirms the validity of old ones. But how do we know which memories are worth writing about? To a certain extent, we must trust our own mental processes to edit and select what is most significant. For example, brief scenes from the past may replay themselves over the years, like film loops, even though the events surrounding those scenes may remain shadowy or completely forgotten. We do not remember everything, but the point is to pay attention to our *own* memories, as Nikki Giovanni does in her poem "Nikki-Rosa."

Nikki-Rosa

childhood remembrances are always a drag
if you're Black
you always remember things like living in Woodlawn
with no inside toilet
and if you become famous or something
they never talk about how happy you were to have your mother
all to yourself and
how good the water felt when you got your bath from one of those
big tubs that folk in chicago barbecue in
and somehow when you talk about home
it never gets across how much you
understood their feelings
as the whole family attended meetings about Hollydale
and even though you remember
your biographers never understand
your father's pain as he sells his stock
and another dream goes
and though you're poor it isn't poverty that
concerns you
and though they fought a lot
it isn't your father's drinking that makes any difference
but only that everybody is together and you
and your sister have happy birthdays and very good christmases
and I really hope no white person ever has cause to write about me
because they never understand Black love is Black wealth and they'll
probably talk about my hard childhood and
never understand that
all the while I was quite happy

NIKKI GIOVANNI

1. Does leaving out the punctuation add to or detract from "Nikki-Rosa"? Does punctuation matter? Is punctuation different for poetry than for prose? (For more discussion of this subject see Chapter 6, Form.)
2. Does the negative-sounding statement at the beginning of the poem get your attention? Does the rest of the poem support that statement? If so, how? If not, then why does Giovanni begin the poem as she does?

We are selective in our memories. We remember what is most useful or interesting, what fits into our scheme for dealing with life, and what gets our attention. Recounting a memory with family members or with friends we sometimes find out that others have different versions of the same events. Besides being selective, memories tend to run in loops, like little movies. Imagine, if we remembered *everything*. In "Funes, the Memorious," a story by the Argentinian writer Jorge Luis Borges, a fall from a horse causes a character to have complete perception and complete memory. A person in this condition would remember every leaf on every tree, the shape of every cloud in the sky, and the face of every person he had ever passed on the street. Borges's fantasy reminds us how selective we really are in what we remember. We do remember a lot. Things that matter to us, things that connect and make meaning, things that rattle our bones and get our attention or blind us with beauty, as well as tiny incidental things seemingly as meaningless as lint in a pocket. Still, consciously at least, we remember only a part of it all. The part we remember, the smell of a great aunt's kitchen, the sound of beach sand squeaking under running feet, or the taste of ice cream eaten with a wooden spoon—that's *our* material. Why? Because we remember it.

Of course what poets want from memory is not only the meaning but the feeling. T. S. Eliot's long poem "The Waste Land" begins with these haunting lines:

> April is the cruellest month, breeding
> Lilacs out of the dead land, mixing
> Memory and desire, stirring
> Dull roots with spring rain.

"Memory and desire," past and future. How powerful the connection between memory and the senses, between the senses and the emotions. The present can disappear in a flood of longing, regret, nostalgia, reminiscence, pain, fondness, and pleasure. There are some memories we relive over and over, as if we were trying to bear them. Some make us so uncomfortable we try not to think of them at all, but the poet must dare to explore both good and bad memories.

In *Remembrance of Things Past,* the French novelist Marcel Proust writes not only about remembered events but about the nature and quality of memory itself. In one famous passage, the narrator dips a piece of cake in tea, and the taste of the tea-soaked cake crumbs looses a flood of memories associated with a particular childhood experience—in a sense recreating the experience itself.

The lesson of Proust, for poets and other writers, is that memory resides in the body and its senses. Which of your senses takes you most readily into memory—taste, smell, sight? Is there a certain odor of food or fabric or gasoline or old books that haunts you like the past itself? Such a sensory memory would be a good starting place for a poem.

Once, after I had conducted a writing workshop that began with the question, "What is your earliest memory?" a psychiatrist in the workshop said that he began his therapy sessions with the same question, since early memory and how a person expresses it are vital clues to the individual's view of himself or herself and the world.

I was not surprised, since poets have always explored the places psychiatrists have been studying in the twentieth century. This does not mean that being a poet and undergoing therapy are the same thing—they clearly are not. But in both cases, small events, fragments out of time, constitute significant parts of the whole. Memories may act as metaphors, messages, or signs. What better place to begin to look for a poem than in memory?

Sometimes it's hard to tell what we actually remember and what we "remember" from photographs or family stories. From a writer's point of view it's all legitimate material. Don't be afraid to lay claim to the collective memories of your family, your tribe. Writing memory poems can be a process of self-definition.

In her poem "Chronicle," Mei-Mei Berssenbrugge tells the story of her birth into a particular family and culture. Explaining how she knows all these things, she says "Grandfather talked to me, taught me" and "my mother tells me."

Chronicle

I was born the year of the loon
in a great commotion. My mother—
who used to pack $500 cash
in the shoulders of her fur gambling coat,
who had always considered herself
the family's "First Son"—
took one look at me
and lit out
on a vacation to Sumatra.
Her brother purchased my baby clothes;

I've seen them, little clown suits
of silk and color.

Each day
my Chinese grandmother bathed me
with elaboration in an iron tub;
amahs waiting in line
with sterilized water and towels
clucked and smiled
and rushed about the tall stone room
in tiny slippers.

After my grandfather
accustomed himself
to this betrayal by First Son,
he would take me in his arms,
walk with me
by the plum trees, cherries, persimmons;
he showed me the stiff robes
of my ancestors and their drafty hall,
the long beards of his learned old friends,
and his crickets.

Grandfather talked to me, taught me.
At two months, my mother tells me,
I could sniff for flowers,
stab my small hand upwards to moon.
Even today I get proud
when I remember
this all took place in Chinese.

MEI-MEI BERSSENBRUGGE

---

1. Why does Berssenbrugge start and end the poem as she does? What makes a
    good beginning and a good ending for a poem?
2. Do you think poets need to explain everything and use common words, or
    is it okay to make the reader work to figure things out? For example, what

are the "*amahs* waiting in line?" Why doesn't Berssenbrugge just use the word "nurse" or "baby's maid" instead of "amah"?

In "Spring Glen Grammar School," Donald Hall uses the image of a box to represent the grade school building itself and perhaps a little model of the building in a glass case, like a "humid" terrarium, along with a model of the town where the school is. The "box" is also memory itself, which contains all the images and experiences associated with the school.

Spring Glen Grammar School

THAT
I remember the moment because I planned, at six in the first grade,
to remember the moment forever. For weeks we memorized
    the alphabet,
reciting it in unison singsong, copying it in block capitals
on paper with wide lines, responding to letters on flash cards—
but we learned no words.
        Then we heard: "Tomorrow we start to read."
Miss Stephanie Ford wrote on the blackboard, in huge letters,
T-H-A-T "That," she said, pointing her wooden stick, "is 'that.'"

POLITICS
Each year began in September with a new room and a
    new teacher:
I started with Stephanie Ford, then Miss Flint, Miss Sudell
whom I loved, Miss Stroker, Miss Fehm, Miss Pikosky . . .
                        At assemblies
I was announcer. I was elected class president in the eighth grade,
not because they liked me—it wasn't a popularity contest—
but because I was polite to grownups, spoke distinctly,
kept my shirt tucked in, and combed my hair: I was presidential.

THE BOX
Eight years of Spring Glen Grammar School. If I should live
to be eighty, this box would contain the tithe of everything.

In the glass case there's a rock garden with tiny snails, mosses,
infinitesimal houses, sidewalks, scissors and crayons, teachers,
and a model of Spring Glen Grammar School.
                                    See, the doors swing
open; see, small pupils gather around a boy in blue knickers.
The box is humid; it continues to continue: nothing escapes.

DONALD HALL

1. Are titles important in poems? What does Donald Hall's title add to his
    poem?
2. Hall divides the poem into three parts with single word subtitles. How would
    the poem have been different if he had simply numbered the three parts, left
    out the divisions entirely, or centered the subtitles? How do you deal with
    titles of poems?
3. What is the importance of the names of the teachers and the name of the
    school in the poem?

These poets make it look easy. Their poems recall (or seem to recall)
childhood events in a spontaneous way. But what if you sit down to write
a poem about your memories and nothing comes? Everyone has had that
frustrating experience at one time or another. Don't worry. Give it time.
Set a specific length of time and just write. Ten minutes, twenty minutes,
an hour—whatever you assign yourself. Don't judge what you're writing
or try to change it at this point. Do whatever it takes to give yourself permission to write.

Think of *free-writing* as a party, an open house of the imagination. You
set the time and the place and send out invitations. You don't know who
will show up. The guests may not even know each other. You just hope
everyone has a good time—and that's why you don't invite the editor.
The editor is that presence that sits in judgment, making snide remarks
about what the guests are wearing and insinuating that you could have
invited a better class of people, when all you really wanted to do was
throw a party and get acquainted. The editor doesn't belong at a free-
write party.

Poet William Stafford has said, if you have writer's block, lower your standards. This is both a daring and a necessary thing to say to writers who have a hard time getting started. Creative writing is a process, not a product. If you work in a shoe factory you know how the shoes are going to turn out, more or less alike. If you begin to write a poem you never know what is going to happen. You start making a tennis shoe and end up with a solar refrigerator. That's poetry.

One thing that can help you write when you finally sit down and find the time and space to do it is to have notes and ideas you've saved when they occur. It's good to have a small notebook to carry around, but writers really do write ideas on napkins in restaurants or any other little scrap that's handy. I've even seen writers jot down ideas on their hands, for lack of scratch paper. I have a small tape recorder that I use to record ideas I get while driving. You'd be surprised at how many possible poems come into your thoughts and then fly out again. The trick is to start recognizing them as good ideas and jot them down.

Besides random notes, journals are also essential writer's memory tools. A journal can be anything you want it to be—an emotional outlet, a memory box, a place to work out thematic connections, an historical record. Here are some possible approaches to journal keeping.

The Factual Journal. Write down things you eat, people you see, car repairs and what they cost, names of books you read, sights that amuse you, trips you make, bits of overheard conversation. This does not mean that you should write down everything that occurs in a day, but do write down a few things that get your attention. Pick one or two factual things to record, no more than would fit into the space of a roomy appointment calendar—an ideal place to record such a journal.

Presumably as an argument for concreteness in poetry, William Carlos Williams says in Book One of his long poem "Paterson," "Say it, no ideas but in things." In the long version of her poem "Poetry," Marianne Moore writes that "the poets among us" must "present for inspection, 'imaginary gardens with real toads in them.'" After a catalog of concrete images representing poetry, Archibald MacLeish, in "Ars Poetica," says, "A poem should not mean / But be." The factual journal deals with toads and other things that "be."

Here is an excerpt from such a journal:

Mar. 18: Went to see H. S. today, haven't seen her for twenty-nine years. Had a flat tire on the way home and changed it myself—first time

I've changed a tire.
> Mar. 19: Called home and visited. B. won a short story contest, picture in the paper.
> Mar. 20: M. left for San Francisco. B. took his roadster to car show. I worked on poem, read some in Margaret Mead's autobiography. Poetry reading tonight.
> Mar. 24: Car lubed and tuned, $76. Sewer crew tore up the road, had to walk in and leave car. Found a deflated helium balloon with note attached, grade school kid's science project. I'll mail him a postcard.
> Mar. 27: Drove to coast. Mt. St. Helens may erupt, but it looked peaceful today.
> Mar. 30: Got back from coast just in time to see Mt. St. Helens erupt, a plume of steam, smoke and ash.

This journal has no poetry yet, but there are possibilities for poems. Looking back at these notes later, one might write about seeing an old family friend after many years, about the experience of driving to the beach in early spring, or about seeing a volcano erupt. Maybe all these things could fit into one poem.

Sometimes it is hard to write about a recent or current experience: either the poetic possibilities escape us or the details are too numerous or emotionally overwhelming. But time has a way of simplifying and isolating the significant configuration, which, along with the help our memory gets from a journal, may make it possible to find a poem in such brief notes. Besides, it is obvious that the daily practice of selecting a few things to write down keeps the mechanism oiled.

The Thematic Journal. This second approach to journal keeping is a little more formal. You'll need a loose-leaf notebook and five to ten dividers, depending on how many subjects you want to explore. Assign to the dividers topics, such as family, dreams, losses, money, or changes. Each day make an entry in one or more of these sections. If you find yourself thinking about something that would fit into one of these sections, write it down; or make a point of writing a brief meditation on one of these topics each day. For your own record, date each entry.

If a topic seems less exciting after a while, or if you find yourself interested in a new topic, change section headings. The point is to use the subjects to comb your thoughts for writing ideas. Anything can be included: experiences, observations, purely imaginary events, comments on the day's news, and so on. The different sections are adaptable to different kinds of explorations. In the dreams section, for example, you might record not only your dreams each night, but also remembered dreams or dreams in the sense of hopes, aspirations, or daydreams. "Family" may consist of character sketches, recalled dialogues among relatives, anecdotes, or more general ideas on the concept of family.

You will not know until after you try it whether this process will help you find subjects for poems, but writing, collecting, and recording help focus the imagination.

The Rough-Draft Journal. This may not be a notebook type journal at all. It may be a box or file folder for scraps of paper on which you jot down bits of first drafts, whether they are lines, words, phrases, or whole poems. To repeat: When you get an idea that sounds like material for a poem—when an interesting word or phrase or description comes into your mind seemingly from nowhere, unless you are swinging by a rope over a pit full of crocodiles—take time to make a note of it. Ideas are slippery. If you don't jot down your ideas, you will find that when you have time to write them out they've vanished.

When you write down ideas, you can, of course, simply say, "Write about the way it felt when lightning struck the house." But if you can, go a step further and write what might actually be a line in a poem: "It threw me out of bed, the sound / I smelled fire. Outside a neighbor screamed." This isn't yet good poetry by any means but it gets you closer to a poem than a simple "write about" statement. If you write a line that actually gets you into the poem, however imperfectly, then, when you have time to work on poems from your notes, you don't have to worry about how to start. Begin free-writing with those words and see what comes.

One way to approach the rough-draft journal is to commit yourself to writing one rough draft a day for a certain length of time. I don't mean just words and phrases. I mean, sit down and write *a complete rough draft for a poem* every single day for a week or a month or however long you are willing to go with it. A *really* rough draft. Scary, isn't it? Since this is an exercise in getting ideas on paper, you shouldn't be concerned with revision at this point. Just make sure you write something that looks and sounds more or less like a poem. After seven days you'll have seven rough drafts and seven choices about what to work on further. Putting off judgment till you have several things to choose from can help you keep going.

You can commit to keeping a rough-draft journal as part of a class or you can make an agreement with a friend that you'll each write at least one rough-draft poem a day for a week or a month or whatever. At the end of the set time, read some entries from your rough-draft journal to one another and talk about ideas for developing the drafts. It's a little daunting, promising to write a poem every day, especially if you're busy and have a hard time writing a poem even once a week, but it can free you up, too.

Imagine: It's ten o'clock at night. You're tired. You need to study for an exam or get up early for work the next day. You'd just as soon fall asleep in front of the television—but you promised you'd write a poem a day for a week. What do you do? At the most, you've got ten minutes to spare. Well, there was that stray dog in the yard. You tried to chase it away but it came back. It looked so pathetic that you decided to feed it, but it growled at you and ran away. Not much there to make a poem? You'd be surprised. The bonus comes when you look at these bits of poems and ideas later and some of them turn out to be better than you thought. Make it really short if you have to, but make it.

The Everything Journal. This is the journal you put together any way you want. Everything goes in it, not just your own writing. You include scraps of paper with ideas for lines and bits of overheard conversations scrawled on them. You include quotations from people you admire. You tape in the message from the fortune cookie you got at dinner the night before and titles of books people tell you they love. You press an occasional flower between the pages and draw small, peculiar pictures of your hands and feet in the margins. When you sit down to write you sometimes find great ideas in this journal. Even if you don't, it keeps you warmed up for writing other things, and that's good.

Suggestions for Writing

1. What is your earliest memory? Write a short paragraph describing it in concrete, sensory language. Deal with specific details, such as sounds, smells, and colors.

   When you have finished describing your earliest memory, write a second paragraph, in which you answer this question: How does your earliest memory fit into the pattern of your life?

   In other words, if your earliest memory is of crossing the street and being scolded for it, is there a parallel in your being a traveler, a rebel, an adventurer? You may feel that there is no pattern to your life. Don't worry; make one up. It could turn out to be true.

When you have completed both of the above exercises, you may find that you have material for a poem, although everything you remember will not necessarily be relevant. Write a poem based on this material.

2.   What was the happiest time in your past? Did you realize at the time how happy you were? If you appreciate this happiness more in retrospect than you did at the time, do you feel regretful, amused, nostalgic?

Do you think you might be making something seem better in memory than it was at the time? Would you go back to that happy time if you could? Considering some of these questions, write a poem about a happy time in your past.

3.   Write a poem about the last time you saw:
     a)   A particular person
     b)   A particular place
     c)   A particular object

4.   Focus on some fragmentary memory. Describe your impressions. Try to recall more than comes easily to mind. Let your imagination embroider the memory. Talk to someone else who was with you and find out how that person's memory coincides with, or differs from, your own. Write about the memory in such a way as to include imagined circumstances or another's point of view. For example, a mother and child may remember an accident or an argument very differently; a husband and wife may remember their first meeting very differently; two friends from high school may remember totally different things either said or did in a particular situation. The discrepancies can be as interesting as the similarities.

5.   Choose at least one of the forms of journal keeping. After a week set aside some time to go back through the journal or collection of notes to look for something that suggests a poem. Make this review at least a weekly habit.

6.   Write a poem in which something in the present reminds you of something in the past.

7.   Write a poem about an experience as it was in the past, but end with some insight that comes from looking back at the experience from any later time in life, whether a week or twenty years later.

8. Write a poem in which you "remember" something that never happened. Use strong sensory images to convince the reader it really happened.

9. Try to remember the names of people you knew in the past, such as children from your first-grade class, your scout troop, your distant relatives. Write a poem using some of these names and telling about the people behind the names.

10. Talk with your parents or someone else who would know about your childhood. Try to find out something you didn't know about yourself and then write about it as if you remembered it.

11. Is there something that happened last week that seems to characterize the week? Write a brief poem about it. Don't try to interpret it—just tell about it and describe it with sensory images: smells, tastes, sounds, sights, textures, temperature, and muscle tension associated with what happened.

3

Catalogs

List making or cataloging can be an organizing principle for the materials of memories and journals. Moreover, the list form itself may give you ideas for poems. Is there anyone who does not make lists? In W. D. Snodgrass's poem, aptly titled "April Inventory," he thinks about the year passing and indirectly asks himself what he has accomplished, what it all means. Here is an excerpt from the poem:

> The tenth time, just a year ago,
> I made myself a little list
> Of all the things I'd ought to know;
> Then told my parents, analyst,
> And everyone who's trusted me
> I'd be substantial, presently.
>
> I haven't read one book about
> A book or memorized one plot.
> Or found a mind I didn't doubt.
> I learned one date. And then forgot.
> And one by one the solid scholars
> Get the degrees, the jobs, the dollars.
>
> And smile above their starchy collars.
> I taught my classes Whitehead's notions;
> One lovely girl, a song of Mahler's,
> Lacking a source-book or promotions,
> I showed one child the colors of
> A luna moth and how to love.

Although this is just part of the longer poem, in these three stanzas it's possible to see Snodgrass's list turning into two contrasting *lists*. His supposed failings such as not reading scholarly criticism ("one book about / a book") and not getting a promotion constitute one list that is balanced by a second, very different list of things he has accomplished. Seeing how the items line up, we come to understand and sympathize with the speaker's feelings about contradictory definitions of success. He doesn't have to interpret for us—his lists do the job.

In subsequent stanzas of Snodgrass's poem, the speaker confronts the question of whether, having failed to complete his "little list," he has indeed made good use of this year of his life. The poem itself has become another list.

Appropriately, Snodgrass refers to the mathematician-philosopher Alfred North Whitehead, who was, as one of my teachers once said, "a poet's scientist." In *Science and the Modern World,* Whitehead begins his second chapter, "Mathematics as an Element in the History of Thought," with the idea that:

> The originality of mathematics consists in the fact that in mathematical science connections between things are exhibited which, apart from the agency of human reason, are extremely unobvious.

These connections have to do with concepts such as quantity and sequence. For instance, what have five fishes, five children, five apples, and five days in common?

Poetry can also draw subtle, unobvious, and previously unseen connections. One way this might happen is through the effects of quantity and sequence, as exhibited by the list. The word "**catalog**" is often used for the list in poetry. Catalogs have appeared in poetry throughout history, as in litanies, which offer a series of invocations, and *epic* literature, which often includes lists of places, supplies, and heroes. A catalog may consist of someone's family tree or of a menu of all the splendid things served at a banquet.

Walt Whitman is the great list-maker in the American poetic tradition. In the following excerpt from "Song of Myself," Whitman gives the impression that he sees everything, everywhere, high and low. He moves quickly from one image to another to give the impression that all these things are happening at once.

> The little one sleeps in its cradle,
> I lift the gauze and look a long time, and silently brush away flies
>   with my hand.

The youngster and the red-faced girl turn aside up the busy hill,
I peeringly view them from the top.

The suicide sprawls on the bloody floor of the bedroom,
I witness the corpse with its dabbled hair, I note where the pistol
    has fallen.

The blab of the pave, tires of carts, sluff of boot-soles, talk of the
    promenaders,
The heavy omnibus, the driver with his interrogating thumb, the
    clank of the shod horses on the granite floor,
The snow-sleighs, clinking, shouted jokes, pelts of snow-balls,
The hurrahs for popular favorites, the fury of rous'd mobs,
The flap of the curtain'd litter, a sick man inside borne to the
    hospital,
The meeting of enemies, the sudden oath, the blows and fall,
The excited crowd, the policeman with his star quickly working his
    passage to the centre of the crowd,
The impassive stones that receive and return so many echoes,
What groans of over-fed or half-starv'd who fall sunstruck or in fits,
What exclamation of women taken suddenly who hurry home and
    give birth to babes,
What living and buried speech is always vibrating here, what howls
    restrain'd by decorum,
Arrests of criminals, slights, adulterous offers made, acceptances,
    rejections with convex lips,
I mind them or the show or resonance of them—I come and
    I depart.

---

1.   Within a poem built by list-making, the poet may construct more than one
    list. What things does Whitman list? What kinds of people? What actions
    does he list?
2.   Describe the overall impression or picture you get from Whitman's lists.
    How does list-making contribute to the idea or subject of his poetry?

    Snodgrass's catalog or "inventory" is in *metered, rhymed verse.* Thus, the
poem seems highly structured, aside from any qualities of list-making. In
Whitman the effect is different. He writes in *free verse,* unrhymed lines of
irregular length without meter, and one of the qualities that gives his poem

structure and unity is that it consists of a list. Otherwise, it is extremely open and flexible, full of variations, changing form to suit content, and moving as freely within the list form as a dancer wearing a loose, voluminous garment. Whitman's extensive catalog continues for many sections and over thirteen hundred lines and optimistically celebrates the democratic state and life in its multiple forms: "Do I contradict myself? / Very well then I contradict myself. / (I am large, I contain multitudes.)" Whitman has had a profound influence on modern and contemporary poetry. If you have not read any of his work, take a break and try his *Leaves of Grass*.

Recalling Whitman, we inevitably think of the long poem, but a catalog or list poem is not necessarily long. The following poem, "Love Poem" by Gary Miranda, is a list whose images interpret the word "angle" variously. Think of Whitehead's words, "Connections between things are exhibited which, apart from the agency of human reason, are extremely unobvious." The connections between the bounce of a ball off a bat, the unintended implications of words, the flight of bats and swallows, the music of eighteenth-century dances, someone picking blueberries, and love are certainly "extremely unobvious" until the poet shows us the connections. To say that the poem is basically a list of examples of ways in which the verb "angle" might be interpreted does not do justice to the feeling of the poem; but it is just such a list. Notice, incidentally, Miranda's unobtrusive, yet effective, use of a formal structure, the division into octave and sestet as in a **Petrarchan sonnet,** and his skillful use of **consonance** and **feminine rhyme** (see Chapter 6).

Love Poem

A kind of slant—the way a ball will glance
off the end of a bat when you swing for the fence
and miss—that is, if you could watch that once
up close and in slow motion; or the chance
meanings, not even remotely intended, that dance
at the edge of words, like sparks. Bats bounce
just so off the edges of the dark at a moment's
notice, as swallows do off sunlight. Slants

like these have something to do with why "angle"
is one of my favorite words, whenever it chances

to be a verb; and with why the music I single
out tonight—eighteenth century dances—
made me think just now of you untangling
blueberries, carefully, from their dense branches.

GARY MIRANDA

1. How does Whitehead's idea of unobvious connections apply to Miranda's poem? What is the connection, for example, between "eighteenth century dances" and baseball?
2. How is sound important in this poem? What kinds of sounds are at the ends of lines, for example, and how do those sounds emphasize the list structure?
3. What is the subject of this poem? How does the list let us know how the speaker feels about his subject?

One of the central concerns of poetry is language, even when that poetry is also about love, death, beauty, time, and other great *themes*. Miranda's poem focuses on the word "angle" to lead him through the associations that express his feelings of love. In the following poem, Lorna Dee Cervantes starts with the word "macho" in the title and makes a list of qualities she associates with that word. Like Miranda, Cervantes addresses an anonymous "you" and in so doing she draws a portrait of someone who embodies the word "macho." What she says finally about the word is not as simple as common usage might indicate. In subject and list structure the poem is comparable to, but very different from, Miranda's "Love Poem."

Macho

Slender, you are, secret as rail
under a stairwell of snow, slim
as my lips in the shallow hips.

I had a man of gristle and flint,
fingered the fine lineament of flexed
talons under his artifice of grit.

Every perfect body houses force
or deception. Every calculated figure
fears the summing up of age.

You're a beautiful mess of thread and silk,
a famous web of work and waiting, an
angular stylus with the patience of lead.

Your potent lure links hunger to flesh
as a frail eagle alights on my chest,
remember: the word for *machismo* is *real*.

LORNA DEE CERVANTES

---

1. What images and other descriptive words does Cervantes use to tell about the person she addresses?
2. Divide the descriptive words from the poem into two contrasting categories, such as "soft" and "hard" or "weak" and "strong." Are the lists in each category about equal or of different length?
3. From the lists of descriptive words, do you know how the speaker in the poem feels about the person she describes? Describe that feeling in your own words.

To go to the opposite extreme in length, Anne Waldman's "Fast Speaking Woman" is a catalog consisting of more than four hundred lines. Waldman's poem is intended for public performance; as the poet reads she chants, varies the tone of her voice, and improvises new lines. The printed version cannot fully convey the quality of such an experience. Nevertheless, one can see how a simple phrase, embellished by imaginative variations, accumulates power and emotional intensity by repetition. In her preface to the poem Anne Waldman acknowledges the inspiration of Mexican Indian religious ceremonies. The following lines, from the beginning, are representative:

Fast Speaking Woman

"I is another"—Rimbaud

because I don't have spit
because I don't have rubbish
because I don't have dust
because I don't have that which is in air
because I am air
let me try you with my magic power:

I'm a shouting woman

I'm a speech woman

I'm an atmosphere woman

I'm an airtight woman

I'm a flesh woman

I'm a flexible woman

I'm a high heeled woman

I'm a high style woman

I'm an automobile woman

I'm a mobile woman

I'm an elastic woman

I'm a necklace woman

I'm a silk scarf woman

I'm a know nothing woman

I'm a know it all woman

I'm a day woman

I'm a doll woman

I'm a sun woman

I'm a late afternoon woman

I'm a clock woman

I'm a wind woman

I'm a white woman

I'M A SILVER LIGHT WOMAN

I'M AN AMBER LIGHT WOMAN

I'M AN EMERALD LIGHT WOMAN

I'm an abalone woman

I'm the abandoned woman

I'm the woman abashed, the gibberish woman

the aborigine woman, the woman absconding

the Nubian Woman

the andeluvian woman

the absent woman

the transparent woman

the absinthe woman

the woman absorbed, the woman under tyranny

the contemporary woman, the mocking woman

the artist dreaming inside her house

I'm the gadget woman

I'm the druid woman

I'm the Ibo woman

I'm the Yoruba woman

I'm the vibrato woman

I'm the rippling woman

I'm the gutted woman

I'm the woman with wounds

I'm the woman with shins

I'm the bruised woman

I'm the eroding woman

I'm the suspended woman

I'm the woman alluring

I'm the architect woman

I'm the trout woman

I'm the tungsten woman

I'm the woman with the keys

I'm the woman with the glue

I'm a fast speaking woman

ANNE WALDMAN

---

1. Would you describe this poem as repetitive or varied? Can it be both?
2. Do the images in the poem grow out of one another by some form of asso-
    ciation or does each one seem entirely new? In other words, are there con-
    nections between the images or does Waldman simply jump around? Explain.

Diane Wakoski, whose "Wind Secrets" appears in Chapter 2, has
written "Ode to a Lebanese Crock of Olives," which incorporates the
listing of delectable food into a statement about the speaker. In the tradition of Whitman, Wakoski makes splendid use of the catalog, piling on
image after image in imitation of the abundance she praises.

Note that this poem is more than one catalog. Besides the list of foods
there are lists of birds, flowers, and images of the California coast. The
speaker's comments and asides explain the meaning of these lists for her and
tie them together in a statement of pleasure in, and acceptance of, her life.

Ode to a Lebanese Crock of Olives

for Walter's Aunt Libby's
diligence in making olives

As some women love jewels
and drape themselves with ropes of pearls, stud their ears
with diamonds, band themselves with heavy gold,

have emeralds on their fingers or
opals on white bosoms,
I live with the still life
of grapes whose skins frost over with the sugar forming inside,
hard apples, and delicate pears;
cheeses,
from the sharp fontina, to icy bleu,
the aromatic chevres, boursault, boursin, a litany of
thick bread, dark wines,
pasta with garlic,
soups full of potato and onion;
and butter and cream,
like the skins of beautiful women, are on my sideboard.

These words are to say thank you
to
Walter's Aunt Libby
for her wonderful olives;
oily green knobs in lemon
that I add to the feast when they get here from Lebanon
(where men are fighting, as her sisters have been fighting
for years, over whose house the company stays in)
and whose recipes for kibbee or dolmas or houmas
are passed along.

I often wonder,
had I been born beautiful,
a Venus on the California seashore,
if I'd have learned to eat and drink so well?
For, with humming birds outside my kitchen window to remind of
    small elegance,
and mourning doves in the pines & cedar, speaking with grace,
and the beautiful bodies
of lean blond surfers,
dancing on terraces,
surely had I a beautiful face or elegant body,
surely I would not have found such pleasure
in food?

I often wonder why a poem to me
is so much more like a piece of bread and butter
than like a sapphire?
But with mockers flying in and out of orange groves,
and brown pelicans dipping into the Pacific,
looking at camelias and fuchsia,
an abundance of rose, and the brilliant purple ice plant
which lined the cliffs to the beach,
life was a "Still Life" for me.
And a feast.
I wish I'd known then
the paintings of Rubens or David,
where beauty was not only
thin, tan, California girls,
but included all abundance.

As some women love jewels,
I love the jewels of life.
And were you,
the man I love,
to cover me (naked) with diamonds,
I would accept them too.

Beauty is everywhere,
in contrasts and unities.
But to you, I could not offer the thin tan fashionable body
of a California beach girl.
Instead, I could give the richness of burgundy,
dark brown gravies,
gleaming onions,
the gold of lemons,
and some of Walter's Aunt Libby's wonderful olives from Lebanon.

Thank you, Aunt Libby,
from a failed beach girl,
out of the West.

DIANE WAKOSKI

1. In the middle of her poem, Wakoski says that a poem is "like a piece of bread and butter" to her. In what way is this poem an example of this? Is it like a meal? Does it give sensory pleasure? Does it satisfy?
2. One type of poetry moves toward understatement, the less-is-more approach. List poems, including this one, tend to be longer and more varied in content. If the list were a little longer or a little shorter, would it make a difference? How does the poet know when a list poem is long enough?

C. K. Williams's "The Modern" also focuses on food, but you may infer that he is talking about more than a tomato. In this list poem, Williams uses long lines in a relatively short poem to focus on a mundane but intense experience and all it suggests.

The Modern

Its skin tough and unpliable as scar, the pulp out of focus, weak,
    granular, powdery blank,
this tomato I'm eating—wolfing, stuffing down: I'm so hungry—is
    horrible and delicious.
Don't tell me, I know all about it, this travesty-sham; I know it
    was plucked green and unripe
then was locked in a chamber and gassed so it wouldn't rot till I
    bought it but I don't care:
I was so famished before, I was sucking sweat from my arm and
    now my tomato is glowing inside me.
I muscle the juice through my teeth and the seeds to the roof of
    my mouth and the hard,
scaly scab of where fruit met innocent stem and was torn free I
    hold on my tongue and savor,
a coin, a dot, the end of a sentence, the end of the long improbable
    utterance of the holy and human.

                                            C. K. WILLIAMS

1. What are the important words and images on this list? Are they all somehow alike or could they be sorted into more than one group?
2. What is the main feeling you get from these words and images?
3. Poets learn to push language to the extreme without losing control or seeming merely grotesque. For example, Williams's tomato skin is not just tough, but "tough and unpliable as scar." How does the list structure contribute to pushing the language and achieving intensity?
4. How would the poem be changed if it were titled "The Tomato"?

You will find lists appearing in other poems in various chapters. It is important to see how the list or catalog can be used to develop, organize, and intensify, without seeming merely wooden and mechanical. With some poems, the rhythms, textures, and colors of words and images invite us to string them together like lights on a Christmas tree. Other times, the process of making a list will suggest a meaning or theme you want to develop, but the list structure itself will become less important.

If meaning comes easily, you are in luck. If not, look for hidden patterns—maybe your list can be edited or forced to give forth meaning.

For example, let us enumerate things of a certain color, such as white:

snow	hospital room
sugar	death sheet
dunes	egg shell
pillow	plaster cast
lady's powder	porcelain
sweet cream	refrigerator
apple meat	ice
egg white	milk shake
sifted flour	chalk
white bread	bridal veil
whipped cream	bandage
vanilla meringue	tissue
beer foam	California stucco
wedding cake	seashell
custard pudding	teeth
white fur underbelly	tendons
white hair	eyeball
surgical gown	maggot

There are a number of food images here, but somehow they lack excitement by themselves. More lively, perhaps, is the connection to snow; the food images might be used to describe the snow rather than to refer to actual food. Thinking of snow as "apple meat" sounds appealing, although the unseasonal context may be too illogical. Perhaps it would be better to pick up the bridal-veil image and attach that to the snow, especially if this list is evolving in the aftermath of a blizzard, with driveways snowed shut and lines down—one might think of a bride married to winter, locked away by a cold groom. What about the alliteration in *bridal* and *bandage?* Could the bride be wearing surgical gauze—a kind of mummy, dressed in her white veil like a death sheet? Or do we want to forget weddings and get back to winter as a chilly feast, drifts of milk shake, vanilla meringue, wedding cake? The maggot definitely does not connect with winter at this point, nor do California stucco and seashells, so let us cross them out. Could winter have a white fur underbelly to be scratched, like a big cat? Maybe we should concentrate on **associations**—white teeth, white fur, white milk in a white saucer—that could also connect with a blizzard. But that would sound too much like Sandburg's "Fog." And so the process goes on.

In some cases, a list can be a poem in itself, but usually it will need a fuller context, as in the earlier examples of this chapter. A list can be unified in a simple or complicated way, depending on what is intended. If we want to use the "white" list to talk about a certain rich feeling after a blizzard, and if we call it "Feast of Snow," we might proceed like this:

> Now is the sweet cream of winter.
> Now is the apple meat of winter,
> the egg white,
> sifted flour,
> white bread of winter;
> this is the whipped cream,
> vanilla meringue,
> beer foam of winter.
> This is the wedding cake,
> the custard pudding weather.

It is still not a poem, but it is closer to one than was the original list because of a continuity in the grouping of images; also, line breaks, syntax, and repeated sounds help create a music. The material could be developed more along this line, or different choices could be made, but still the inspiration would come from the original catalog of images.

A list from which one might make a poem can be purely associative and loosely defined, like this "white" list, or it can be more definite in its aims. For example: make a list of objects on your desk that show what kind of person you are. You could turn a list into a narrative poem, a story woven around images of red objects or the names of exotic places. You could subtly incorporate a list into a lyric poem, so that one would hardly recognize it as such, but so that it was an accent, like the periodic glittering of metallic thread woven into a piece of earth-colored fabric. Create parallel or opposing lists: what we loved and what we hated, sounds of night and sounds of day, then and now. Look for the connections between things.

Suggestions for Writing

1. Write a poem based on one of the following ideas for lists.
    a) *Future lists.* List strange, exotic things you want to do; things you want to accomplish in life; things you want to do tomorrow; things you would like to do with, or to, someone or something; things you expect your future to bring.
    b) *Past lists.* List your earliest memories, more than just one this time; things you regret doing or not having done; your most memorable meals; the food and all the surrounding details of one memorable meal; all the houses or apartments or towns where you have lived; friends with whom you have lost contact; all the names you can remember from your first-grade class; all the pets you have ever owned; strange sights you have seen.
    c) *Object lists.* List things in your favorite room; things in a room you dislike; things on your desk, in your pockets, in your purse; things in someone's attic, storage room, or closet; things you have seen in a pawnshop window or in some other sort of business—a flower shop, a bookstore, an all-night truck stop, or foreign restaurant; list all the objects you can remember having lost in your lifetime.
    d) *Dream lists.* List recurring dreams or fantasies.
    e) *Favorites lists.* Make lists of heroes, favorite foods, favorite clothes, favorite possessions, friends, most enjoyable places you have ever been.

f) *Dislikes lists.* Make lists of foods you dislike, bad habits (your own or other people's), most boring days or events in your life, chores you dislike to do, times in history you are glad you do not live in.

g) *Random lists.* Make a list by some arbitrary method: close your eyes and put your finger down at various points in the index of a mail order catalog; open a dictionary several times and write down the word that appears in the upper right-hand corner of the right-hand page; or twirl the radio or television dial and make a list of the first words you hear at each change.

h) *Word lists.* Collect words that appeal to you for some reason. Collect them from overheard conversations, by browsing through the dictionary, or by going to some sort of specialized publication. Think about familiar words that seem particularly beautiful or interesting to you.

i) *Sensory lists.* Give yourself five or ten minutes to make a list of things all of one color; or define a list in some other sensory way—white, cold things; red, shiny things; yellow, fragrant things; noisy, tasty things; dry, crumbly things. Or simply make a list of things with an intense appeal to one of the senses, various pungent-smelling things, for example.

2. Select five or six of the most intriguing items from one of these lists. Try to choose items that do not seem related in any other way than by the topic of the list. Work them into a poem that shows some surprising connection.

3. Work into a poem as many items as possible from one of your lists. Let the items determine what the poem is about.

4. Turn a list into a chant by the use of some basic statement or construction, such as "I want," "I remember," "The color was red, like. . . ." Read your completed chant aloud to someone.

5. Incorporate a list into a narrative poem. Make the list first, then create the narrative.

6. Write a two-part poem, using two opposed or contrasting lists to make a point.

7.   Choose some object, a piece of food such as Williams's tomato, for example, and make a list of everything you notice about it. Push your descriptions and observations to the extreme. Whether your feelings about the object are intense or not, make the descriptions intense. Use far-out *similes* and extreme *metaphors* in your list. Give the impression that your list is going wild.

8.   Choose some word that interests you. Write a poem in which you assemble into a list the associations the word suggests to you. It can be a very simple word such as home, feet, or danger. (Imagine writing this poem as taking a long, roundabout way to get somewhere.)

4

Observation

You must become an ignorant man again
And see the sun again with an ignorant eye
And see it clearly in the idea of it.

In these lines from "Notes Toward a Supreme Fiction," Wallace Stevens suggests that learning about things can actually get in the way of seeing them. Surely, by learning about a thing—the parts of a plant or the history of a place—we are better able to perceive that thing. And lack of education or experience may hamper our ability to express what we perceive. But maybe that is not Stevens's point. Perhaps he means that we originally see things for ourselves before our originality becomes obscured by repetition and other people's ideas. In writing poetry we must work to get that originality back. We must somehow manage both the kind of innocence or openness that lets us see for ourselves and the kind of sophistication that allows us to judge and perfect our own work—imaginative openness on the one hand; vigilant self-criticism on the other. This chapter deals primarily with the former.

Make some notes on what you see out of the window. Name at least three things. Make a simple descriptive statement about each one, and arrange the statements in the form of lines of poetry. You could arrive at something like this:

The rotten apples look like rust in the snow
where rabbits have been digging to eat them.
The bare willow tree is starting to turn yellow,
then green.
Snow is melting.
The red plastic sled
is leaning against the fence.

This is not much like a poem, but at least it contains some images, a suggested subject (change of seasons), and a minimal landscape.

See what William Carlos Williams has done with a minimal landscape in the following:

The Red Wheelbarrow

so much depends
upon

a red wheel
barrow

glazed with rain
water

beside the white
chickens.

WILLIAM CARLOS WILLIAMS

---

1. When you first read the poem, which words stay in your memory most clearly? How are these words important to the poem?
2. In another poem, Williams stated that there are "no ideas but in things." How does that apply to this poem?

"The Red Wheelbarrow" is no doubt one of the two most quoted **imagist** poems in the English language. The other is by Ezra Pound.

In a Station of the Metro

The apparition of these faces in the crowd;
Petals on a wet, black bough.

EZRA POUND

1. What different things are compared in this poem? Which sense or senses are involved in the comparison?
2. How would you express what Pound says here in different words? Is anything lost by changing the words?
3. Does the poet seem to feel any emotion in this poem? Do the words give you any particular feeling or emotion?

Williams, Pound, and others promoted the idea that poetry should present direct images with primal clarity, that the thing itself is the essence of poetry. Therefore we do not say that the red wheelbarrow stands for hope, or life, or work, or blood, or the industrial revolution. We do not say that the white chickens are purity, or life, or nature, or the agrarian way of life. The wheelbarrow stands before us, "red" and "glazed with rain," in concrete juxtaposition with the "white / chickens." What we see, it seems, is what we get. "No ideas but in things."

Whenever we talk about poetry we cannot escape talking about images, words which stimulate the senses. An image word makes us see, smell, taste, touch, hear, or respond with muscle tension, kinesthetically. Verbal images allow us to simulate the experience. Instead of just talking generally about a good meal—"The salad was mighty tasty"—we try to recreate the experience in words: "It was Boston lettuce, very tender, delicate green, with feta cheese, a sprinkling of oregano and freshly ground pepper, olive oil, red-wine vinegar, and three wedges of firm, vine-ripened tomato." If our images are clear and evocative, we do not have to say "mighty tasty"; the reader knows.

There is something cleanly satisfying and modern about this approach. Out with the Victorian bric-a-brac. Let form follow function. It is like the single stroke of a Chinese paintbrush that creates a bird's wing or like the black and white photography of Paul Strand.

This does not mean, however, that modern poems are not complex. In "The Red Wheelbarrow," for example, the words "so much depends" create **ambiguity.** Ambiguity has to do with vagueness or uncertainty, the possibility that something means more than one thing. If you are writing a land-sale contract or instructions on how to remove an appendix, ambiguity isn't a good thing, but in poetry it creates mystery and mood by letting the writer suggest several meanings at one time. Ambiguity can give a sense of openness and richness to a poem.

"In a Station of the Metro" is also somewhat ambiguous, but because of the way Pound juxtaposes two different images, the faces and the fallen petals, it is easier to draw a conclusion from this poem. Juxtaposing the two images in this way creates a **metaphor,** an implied comparison between two things. Implying that faces in a crowd are like fallen petals in a rainstorm gives us simultaneous feelings of pity and beauty.

When such a comparison is not simply implied but is actually stated using "like" or "as," the comparison is called a **simile.** Metaphors and similes work in more or less the same way but because a metaphor is implied rather than stated, metaphors are apt to be more ambiguous and thus potentially richer and more complex.

Notice the way in which images and comparisons work in the following poem by Galway Kinnell. The poem consist of careful but not elaborate description of the behavior of starfish on tidal flats.

Daybreak

On the tidal mud, just before sunset,
dozens of starfishes
were creeping. It was
as though the mud were a sky
and enormous, imperfect stars
moved across it as slowly
as the actual stars cross heaven.
All at once they stopped,
and as if they had simply
increased their receptivity
to gravity they sank down
into the mud; they faded down
into it and lay still; and by the time
pink of sunset broke across them
they were as invisible
as the true stars at daybreak.

GALWAY KINNELL

---

1.   Which words in "Daybreak" simply state observations? Which words express similes?

The poems we have been looking at so far use simile and metaphor in a fairly understated way. Here is a poem by an earlier writer, Thomas Campion (1567–1620), which uses *extended metaphor,* that is, an implied comparison developed in various images throughout the entire poem.

There is a garden in her face

There is a garden in her face
Where roses and white lilies grow;
  A heav'nly paradise is that place
Wherein all pleasant fruits do flow.
    There cherries grow which none may buy
    Till "Cherry-ripe" themselves do cry.

Those cherries fairly do enclose
Of orient pearl a double row,
  Which when her lovely laughter shows,
They look like rose-buds filled with snow;
    Yet them nor peer nor prince can buy,
    Till "Cherry-ripe" themselves do cry.

Her eyes like angels watch them still;
Her brows like bended bows do stand,
  Threat'ning with piercing frowns to kill
All that attempt, with eye or hand
    Those sacred cherries to come nigh
    Till "Cherry-ripe" themselves do cry.

THOMAS CAMPION

---

1. Identify the metaphors and similes in "There is a garden in her face."
2. Would it make any difference if Campion had written, "Her face is *like* a garden?" Does a metaphor or simile seem stronger as a figure of speech?
3. If you didn't know when Campion lived, would you think this was a modern poem? Why or why not?

The following poem is just what its title indicates, a response to an old photograph. Sharon Olds is a younger poet known for the startling frankness of her observations. Another of her poems, "His Stillness," appears in Chapter 1. One of Olds's techniques for achieving intensity is to seem to violate the privacy of her subjects. As she observes them closely, she sees, and then says, things that are so private that we are shocked by the vulnerability of the people she is writing about (including herself). Her language is vividly descriptive but plain spoken.

Photograph of the Girl

The girl sits on the hard ground,
the dry pan of Russia, in the drought
of 1921, stunned,
eyes closed, mouth open,
raw hot wind blowing
sand in her face. Hunger and puberty are
taking her together. She leans on a sack,
layers of clothes fluttering in the heat,
the new radius of her arm curved.
She cannot be not beautiful, but she is
starving. Each day she grows thinner, and her bones
grow longer, porous. The caption says
she is going to starve to death that winter
with millions of others. Deep in her body
the ovaries let out her first eggs,
golden as drops of grain.

SHARON OLDS

1. One of the challenges to a poet is to choose just the right word. The right word doesn't need to be fancy, it just has to be "right." Look at the words Olds uses, such as "dry pan," "stunned," "radius," "caption," "eggs," and "golden." What do these and other words do for the poem? Would synonyms work as well?
2. Why does Olds break line ten after the words "she is?"

3. At what point in the poem does Olds move from what she actually sees in the photo to what she infers from it?
4. Compare the images in this poem to those in Campion's. Both poems look at individual women closely. How are the two poems alike and how are they different?

Even when writing about a subject in a seemingly objective way, mainly presenting images without much commentary, a poet is not necessarily being objective. By choosing images and words, the poet is shaping the feeling of the poem. In the following poem, for example, C. K. Williams writes about something he apparently witnessed in a public place. Although he interprets the scene in a limited way, it would be hard to find any phrase or line that tells us how Williams feels about what he sees. Nevertheless the poem communicates emotion.

Will

The boy had badly deformed legs, and there was a long, fresh,
  surgical scar behind one knee.
The father, frankly wealthy, quite young, tanned, very board-room,
  very well-made, self-made,
had just taken the boy's thin arm the way you would take the arm
  of an attractive woman,
with firmness, a flourish of affection; he was smiling directly down
  into the boy's face
but it was evident that this much companionability between them
  wasn't usual, that the father,
whatever else his relation to the boy consisted of, didn't know that
  if you held him that way
you would overbalance him, which, when the boy's crutches
  splayed and he went down, crying "*Papa!*"
must have been what informed his voice with such shrill petulance,
  such anguished accusation.

C. K. WILLIAMS

1. What do you think the title of this poem means? Does the title help us understand the poem?
2. Do you get the impression that this is something Williams really observed? If so, does that add to the poem?

Yusef Komunyakaa's book of poetry, *Dien Cai Dau,* deals with his experiences as a military combat correspondent in Vietnam. "Facing It," the final poem in that book, describes what he sees as he meditates upon the Vietnam Veteran's Memorial in Washington D.C.

Facing It

My black face fades,
hiding inside the black granite.
I said I wouldn't,
dammit: No tears.
I'm stone. I'm flesh.
My clouded reflection eyes me
like a bird of prey, the profile of night
slanted against morning. I turn
this way—the stone lets me go.
I turn that way—I'm inside
the Vietnam Veterans Memorial
again, depending on the light
to make a difference.
I go down the 58,022 names,
half-expecting to find
my own in letters like smoke.
I touch the name Andrew Johnson;
I see the booby trap's white flash.
Names shimmer on a woman's blouse
but when she walks away
the names stay on the wall.
Brushstrokes flash, a red bird's
wings cutting across my stare.
The sky. A plane in the sky.

A white vet's image floats
closer to me, then his pale eyes
look through mine. I'm a window.
He's lost his right arm
inside the stone. In the black mirror
a woman's trying to erase names:
No, she's brushing a boy's hair.

YUSEF KOMUNYAKAA

---

1. Why does Komunyakaa tell the exact number of names on the monument?
2. How does color play a part in the poem?
3. How does Komunyakaa help you see what he is seeing, including the illusion that the people coming to visit the monument are inside it?
4. What does the title mean?

In the previous poems the writers use image words to describe their observations. By comparing different images or by implying comparison, they communicate feelings that are difficult to express directly. In the following poem, D. H. Lawrence uses these poetic techniques, but he also allows himself to comment directly, interpreting and judging what he observes and what he himself does. As you read "Snake," notice particularly the close, detailed description in the poem and how Lawrence uses images to establish the reality of his subject before he comments.

Snake

A snake came to my water-trough
On a hot, hot day, and I in pyjamas for the heat,
To drink there.

In the deep, strange-scented shade of the great dark carob-tree
I came down the steps with my pitcher
And must wait, must stand and wait, for there he was at the trough
    before me.

He reached down from a fissure in the earth-wall in the gloom
And trailed his yellow-brown slackness soft-bellied down, over the
    edge of the stone trough
And rested his throat upon the stone bottom,
And where the water had dripped from the tap, in a small
    clearness,
He sipped with his straight mouth,
Softly drank through his straight gums, into his slack long body,
Silently.

Someone was before me at my water-trough,
And I, like a second comer, waiting.

He lifted his head from his drinking, as cattle do,
And looked at me vaguely, as drinking cattle do,
And flickered his two-forked tongue from his lips, and mused
    a moment,
And stooped and drank a little more,
Being earth-brown, earth-golden from the burning bowels of the
    earth
On the day of Sicilian July, with Etna smoking.

The voice of my education said to me
He must be killed,
For in Sicily the black, black snakes are innocent, the gold are
    venomous.

And voices in me said, If you were a man
You would take a stick and break him now, and finish him off.

But must I confess how I liked him,
How glad I was he had come like a guest in quiet, to drink at my
    water-trough
And depart peaceful, pacified, and thankless,
Into the burning bowels of this earth?

Was it cowardice, that I dared not kill him?
Was it perversity, that I longed to talk to him?

Was it humility, to feel so honoured?
I felt so honoured.

And yet those voices:
If you were not afraid, you would kill him!

And truly I was afraid, I was most afraid,
But even so, honoured still more
That he should seek my hospitality
From out the dark door of the secret earth.

He drank enough
And lifted his head, dreamily, as one who has drunken,
And flickered his tongue like a forked night on the air, so black,
Seeming to lick his lips,
And looked around like a god, unseeing, into the air,
And slowly turned his head,
And slowly, very slowly, as if thrice adream,
Proceeded to draw his slow length curving round
And climb again the broken bank of my wall-face.

And as he put his head into that dreadful hole,
And as he slowly drew up, snake-easing his shoulders, and entered
    farther,
A sort of horror, a sort of protest against his withdrawing into that
    horrid black hole,
Deliberately going into the blackness, and slowly drawing himself
    after,
Overcame me now his back was turned.

I looked round, I put down my pitcher,
I picked up a clumsy log
and threw it at the water-trough with a clatter.

I think it did not hit him,
But suddenly that part of him that was left behind convulsed in
    undignified haste,
Writhed like lightning, and was gone

Into the black hole, the earth-lipped fissure in the wall-front,
At which, in the intense still noon, I stared with fascination.

And immediately I regretted it.
I thought how paltry, how vulgar, what a mean act!

I despised myself and the voices of my accursed human education.

And I thought of the albatross,
And I wished he would come back, my snake.

For he seemed to me again like a king,
Like a king in exile, uncrowned in the underworld,
Now due to be crowned again.

And so, I missed my chance with one of the lords
Of life.
And I have something to expiate;
A pettiness.

Taormina.

D. H. LAWRENCE

---

1. What are some of the strong image words in the poem?
2. Sometimes a poet presents images without commenting on them. Other times, as in "Snake," the poet adds some sort of commentary to help explain the meaning of the images. What sort of commentary does Lawrence provide and how does it help the reader respond to the images in the poem?

When you were a child, did you ever think that a tree at night looked like a monster with arms held out to grab you, that a shadow was a menacing, or playful, moving figure, that fried eggs looked like eyes, that broccoli looked like little trees, or that mashed potatoes and gravy were mountains running with volcanic lava? The last three are not just playing with food—they are metaphorical thinking. Children are natural metaphorical thinkers. Meeting a new experience, seeing a new object, they compare it to something they already know. The problem is that repetition and the influence of others may dull us. Red as a rose. Black as night. Ham and eggs for breakfast again. Big deal.

You can exercise your ability to make images, original observations and comparisons, metaphors, and similes by writing **meditations.** The word "meditation" suggests getting away from our daily, distracted, decision-making involvement with the world, repeating a mantra to ourselves, staring into a fire, or taking a long walk on a beach. It suggests a prayerful attention to the moment. These things are not exactly what is meant by the written meditation, but they do have some of the quality of focused yet free-floating attention. A written meditation is a discourse, reflections and variations on an object or event, as Sharon Olds meditates in "Photograph of the Girl" or D. H. Lawrence meditates in "Snake."

The first step is close attention. What does the thing look like? What does it smell, taste, feel like? What does it do? The second step is *whatever comes.* So maybe it's slow in coming at first. Or maybe it's not as astonishing as you would like. That's okay. A writer has to learn to trust the process of association. Sometimes it gets easier, but you can never really predict *what* will come. What you can count on is that close observation is a good place to begin.

Following are some additional poems of observation. As you read through them, imagine how each poet might have gotten the idea for the poem from something he or she observed. In each one something is observed immediately or in memory, and the poem proceeds from that observation. You will find, however, that the poems are very different from one another. In some cases the writer is concerned mainly with a visual effect. Sometimes a philosophical point is implied or stated outright. Marge Piercy's "A Work of Artifice," for example, is an extended metaphor about the potential for growth in living things and how it may be stunted.

A Work of Artifice

The bonsai tree
in the attractive pot
could have grown eighty feet tall
on the side of a mountain

till split by lightning.
But a gardener carefully pruned it.
It is nine inches high.
Every day as he
whittles back the branches
the gardener croons,
It is your nature
to be small and cozy,
domestic and weak;
how lucky, little tree,
to have a pot to grow in.
With living creatures
one must begin very early
to dwarf their growth:
the bound feet,
the crippled brain,
the hair in curlers,
the hands you
love to touch.

MARGE PIERCY

1. How do you know that Piercy is writing about a woman as well as about a bonsai tree?
2. Using contrasting images is one way that a poet gets across the point of the images. What are the contrasting images here? What does Piercy imply by the nature of the contrast?

William Carlos Williams's "Spring and All" contains beautiful and convincing images of the early spring landscape. Besides portraying the season in realistic detail, the poet personifies spring as someone waking, coming back to consciousness: "sluggish / dazed spring approaches." The personification extends to the rebirth of the weeds and grasses: "They enter the new world naked." Perhaps there is also an implied association between the landscape and "the contagious hospital." Plants recover like patients; or the patients, even though they are not in the poem directly, are like the plants: "the profound change / has come upon them."

Spring and All

By the road to the contagious hospital
under the surge of the blue
mottled clouds driven from the
northeast—a cold wind. Beyond, the
waste of broad, muddy fields
brown with dried weeds, standing and fallen

patches of standing water
the scattering of tall trees

All along the road the reddish
purplish, forked, upstanding, twiggy
stuff of bushes and small trees
with dead, brown leaves under them
leafless vines—

Lifeless in appearance, sluggish
dazed spring approaches—

They enter the new world naked,
cold, uncertain of all
save that they enter. All about them
the cold, familiar wind—

Now the grass, tomorrow
the stiff curl of wildcarrot leaf
One by one objects are defined—
It quickens: clarity, outline of leaf

But now the stark dignity of
entrance—Still, the profound change
has come upon them: rooted, they
grip down and begin to awaken

WILLIAM CARLOS WILLIAMS

---

1. If you were to sketch a picture based on Williams's poem, would it be easy
   to know what to put in the picture? What colors would you need? How
   would you picture "sluggish / dazed spring"?

2. Besides image words, Williams makes use of less concrete language, strong **abstract** words such as the adjective "contagious" and the abstract noun "dignity." Look for other examples of abstract language that add to the poem.

In "Umbrella" the author thinks that an umbrella looks like a black flower, a flower that blooms in the rain and wilts in the sun. There is also an element of personification here. The umbrella "broods" and "consents" and is likened to a mourner. (**Personification** is a figure of speech in which the nonhuman—for example, animals, ideas, and objects—is given human attributes.)

Umbrella

I press a button,   .
and this black flower
with its warped pistil
broods over me,
tears dripping from a dozen
silver stamens.
It catches water, this flower,
and sheds it,
consents to wilt in a closet
like some wrinkled mourner
between funerals.

DUANE ACKERSON

---

1. Would you understand this poem without the title?
2. Is observation the whole point of this poem or is there some other meaning to it?

Merwin's "Crossing Place" is very subtle and understated. I will not try to paraphrase the poem. Simply think about someone arduously trying not to spill water back into the stream from which it came.

Crossing Place

I crossed the stream
on the rocks
in the summer
evening
trying not to spill
the pitcher of water
from the falls

W. S. MERWIN

---

1. What senses do the images appeal to in this poem?
2. How is "Crossing Place" like "Umbrella" and how is it different? For example, look at how each poem begins. Are there concrete images in both poems? Do the authors comment or interpret?
3. "Crossing Place" seems simply to state the facts. Does there seem to be any other meaning to it?
4. What is the advantage or disadvantage in simply putting the images before the reader without telling the reader how to interpret the images? Do you like poets to come out and state their "messages" or do you like them to be more mysterious?

Seamus Heaney, who is from Northern Ireland, has written a series of poems based on the bog people of Northern Europe, so called because the bodies of many of them have been found remarkably well-preserved in peat bogs. The body of the Grauballe man, who probably died by ritual murder in about 100 B.C., was discovered in Denmark in 1952. Preserved by the acid waters of the peat bogs and transformed to a blackened leathery state, these and other similar human remains are at once horrifying, pathetic, and fascinating. Notice how Heaney uses comparison after comparison to re-create the image of "The Grauballe Man" in words. You can see a picture of the subject, along with a passage from Heaney's poem, in *National Geographic* magazine, March 1987. After you have read the poem, it would be interesting to compare the image Heaney gives in words with the pictorial image.

The Grauballe Man

As if he had been poured
in tar, he lies
on a pillow of turf
and seems to weep

the black river of himself.
The grain of his wrists
is like bog oak,
the ball of his heel

like a basalt egg.
His instep has shrunk
cold as a swan's foot
or a wet swamp root.

His hips are the ridge
and purse of a mussel,
his spine an eel arrested
under a glisten of mud.

The head lifts,
the chin is a visor
raised above the vent
of his slashed throat

that has tanned and toughened.
The cured wound
opens inwards to a dark
elderberry place.

Who will say 'corpse'
to his vivid cast?
Who will say 'body'
to his opaque repose?

And his rusted hair,
a mat unlikely

as a foetus's.
I first saw his twisted face

in a photograph,
a head and shoulder
out of the peat,
bruised like a forceps baby,

but now he lies
perfected in my memory,
down to the red horn
of his nails,

hung in the scales
with beauty and atrocity:
with the Dying Gaul
too strictly compassed

on his shield,
with the actual weight
of each hooded victim,
slashed and dumped.

SEAMUS HEANEY

1. Heaney describes the figure of the Grauballe man and then, in stanzas 8 and 9, tells when he first saw him. Imagine reversing stanzas 1–7 and 8–12. Would the poem work as well?
2. What are some of the images that help you "see" what Heaney sees? Are the images mainly visual or do they appeal to other senses? Explain.

Suggestions for Writing

1. Choose some small object or entity for close observation: a stone, a fungus, a wristwatch, an onion, a ladybug, a sewing needle, a drop of pond water or a piece of your own hair as seen under a microscope,

a scab, a toenail, or an ice cube. Start with the first object you see, or pick something with great care because it attracts you. Make this a treasure hunt if you like. Go outside and look around to find a candy-bar wrapper, a pine cone, a leaf, a frog, or a styrofoam cup.

Whatever you choose, give it your closest attention. Describe in writing all your sensory impressions of this object, all the details you can muster. You can start with prose or write your observations in loosely broken lines, whichever seems easier.

When you feel that you have a solid foundation of specific, concrete images, the second half of the writing exercise begins: generalize from the things you observe to some meaning drawn from your observations. For example, describe a rock in great detail. Then make a generalization about life, or time, or the human condition, based on that description. Don't be afraid to overdo it. You can cut back in revision. Finally, experiment with making your prose or poetry rough draft into a polished poem.

2. Look at or write about something very small—all its features, actions, and so on. Write a poem showing how it is like something very large. Or relate something nearby to something faraway.

3. Read the descriptions in a book of natural history: a guidebook to birds, mushrooms, or wildflowers, for example. Then write a poem of *identification* about a plant, bird, animal, rock, fish, protozoan, constellation, geological formation, mountain peak, or something else from the natural world. The poem may be very abstract but the reader should be able to recognize the subject.

4. Write a poem about a scene: something you came upon suddenly, something that surprised you, or something that stays in your memory. Don't explain what it means. Let the reader see what you see, what happens, what is there.

5. Write a poem in terms of the smallest parts of a thing or entity, instead of dealing with the whole. For example, the eye of a rabbit or lizard, a leaf bud on an apple tree, the battery in your electric watch.

6. Think of some encounter with a work of art: a painting, a certain opera singer's performance, a piece of music you know and love or one that you heard for the first time, a statue, a building, or some other work. Write a poem that is a meditation on that work.

7. Choose a picture, such as an old family photo or a portrait or scene from a book or magazine. Try to choose a picture with dramatic possibilities. Write a meditative poem describing the picture. What inferences can you draw from the picture beyond its surface appearance?

8. Choose one of the observation poems in this chapter and use it as a model for writing a poem on a different subject. For example, if you model your poem on "The Grauballe Man," you might use a series of four-line stanzas in which you develop one simile after another to describe the appearance of your subject.

5

Address

When you write a poem do you imagine an audience? It is all very well to argue that a genuine writer is impelled from within and would write whether or not an audience existed, but even the extremely reclusive, publicity-shy poet Emily Dickinson seems to be addressing someone in this poem:

I'm Nobody! Who are you?
Are you—Nobody—too?
Then there's a pair of us!
Don't tell! they'd banish us—you know!

How dreary—to be—Somebody!
How public—like a Frog—
To tell your name—the livelong June—
To an admiring Bog!

Dickinson also said, "This is my letter to the world, / That never wrote to me." When you write poetry, think about whether you are addressing a friend, a stranger, or an accomplice in obscurity, whether you are sending a "letter to the world." Defining an audience can help you find subjects and strengthen the focus of your poems. Addressing someone else also takes some of the burden off the pervasive "I."

A **poem of address** may name someone and thus designate an audience. The poem may address a pretended audience for rhetorical effect—for example, "To My Cat"—or it may simply imply a listener, an anonymous "you," as is the case in the following poem, by William Carlos Williams. "This Is Just to Say" sounds a little like a note left in a kitchen—the situation is clear enough. The reader does not know the identity of "you," but the speaker wants to shift emphasis away from himself by bringing in someone else. He is guilty, but he says, "Forgive me," not "I am sorry." He is, of course, not at all sorry—"They were delicious."

This Is Just to Say

I have eaten
the plums
that were in
the icebox

and which
you were probably
saving
for breakfast

Forgive me
they were delicious
so sweet
and so cold

WILLIAM CARLOS WILLIAMS

1. What would have been different in the poem if Williams had said "which she" (or "he" or "my roommate" or "the cook") "was saving" and "I hope [she or he] forgives me"?
2. Tone is an expression of attitude or feeling toward a subject. How does speaking directly to an individual change the tone of the poem?

In the following poem, the writer also addresses someone who is not present. We do not understand the specifics of the situation. Someone seems to be waiting for a call. Whether the caller will come seems to be very important to the speaker. The cold, still landscape and the ice rose from the speaker's breath that blooms on the window glass establish a lonely, haunting scene:

#5

Another winter morning
I'm expecting your call
I stand close to the window and watch
my breath form a rose on the glass
I scratch your name on it
then wipe it away with my sleeve
listening for your tires
to crunch through the ice on the drive
I notice how snow glistens on the pine boughs
that there's no wind at all
It's too cold for my walk
Nothing dares disturb this stillness
I know you aren't coming
I press my cheek to the window
The telephone rings
My breath forms a rose on the glass

DAN GERBER

---

1. Do we need to know who "you" is to understand this poem? Does not naming the person make the poem feel more or less personal?
2. When the poet addresses "you," does the reader feel involved? Does the reader feel as if the poet is speaking to him or her? How does that affect the tone of the poem?

Such a poem resembles the conversations we sometimes carry on in our heads. Unlike real conversations, in which words are blurted out or jumbled or not said at all, the ones in our heads are continually polished and revised. All the things we wish we could say, or have said, or might say go around and around. In a poem the imaginary conversation becomes even more perfect; and, what is better, because a poem is written down, it can actually make its point.

A poem of address is at the same time intimate and distant. Although it purports to address a particular person, it is intended to be overheard by the rest of the world. This allows the writer to be direct yet dramatic and helps focus the poem on its intention.

The preceding examples spoke to an anonymous "you." An *epistolary,* or letter, poem is more specific. It is in the form of a letter addressed to a particular friend, or enemy, or stranger; someone living or dead, real or fantastic; the President, or a movie star, or Anne Boleyn, or even a part of your own body. You could write a letter to the back of your head or an apologetic letter to your broken leg.

A good letter addresses the one to whom it is written in such a realistic way that it seems like one side of a conversation with someone who is actually present. For some people, the letter is freer than face-to-face conversation. There are no interruptions, for one thing. And things can be written in a more formal, literary way than they can be said. Revision is possible, and if one has last-minute doubts about content, the letter can be burned.

Richard Hugo has published a number of letter poems addressed to friends and fellow poets in a book titled *31 Letters and 13 Dreams.* The letter poems are interspersed with dream poems that sometimes underscore the imagery of the letters and sometimes offset the letters by contrast. Often the place where they were written is the starting point for a string of associations, meditations, or memories. In "Letter to Simic from Boulder," for example, Hugo muses on the appalling fact, learned years later, that the poet Charles Simic, now living and writing in the United States, was a child in Belgrade at the time Hugo was bombing the city during the Second World War. Hugo says, "Dear Charles, I'm glad you avoided the bombs, that you / live with us now and write poems."

In the following poem, Hugo addresses an old school friend, now also a poet and college writing teacher; he considers the subjects of the past and of time passing. Notice how the line endings work less as emphatic stops than as a gentle restraining that formalizes the flow of emotions and associations. Often the letter form provides a loose, flexible shape that can contain the swarm of thoughts passing through a writer's mind.

Letter to Haislip from Hot Springs

Dear John: Great to see your long-coming, well-crafted book
getting good reviews. I'm in a town that for no reason

I can understand, reminds me how time has passed since we
studied under Roethke, Arnold Stein, Jack Mathews and
Jim Hall at Washington. Two of them are gone already.
I think of that this morning and I get sad. This motel
I took for the night, hoping to catch the morning fishing
at Rainbow Lake, is one that survived after most others
went broke when they discovered the hot springs simply didn't
work. No therapeutic value. None of that. The old climbed
up out the steaming water still old. The cripples still limped
after three weeks of soaking. I'm a little lame myself
these days. Bad hip from a childhood accident. Skeletal
problems show up as we enter middle age. Our bones
settle in and start to complain about some damn thing that
happened years ago and we barely noticed it then.
Who thought 25 years ago we'd both be directors
of Creative Writing, you at Oregon, me here at
Montana, fishing alone in the Flathead wind, in lakes
turned silver by sky, my memories so firm, my notion
of what time does to men so secure I wish I'd learned to
write novels. Now I can understand the mind that lets Sam
wander off to Peru on page 29 and come back
twenty years later in the final chapter, a nazi.
I know why I always feel sad when I finish a novel.
Sometimes cry at just the idea that so much has happened.
But then, I'm simply a slob. This is no town for young men.
It sets back off the highway two miles and the streets stand bare.
When I drive in, I feel I'm an intrusion. When I leave,
I feel I'm deserting my past. I feel the same sadness
I feel at the end of a novel. A terrible lot has happened
      and is done. Do you see it happening to students?
I do and say nothing, and want to say when some young poet
comes angry to my office: you too will grow calm. You too
will see your rage suffer from skeletal weakness you picked
up when young, will come to know the hot springs don't work,
      and love
empty roads, love being the only man casting into
a lake turned silver by sky. But then, maybe he won't,
no matter. The morning is clear. I plan to grab breakfast
at the empty cafe, then head to the lake, my Buick

purring under the hood as Stafford would say. And I plan
to enjoy life going by despite my slight limp. Best. Dick.

RICHARD HUGO

---

1. There are a number of personal **allusions** in the form of references to people, places, and events in the poet's life. Does it matter that the reader probably won't recognize many of these references? How do these references
   emphasize that this is a poem of address?
2. How does Hugo use the letter form to give him freedom in developing the
   form and content of the poem?
3. Does there seem to be a central, unifying idea (or *theme*) in this poem?
   Explain.

Although a letter poem is addressed to a specific audience, the intention is usually that it be read by others as well. In this sense, the letter
form is a rhetorical device. The personal feeling is genuine, but the true
audience is not necessarily the person addressed. Like the general poem of
address, the letter poem can convey a tone of intimacy while maintain-
ing some distance from its object.

A letter poem is somewhat like a soliloquy in a play, such as Hamlet's famous "To be, or not to be" speech. A soliloquy lets the audience
know what is going on inside a character's mind or presents other information that is not presented dramatically. It is one form of the **monologue,** a speech by one person (**dialogue** is the name for speech between
two or more people). The letter form is another kind of monologue.

Address poems need not be restricted to the **persona,** or character,
of the poet. The poet may adopt a different persona, as in the following
"letter," in which Ezra Pound writes in the character of a young wife.
This love poem about separation derives much of its intensity from the
intimacy established by the direct address of the wife to the husband. Of
course, he is gone. He may never get the letter. Maybe he is dead, never
coming back. We do not know. But the extraordinary imagery of the
poem would not be as powerful had the husband been spoken of in the
third person, as "he."

The River-Merchant's Wife: A Letter

While my hair was still cut straight across my forehead
I played about the front gate, pulling flowers.
You came by on bamboo stilts, playing horse,
You walked about my seat, playing with blue plums.
And we went on living in the village of Chokan:
Two small people, without dislike or suspicion.

At fourteen I married My Lord you.
I never laughed, being bashful.
Lowering my head, I looked at the wall.
Called to, a thousand times, I never looked back.

At fifteen I stopped scowling,
I desired my dust to be mingled with yours
Forever and forever and forever.
Why should I climb the look out?

At sixteen you departed,
You went into far Ku-to-yen, by the river of swirling eddies,
And you have been gone five months.
The monkeys make sorrowful noise overhead.

You dragged your feet when you went out.
By the gate now, the moss is grown, the different mosses,
Too deep to clear them away!
The leaves fall early this autumn, in wind.
The paired butterflies are already yellow with August
Over the grass in the West garden;
They hurt me. I grow older.
If you are coming down through the narrows of the river Kiang,
Please let me know beforehand,
And I will come out to meet you
        As far as Cho-fu-Sa.

RIHAKU
Translated by Ezra Pound

1. How do we know who is speaking in this poem? What do we know about
    the speaker?
2. Is the personal feeling of the address poem changed in any way when the
    speaker is a character other than the poet?

The term **apostrophe** describes an address to any imaginary object,
abstract idea, personified thing, or person who is absent. Originally,
"apostrophe" meant turning away, that is, a turning away from one's audience to speak directly to a person. This rhetorical device is very old.
The index of any large anthology of poetry will usually contain a number of "To" poems: "To a Skylark," "To a Mouse," "To an Athlete Dying Young," "To Autumn," "To a Waterfowl," and so on.

In the fourteenth century, Geoffrey Chaucer wrote the "Complaint
to His Purse," in which he tells his empty purse to be full, as if it were a
sweetheart for whom he pines: "Beeth heavy again, or elles moot I will
die." The poem was actually addressed to Henry IV, as a plea that
Chaucer's allowance be increased.

Complaint to His Purse

To you, my purs, and to noon other wight,
Complaine I, for ye be my lady dere.
I am so sory, now that ye be light,
For certes, but if ye make me hevy cheere,
Me were as lief be laid upon my beere;
For which unto youre mercy thus I crye:
Beeth hevy again, or elles moot I die.

Now voucheth sauf this day er it be night
That I of you the blisful soun may heere,
Or see youre colour, lik the sonne bright,
That of yelownesse hadde nevere peere.
Ye be my life, ye be myn hertes steere,
Queen of confort and of good compaignye:
Beeth hevy again, or elles moot I die.

Ye purs, that been to me my lives light
And saviour, as in this world down here,
Out of this tonne helpe me thurgh your might,
Sith that ye wol nat be my tresorere;
For I am shave as neigh as any frere.
But yit I praye unto youre curteisye:
Beeth hevy again, or elles moot I die.

Envoy to Henry IV
O conquerour of Brutus Albioun,
Which that by line and free eleccioun
Been verray king, this song to you I sende:
And ye, that mowen alle oure harmes amende,
Have minde upon my supplicacioun.

GEOFFREY CHAUCER

---

1. There is always a certain artificiality in the poem of address, for the poet pretends to speak to one person and yet intends others who read the poem to be part of the audience also. In "Complaint to His Purse," Chaucer pretends to speak to his money purse but of course intends the complaint to reach the ears of his patron and employer, the king. Why does he adopt this pretense? Why not address the poem directly to Henry IV? After all, the *envoy* makes his true intended audience clear.
2. What are some reasons for addressing a poem to a particular person or thing when you really want the poem to speak to someone else?

In the manner of Chaucer, one might use such a device to write, for example, a poem to a chair where someone dear once sat or a poem to a well-liked but disorderly roommate: "Complaint to Betsy's Shoe, Found in a Bowl of Popcorn at 8 a.m."

The apostrophe sometimes teeters between humor and seriousness, and a grandiose address to some common object can end up sounding ludicrous. However, Karl Shapiro uses such discrepancy intentionally and with memorable effect in the following poem.

The Fly

O hideous little bat, the size of snot,
With polyhedral eye and shabby clothes,
To populate the stinking cat you walk
The promontory of the dead man's nose,
Climb with the fine leg of a Duncan-Phyfe
   The smoking mountains of my food
     And in a comic mood
   In mid-air take to bed a wife.

Riding and riding with your filth of hair
On gluey foot or wing, forever coy,
Hot from the compost and green sweet decay,
Sounding your buzzer like an urchin toy—
You dot all whiteness with diminutive stool,
   In the tight belly of the dead
     Burrow with hungry head
   And inlay maggots like a jewel.

At your approach the great horse stomps and paws
Bringing the hurricane of his heavy tail;
Shod in disease you dare to kiss my hand
Which sweeps against you like an angry flail;
Still you return, return, trusting your wing
   To draw you from the hunter's reach
     That learns to kill to teach
   Disorder to the tinier thing.

My peace is your disaster. For your death
Children like spiders cup their pretty hands
And wives resort to chemistry of war.
In fens of sticky paper and quicksands
You glue yourself to death. Where you are stuck
   You struggle hideously and beg,
     You amputate your leg
   Imbedded in the amber muck.

But I, a man, must swat you with my hate,
Slap you across the air and crush your flight,
Must mangle with my shoe and smear your blood,
Expose your little guts pasty and white,
Knock your head sidewise like a drunkard's hat,
  Pin your wings under like a crow's,
    Tear off your flimsy clothes
And beat you as one beats a rat.

Then like Gargantua I stride among
The corpses strewn like raisins in the dust,
The broken bodies of the narrow dead
That catch the throat with fingers of disgust.
I sweep. One gyrates like a top and falls
  And stunned, stone blind, and deaf
    Buzzes its frightful F
And dies between three cannibals.

KARL SHAPIRO

---

1. Since there is no chance at all that a fly would read Shapiro's poem, why pretend to address a fly at all? Does it make the poem more intense? More humorous? More shocking?
2. How does the address to the fly provide a framework (beginning, middle, end, arrangement of ideas and images) for developing the poem?

The speaker in Norman Hindley's "Wood Butcher" uses a kind of *interior monologue* to work out a problem of self-acceptance. He confronts his father after many years and acknowledges the need for his father's praise. What sort of poem might you write to someone whom you felt you had disappointed years ago or to someone who had misunderstood you?

Wood Butcher

For my Father

After the Navy and the war
You drafted big prints and started a summer house
in Bay Springs. I was your helper, and that first year
We worked weekends through most of the winter.
The wind, your cold immaculate tools, the hole
In the floor of the Ford we traveled in . . .
I hated it all. Especially my carpentry. I ruined doors,
My tape never returned,
I couldn't saw. "Measure twice, cut once."
You said it a hundred times.
I tried everything to please you,
You my ex-flyboy, the perfectionist.
Even your smile was mitered. Your hands cool and silky
On the tools, brown as the lining
Of your flight jacket. Mine were white,
Mitts of a wood butcher.
You never said that,
But when you came across the scarred paneling,
The wrong nail, the split grain,
Doughnut grease on the new glass,
I'd watch your eyes, the drained bluebirds
That flew your face.

I fouled some screens up once,
Wrinkles, wavy frames,
You broke them out with a chair.
My best day I spent hauling dry wall,
Holding while you fitted and tacked.
For years I would devote myself
To carrying and fetching.
Strong, good with mortar, but squirrelly.
A world class gofer.

I want you to know
that today I finished a boat, designed it,

22 feet, foredeck, wheel,
A transom you could hang a Pratt & Whitney on.
But none of this is challenge or revenge,
The boat is a way of speaking, a tongue
Saying I still want to please you
That it's your disappointment that drives me.

NORMAN HINDLEY

---

1. How does Hindley use "Wood Butcher" to say things to his father he might never have told him directly? How does he feel about working for and with his father?
2. What might the poem have been like from the father's point of view, addressed to the son?

Sandra McPherson's poem "For Elizabeth Bishop," tells about her student-teacher relationship with the poet Elizabeth Bishop and uses a memory to turn the address into an **elegy,** an expression of sorrow for someone who has died. American born, Bishop lived much of her adult life in Brazil but traveled sometimes to the United States to teach. Some of Bishop's books included *North and South, Questions of Travel,* and *Geography III.* These geographical themes certainly help shape the following poem.

For Elizabeth Bishop

The child I left your class to have
Later had a habit of sleeping
With her arms around a globe
she'd unscrewed, dropped, and dented.
I always felt she *could* possess it,
The pink countries and the mauve
And the ocean which got to keep its blue.
Coming from the Southern Hemisphere to teach,

Which you had never had to do, you took
A bare-walled room, alone, its northern
Windowscapes as gray as walls.
To decorate, you'd only brought a black madonna.
I thought you must have skipped summer that year,
Southern winter, southern spring, then north
For winter over again. Still it pleased you
To take credit for introducing us,
And later to bring our daughter a small flipbook
Of partners dancing, and a ring
With a secret whistle.—All are
Broken now like her globe, but she remembers
Them as I recall the black madonna
Facing you across the room so that
In a way you had the dark fertile life
You were always giving gifts to.
Your smaller admirer off to school,
I take the globe and roll it away: where
On it now is someone like you?

SANDRA McPHERSON

---

1. Does McPherson "tell" Bishop things she might already know?
2. How does addressing the poem to Elizabeth Bishop emphasize its elegiac qualities?

From these examples you may begin to see that the possibilities for writing a poem of address are virtually unlimited. You can address a person who you know would never read the poem, or a part of the body, or even the anonymous reader. One other way of developing a poem of address, although not as an apostrophe or a poem to a particular listener, is by answering a question posed by yourself or someone else. This device for eliciting and shaping a poem is discussed here because, like the poem of address that confronts an audience, it depends on the poet's confronting an external impetus, namely, a question.

Make up a question you would like to answer or pretend that some-one else has asked you a question and answer that. For example:

Why haven't I answered your call?
I'll tell you why:

Or,

Why do I always wear this small, cheap ring?
Once, years ago ...

You get the idea.

Suggestions for Writing

1. Write a poem addressed to another self, your alter ego, or to your image in the mirror, but don't explain that you are addressing your-self. Let that come out in the poem.

2. Write a poem to an anonymous "you" suggesting some secret con-nection in a mysterious and unique way.

3. Write a poem addressed to an anonymous "you" evoking a particu-lar mood or emotional state by concrete images. Suggest:
   a) Loneliness
   b) Anger
   c) Guilt
   d) Hilarity

4. Write a poem addressed to some part of your body. Be sure that the poem displays some consistent attitude or strong feeling.

5. Write an apostrophe to an animal or object. Consider whether the tone should be comic, serious, or something in between.

6. Write a letter poem:
   a) To a friend
   b) To an enemy
   c) To someone who is dead
   d) To a stranger
   e) To a celebrity

7. Write a poem in answer to a question you imagine someone else asking you.

8. Write a poem to someone telling them something you want to say but would have a hard time telling them directly.

6

Form

The word **form** is used to mean the structure of a poem, whether prescribed and **regular** like the **sonnet** form or **irregular** as in *free verse*. (*Irregular* does not mean chaotic, but rather that the poet improvises form *organically* from the content of the poem as the poem is written.) Line length, sound patterns, rhythms, stanza breaks, and organization of content are all elements in form, whether regular or irregular. We have, of course, been dealing with form all along, and most of the examples in this book have *organic form*, from the *catalog poem* to the *concrete* representation of a lilac blossom. This means that the poem is a whole system, rather than merely an idea dressed up in arbitrary rhymes, rhythms, and stanza breaks. We can see how form works in "Poem" by William Carlos Williams, where the poem describes the movement of a cat picking its catlike way.

Poem

As the cat
climbed over
the top of

the jamcloset
first the right
forefoot

carefully
then the hind
stepped down

into the pit of
the empty
flowerpot

WILLIAM CARLOS WILLIAMS

---

1. How many words are in each **line** of Williams's "Poem"?
2. How many syllables are in each line of the poem?
3. How many stressed or accented syllables are in each line?
4. How many lines are in each **stanza**?
5. Read the poem aloud. Do you hear any particular *sounds* being repeated throughout the poem? At the ends of lines?
6. Are there pauses for punctuation or meaning at the ends of lines or do the lines run on without pauses?
7. In what way might the line breaks help the reader see the subject?
8. In a summary based on the previous seven questions, describe the form of Williams's "Poem."

Using form to express a particular subject or mood is bound to be a somewhat subjective process, but the effect of form on this poem is dramatically clear when we imagine Williams's "Poem" broken in another way:

As the cat climbed over the top of
the jamcloset first the right forefoot
carefully then the hind stepped down
into the pit of the empty flowerpot

Now the rhythm sounds more like a galloping horse than a delicate cat. Yet even though this version horribly distorts the original, we can note some formal aspects. Arranged this way, there is a fairly regular pattern of stresses in each line with a variable number of unstressed syllables, and the sounds of "forefoot" and "flowerpot" create a *consonant rhyme* with the added effect of **alliteration** to link the ends of the lines. Thus, this example should point out that free verse is not in any sense formless. Williams's poem has form, but it is not *a* form.

Now look at the following by Phyllis McGinley, a poem that is a form, a ballade. A **ballade** is a French form with twenty-eight lines of no set length, divided into three *octaves* (eight-line stanzas) and a *quatrain* (four-line stanza) called the *envoy*. There are only three rhymes in a ballade, here established by "hair with," "hose," and "Spanish." The rhyme scheme for each of the eight-line stanzas is *a b a b b c b c*.★ The rhyme scheme of the envoy is *b c b c*. The last line of each stanza consists of a *refrain*, or repeated line. McGinley's refrain is repeated with small changes that give a pleasant sound of variation within a set pattern.

Ballade of Lost Objects

Where are the ribbons I tie my hair with?
   Where is my lipstick? Where are my hose—
The sheer ones hoarded these weeks to wear with
   Frocks the closets do not disclose?
Perfumes, petticoats, sports chapeaux,
   The blouse Parisian, the earring Spanish—
Everything suddenly ups and goes.
   And where in the world did the children vanish?

This is the house I used to share with
   Girls in pinafores, shier than does.
I can recall how they climbed my stair with
   Gales of giggles, on their toptoes.
Last seen wearing both braids and bows
   (But looking rather Raggedy-Annish),
When they departed nobody knows—
   Where in the world did the children vanish?

Two tall strangers, now I must bear with,
   Decked in my personal furbelows,
Raiding the larder, rending the air with

★As a notational convention, rhymes are assigned letters in order of appearance at the end of lines, and each time a rhyme recurs, the letter is repeated.

Gossip and terrible radios.
Neither my friends nor quite my foes,
Alien, beautiful, stern, and clannish,
Here they dwell, while the wonder grows:
Where in the world did the children vanish?

Prince, I warn you, under the rose,
Time is the thief you cannot banish.
These are my daughters, I suppose.
But where in the world did the children vanish?

PHYLLIS McGINLEY

---

1. How would you describe the tone of the "Ballade of Lost Objects"? That is, does the rhyme pattern make the poem sound serious, playful, sad, ironic, or what?
2. McGinley seems at first to be writing a poem simply about the things her daughters borrowed, but as she moves through the stanzas, we realize she is also writing about the bittersweet experience of seeing her children grow up. How does the repetition of the ballade lend itself to this expression of mixed feelings?

Again, let us consider an alternate version to see whether form and content are likewise indivisible in a set form. In a free-verse revision, we would dispense with words and arrangements particularly suited to the ballade.

Where are my hair ribbons?
Where is my lipstick, my hose—
The sheer ones I kept to wear
with dresses not in my closet?
Perfumes, petticoats, sports hats,
The Parisian blouse, the Spanish earring—
Everything's gone.
Where did the children go?

Basically, the sense is here, but the fun is gone, and with it the bittersweet, humorous, rueful tone of the poem, which obviously has as much to do with the ballade form as with the content.

Sometimes free verse, which is the predominant form of poetry today, is seen as antagonistic to set traditional forms and even to improvised forms which use regular rhyme and meter—that is, the new versus the old, the permissive versus the strict, the liberal versus the conservative, the *open* versus the *closed,* the **formal** versus the **informal,** and other dichotomies. It is true that the most vital movement in modern forms has been into experimentation and free verse, and there seems to be little point in imitating the poetry of past centuries. But it would be a mistake to ignore tradition and the existence of poetic conventions, just as it would be a mistake to believe that a work is not a poem unless it rhymes.

In this chapter we will study some ideas about form, including repetition (of which rhyme is one example), **rhythm** (both metered and irregular), and line breaks. We will also look at **traditional forms,** but since that is a lengthy subject, one should consult the many useful books on the topic for more exhaustive lists of such forms.

Relevant to the writing of poetry, one sometimes hears the idea that every student poet ought to start out by writing in strict forms and progress to freer verse from there. If not expressed in this way, the idea comes up that every poet ought to write at least one sonnet, sometime, perhaps in order to pay homage to all writers in English, particularly Shakespeare, who have done it so well. The **sonnet** is a fourteen-line poem written in rhymed **iambic pentameter** verse, and it is a form that lends itself especially well to innovation and flexibility. Still, it seems unfair to make the sonnet, or any form, into a poetic version of a Red Cross swimming test. You do not *have* to write in forms such as a sonnet, but you might want to consider it.

Before progressing further, let us summarize a few of the basics of scansion of formal verse. To **scan** a line of formal poetry is to examine or analyze its structure in terms of a repeated stress pattern, or meter. A syllable or group of syllables constituting a single metrical unit is called a **foot.** The syllables in a unit are described as stressed (ˉ) or unstressed (ˇ), so that common metrical feet are as follows:

iamb (ˇˉ)
trochee (ˉˇ)

anapest (˘˘¯)
dactyl (¯˘˘)
spondee (¯¯)
pyrrhic (˘˘)

This means that the iamb consists of one unstressed syllable followed by one stressed syllable, the trochee of one stressed syllable followed by one unstressed, and so on. The pyrrhic is not always considered a foot, since it serves to mark a flat or unstressed pair of syllables in a line; but it could be used to mark two unstressed syllables between or with regular, stressed feet. In any case, the number of stressed or accented syllables is what we listen for in any line, even where there is no regularity of stressed syllables and varying numbers of unstressed syllables.

Besides the kind of foot in a line, we may count how many feet are in a line. Thus we have monometer (one foot), dimeter (two feet), trimeter (three feet), tetrameter (four feet), pentameter (five feet), and hexameter (six feet), and on through heptameter and octameter, if a line is that long. Try to beat out the rhythm of a line that would be, say, iambic octameter (eight iambs). You will find that such a regular meter feels thin, hard to sustain, when stretched over a very long line. Here is a long line from a Roethke poem "The Meadow Mouse," broken only for lack of space:

> Now he's eaten his three kinds of cheese and drunk from
>   his bottle-cap watering trough—

The predominant foot is the anapest, of which there are five with one amphimacer ("kinds of cheese" ¯˘¯) one iamb ("and drunk") in the middle, a seven-foot line, or almost pure anapestic heptameter. But not all of the lines of this poem are so long. Notice that a seven-foot line of anapestic feet would be seven syllables longer than a seven-foot line of iambic feet. But meter in a very long line is not heard as emphatically as it is in a pentameter line, for instance.

On the other hand, if a line is very short, there is scarcely room to hear meter at all. We can hardly get a running start on one foot, and two will just get us to the next line. Perhaps for these reasons tetrameter and pentameter seem to be most common. In "The Lifeguard," James Dickey counts stresses instead of feet and uses a three-stress line very effectively to give a feeling of hypnotic movement:

In a stable of boats I lie still,
From all sleeping children hidden.
The leap of a fish from its shadow
Makes the whole lake instantly tremble.

There is a feeling that lines with an even number of feet or stresses are more stable and complete, whereas lines with an odd number of feet or stresses pull us on, the uneven foot or stress creating an imbalance to be fulfilled. Perhaps this is somewhat subjective, but does it seem to apply to Dickey's three-stress lines? Check various poems to see whether or not it is true that a tetrameter line feels more self-contained than a pentameter line. If it is true, this adds a degree of subtlety to the pentameter line, complete in itself yet always pushing on to the next line.

Let us now return to the sonnet. As we have mentioned, the traditional sonnet is a fourteen-line poem in rhymed iambic pentameter. Sonnets are usually classified according to their pattern of end rhymes and stanza breaks; the standard sonnet forms are as follows:

Shakespearean. Three quatrains (four-line stanzas) are followed by a *heroic couplet* (lines rhymed in pairs), with a rhyme scheme of *a b a b, c d c d, e f e f, g g.*

Petrarchan (or Italian). This sonnet consists of an octave (eight-line stanza) and a sestet (six-line stanza), which usually rhyme *a b b a a b b a, c d e c d e,* although the sestet may be varied, *c d c c d c* or *c d e d c e,* for example.

Spenserian. This consists of three rhyme-linked quatrains and a rhymed **couplet,** *a b a b, b c b c, c d c d, e e.*

The sonnet form has perhaps been so widely used because its length is not too short, not too long. The iambic-pentameter lines are long enough to allow for complex and continuing thought and sound structures. In writing a sonnet, the idea would be to find the most freedom possible within the form. In general, original content and innovations of style create an energizing tension against the restraints and traditions of the form. If you write a sonnet that sounds like "Shall I compare thee to a summer's day?" however, with all respect to Shakespeare, you are on the wrong track.

One subtlety that modern poets introduce in using the sonnet is to write it in some variation, so that the reader scarcely notices the form, perhaps not at all on first reading. For example, look back at Gary

Miranda's "Love Poem" in Chapter 3. Although the rhyme scheme is not conventional and the iambic pentameter is irregular after the first line, the poem is like a Petrarchan sonnet in that it is divided into an octave and a sestet. Instead of using the more common **vowel rhymes,** Miranda uses consonant rhyme, slant rhyme, and feminine rhyme. *Consonant rhyme* means that the final consonants are the same, but the vowels preceding them are different, as in "glance" and "fence." *Feminine rhyme* is a rhyme consisting of two syllables, the first stressed and the second unstressed, as in "chances" and "dances". *Slant rhyme* is the intentional use of approximate rhyme, very common in modern poetry. Here, "dances" and "branches" are approximate, feminine rhymes. In the Roethke poem "The Meadow Mouse," mentioned earlier, approximate rhymes—such as "stocking, him in," and "trembling" and "rising" and "forsaken"—yield a light, musical touch.

In Phyllis McGinley's ballade most of the rhymes are *masculine,* that is, the rhyme is in the final accented syllable, as in "bows" and "knows." But she also uses a feminine rhyme in "Spanish" and "vanish." You will notice that her direct masculine rhyme is more emphatic and obvious than the more oblique consonance used by Gary Miranda.

Here is another modern example, Archibald MacLeish's "The End of the World."

The End of the World

Quite unexpectedly as Vasserot
The armless ambidextrian was lighting
A match between his great and second toe
And Ralph the lion was engaged in biting
The neck of Madame Sossman while the drum
Pointed, and Teeny was about to cough
In waltz-time swinging Jocko by the thumb—
Quite unexpectedly the top blew off:

And there, there overhead, there, there, hung over
Those thousands of white faces, those dazed eyes,
There in the starless dark the poise, the hover,

There with vast wings across the canceled skies,
There in the sudden blackness the black pall
Of nothing, nothing, nothing—nothing at all.

ARCHIBALD MacLEISH

---

1. Practice scanning the poem. Which syllables are stressed and which are un-stressed? Is the pattern regular?
2. What pattern do you see in the end rhymes? Letter them accordingly.
3. What happens between the first and second stanzas in terms of content?
4. Does form mirror content in this poem? Explain.

As you will have noticed, the rhyme scheme matches exactly the traditional pattern of a Shakespearean sonnet, although the stanza division is into an octave and sestet. This does not make much difference, however, because the rhymes make a pattern of three quatrains and a rhymed couplet. It is just that MacLeish turns, or changes direction, between lines 8 and 9 instead of between lines 12 and 13. One of the characteristics of the sonnet is that there is a break or change of feeling or view at some point.

"The End of the World" starts off more or less as iambic pentameter, although it is quite a feat to scan a word like "ambidextrian," but then the meter varies to suit the sense and the two stressed syllables of "there, there" in line 9 finally bring the meter appropriately to a stunned halt for emphasis. There is an extra syllable in line 9, as well as two extra stresses. Well, why not? The world is ending in that line. Stop and be amazed.

Sometimes a poem is clearly not a sonnet but has the feeling of one. It may be broken into two parts that mirror an octave and sestet; it may be approximately fourteen lines long with a ten-syllable line predominating; it may have a progression of images turned around somehow by a final couplet or even a single epigrammatic line. The following ten-line poem, with short lines and no apparent rhyme scheme, which also deals with the end of a world, is not a sonnet, yet it is balanced like a Shakespearean sonnet.

The Epitaph Ending in And

In the last storm, when hawks
blast upward and a dove is
driven into the grass, its broken wings
a delicate design, the air between
wracked thin where it stretched before,
a clear spring bent close too often
(that Earth should ever have such wings
burnt on in blind color!), this will be
good as an epitaph:

Doves did not know where to fly, and

WILLIAM STAFFORD

---

1. With no other stanza breaks, why does Stafford set off the final line of the poem?
2. How do you feel about Stafford's ending the poem with an incomplete statement?

Stafford's poem brings up an interesting subject related to form in poetry, that is, the subject of **closure.** Closure in a poem is simply its being finished or closed. You will no doubt have noticed that some poems end with a very definite punch, and others seem to trail off or end with unresolved sounds and feelings. In "The Epitaph Ending in And," Stafford deliberately uses our expectation that a poem will end in a conclusive way to create an uneasy feeling when his poem does not. The world ends, but there is no way to provide a comfortable final word, no neat couplet or rousing cry to resolve our feelings. How should one finish a poem? Should the ending be like a blow to the stomach? Should it wrap everything up and suddenly make the poet's intentions clear? Should it somehow return us to the beginning of the poem, the initial problem or hypothesis, persuading us like a debater's argument?

Like other aspects of form, closure can be very definite, formal, and resolved, or it can be soft, ambiguous, and low-keyed. Look at some of the poems in this chapter and other chapters and notice how different

poets close their poems. For example, why does Williams end his "Poem"
with the cat stepping into "the empty / flowerpot"? Look at Paula Gunn
Allen's poem, which follows. As you study the poem for other elements
of form, notice where she ends it.

Taking a Visitor to See the Ruins

for Joe Bruchac

He's still telling about the time he came west
and was visiting me. I knew he
wanted to see some of the things

everybody sees when they're in the wilds of New Mexico.
So when we'd had our morning coffee
after he'd arrived, I said,

Would you like to go see some old Indian ruins?
His eyes brightened with excitement,
he was thinking, no doubt,

of places like the ones he'd known where he came from,
sacred caves filled with falseface masks,
ruins long abandoned, built secure

into the sacred lands; or of pueblos
once home to vanished people but peopled still
by their ghosts, connected still with the bone-old land.

Sure, he said. I'd like that a lot.
Come on, I said, and we got in my car,
drove a few blocks east, toward the towering peaks

of the Sandias. We stopped at a tall
high-security apartment building made of stone,
went up a walk past the pond and pressed the buzzer.

They answered and we went in,
past the empty pool room, past the empty party room,
up five flights in the elevator, down the abandoned hall.

Joe, I said when we'd gotten inside the chic apartment,
I'd like you to meet the old Indian ruins
I promised.

My mother, Mrs. Francis, and my grandmother, Mrs. Gottlieb.
His eyes grew large, and then he laughed
looking shocked at the two

women he'd just met. Silent for a second, they laughed too.
And he's still telling the tale of the old
Indian ruins he visited in New Mexico,

the two who still live pueblo style in high-security dwellings
way up there where the enemy can't reach them
just like in the olden times.

PAULA GUNN ALLEN

---

1. We have been using the term "formal" to describe poetry that uses more regular, sometimes traditional structure. In contrast, "informal" would describe poetry with a more irregular, organic form. Would you describe "Taking a Visitor to See the Ruins" as more formal or informal? Break your answer down into categories including stanza length, line length, rhythm, and rhyme or other sound structures.
2. Gunn uses enjambed or run-on lines. Look for examples of **enjambment**. How does this affect the tone of her poem?
3. Why does Allen end her poem as she does? How would it have changed the poem had she deleted the last three lines?

Besides rhyme, meter, stanza breaks and closure, other structural elements in poetry include repetend, alliteration, internal rhyme, beginning rhyme, and things having to do with line breaks, such as enjambment, syllable count (the meter is determined by the number of syllables in a line, rather than by the number and kind of feet), and breath length. Perhaps we should also include paragraphs, since prose poems do not break lines at all, except as prose does, by page margins.

First let us look at all of these that concern repetition: internal rhyme, beginning rhyme, alliteration, and repetend. Listening to poetry, we hear similarities and repetitions in sound. Like sounds pull together, whether at the end or in the middle of a line. Rhymes seem more emphatic at the end of a line. If the line is end stopped, that is, if punctuation and completion of sense both occur at the end of a line, then a rhyme there is even more emphatic. Look at these lines from the beginning of Edgar Allan Poe's "Sonnet—To Science."

> Science! true daughter of Old Time thou art!
>   Who alterest all things with thy peering eyes.
> Why preyest thou thus upon the poet's heart,
>   Vulture, whose wings are dull realities?

If we give one point for punctuation at the end of a line, one point for the line break itself, and one point for a rhyme, then lines 1 and 3 would each have three-point stops. Since "eyes" and the last syllable of "realities" are only approximate rhymes—unless Poe meant them to have an unfamiliar, antique-sounding pronunciation—perhaps we should give that rhyme only a half of a point, so that lines 2 and 4 would have two-and-a-half-point line endings. By contrast, "things" and "wings," in the middle of lines 2 and 4, respectively, would each get just one point. We do not stop for the rhyme of "things" and "wings," since it is not punctuated nor at the end of the line, yet the rhyme still tugs at the ear.

There is no need to proceed with this measuring system, but we should be conscious of the different values and gradations of such pulls and tensions in poetry. Undoubtedly a whole network could be drawn consisting of lines between the same or similar sounds in a poem and elements such as punctuation, line breaks, stanza breaks, and pauses in the sense to show the tensions pulling the poem together, pushing it on. It is this sense of structure that is more important in modern poetry than set patterns. Notice how structure functions in Stafford's "The Epitaph Ending in And" as compared to Poe's poem.

Stafford uses a device called **enjambment,** the run-on-line, which can have a very pleasing, subtle effect. Enjambment means that the sense of the line continues on into the next line, or further. The end of the line says stop, the sense of the language says go. Feel the pull in the line "blast upward and a dove is," for example. This would be a one-point line ending at most. Notice that the poem is one uncompleted sentence. The heaviest stop is the colon in the next-to-the-last line, an appropriate stop, after the word "epitaph."

Even though "The Epitaph Ending in And" does not rhyme, notice the pleasing effect of the similarities in sound of "design," "thin," "spring," and "blind" down the center of the poem. Identical words are not considered rhymes in English, but of course we hear the repetition of "wings" at the end of the two lines. **Repetend** is a poetic device that repeats a word or phrase regularly or irregularly throughout a poem. Like rhyme, repetend gives unity and a musical quality by repetition of sound. Like Phyllis McGinley's repeated line, or refrain, "And where in the world did the children vanish?" repetend emphasizes a particular content. The repetition of "wings" in "The Epitaph Ending in And" focuses on the effort to fly, and that "Doves did not know where to fly, and." The recurrence also gives a kind of music to a nonrhyming poem.

In the following poem, repetend in the words "move" and "moves" plays a small but important role.

Verge

(for Roger Pfingston)

This morning comes like Spain
to my house:
suddenly the sun slashes
between the two houses across the field
and strikes through my kitchen window,
across my table, and into the sink.
The goldfish is stunned in the bowl.
On the orange crate
the odor of thick woods
waits in the fern's leaves.
My pencil is suspended above clean paper.
The ocean has pushed out one bright drop
that hangs from the spigot.
I will move
when the fish moves.

RICHARD THOMAS

1. How does the closure of this poem compare to that of other poems in this chapter, particularly "The End of the World" and "The Epitaph Ending in And?" Is it more or less definite?
2. Does the ending of this poem clarify its meaning? Do the endings of other poems in this chapter clarify meaning? Do you want the end of a poem to somehow clarify or sum up the whole poem? Explain.

This poem would be quite different and not nearly as strong if it ended "I will move / when the fish does." The emphasis of "move" and "moves" not only links the fish and man more closely, but the sound of the word turns into something like an order, "Move, move!" But the transfixed beings in the poem are still.

Poe's "Ulalume" is often cited as a prominent example of repetend. Here are a few lines:

> The skies they were ashen and sober:
>   The leaves they were crisped and sere—
>   The leaves they were withering and sere—
> It was night in the lonesome October
>   Of my most immemorial year;
> It was hard by the dim lake of Auber,
>   In the misty mid region of Weir—
> It was down by the dank tarn of Auber,
>   In the ghoul-haunted woodland of Weir.

Poe's repetition of "they were," "The leaves they were," "and sere," and so on is extreme and the poem is melodramatic and gloomy, though these are not necessarily qualities of repetend. Poe's use of the device emphasizes the dramatic qualities in the poem. In modern poetry, repetend is apt to be used more lightly and naturally. After all, common sounds and words reappear even in *non-poetic* speech.

Sometimes the simple **repetition** of sounds within lines is enough to give a poem a musical, unified feeling. In Judith Root's "The Rose and the Serpent," a poem about aging, unrhymed lines incorporating informal repetition of sounds and leading to a rhymed closure create an improvised structure. Notice the way in which the title draws attention to the contrasting images and thus to the structure and meaning of the poem.

The Rose and the Serpent

I want to shed them all,
my lives, like skin,

sink below 30
and catch the spark
that brought me here

instead

of boxed and scented
like a rose my mother
picked and tended.

JUDITH ROOT

1. Look for examples of alliteration in the poem. Do the repeated sounds cluster together or are they scattered throughout the poem?
2. What kind of rhyme is represented by "scented" and "tended"?
3. How does the **sound structure** of the poem reflect content? For example, are the first five lines snakelike in any way? Are the last three more "boxed"? Can you find any other example of form reflecting content?

Implicit in the discussion of structure has been the idea of the line break. Traditional forms break the line after the appropriate number of feet—say, once every five feet in iambic pentameter. But free verse is improvisational, and one of its distinguishing features is the line of variable length. The poet varies the rhythms and sound patterns for desired effect, rather than following a set pattern. But since that would also describe prose, how do we distinguish between prose and free verse?

There are differences. Like other kinds of poetry, free verse is rhythmically focused and calculated. Line breaks are used for emphasis. There may be internal rhymes or alliteration, but above all the poet tries to hear the rhythms in the language. Consider such lines as these:

I celebrate myself and sing myself
And what I assume you shall assume,
For every atom belonging to me as good belongs to you.

I loafe and invite my soul,
I lean and loafe at my ease observing a spear of summer grass.

Although these lines from Walt Whitman's "Song of Myself" do not have regular meter, they certainly have patterns of stress or accent. Even the pause at the end of each line is part of the poem's rhythm. Incidentally, Whitman also uses repetend. Unlike Stafford's and Thomas's free-verse poems, poems by Whitman commonly use very long lines with pauses or stops at the ends of lines, rather than enjambment or run-on.

One idea about free verse that has been expressed is that the line breaks represent pauses for breath. Obviously that cannot always be true, since free verse is sometimes written in short lines, unless we believe that the poets were short of breath. As we saw in Williams's "Poem," at the beginning of the chapter, the lines were short and the line breaks arose organically. There does seem to be a relationship, however, between the breath and line breaks in Whitman.

But to think of the breath line only in terms of the long line would be a mistake. There is always a physical sense of the breath in the formation of words, and the end of any line of poetry, even a short one, evokes that physical sense, whether it is a deep breath, an exhalation, or a sort of catch, barely perceptible.

To develop a sense of effective line breaks in free verse, you might practice on prose, as in **found poetry** (Chapter 8). Can you break up the lines in a prose passage to emphasize rhythms inherent in the language? Or try to rearrange as prose examples of poems presented earlier. Does it matter whether the following are broken into lines or not?

I'm a shouting woman I'm a speech woman
I'm an atmosphere woman I'm an airtight
woman I'm a flesh woman I'm a flexible woman

ANNE WALDMAN
From "Fast Speaking Woman" (Chapter 3)

A snake came to my water-trough on a hot, hot day, and I
in pyjamas for the heat, to drink there. In the deep, strange-scented
shade of the great dark carob-tree I came down the steps
with my pitcher and must wait, must stand and wait, for there
he was at the trough before me.

D. H. LAWRENCE
From "Snake" (Chapter 4)

Could you line out the poems according to their original breaks just by looking at these passages? The Waldman poem would be easier than the Lawrence poem, of course, once you realized her system. The mid-sentence capital letters that appeared at the beginning of lines in "Snake" have been changed to small letters, to eliminate that clue. In modern poetry it is not as common as it once was to use capital letters at the beginning of each line. Capital letters at the beginning of a line reinforce an artificiality and serve to call attention to the fact of the poem's being broken into poetic lines, whereas modern poetry tries to be less consciously "poetic" and to use the style and rhythms of prose in a poetic way.

A form that carries this idea to its logical conclusion is called the **prose poem.** Following are two examples of the prose poem, one by Russell Edson (see also Chapter 9) and the other by Vern Rutsala (see also Chapter 1).

Counting Sheep

A scientist has a test tube full of sheep. He wonders if he should try to shrink a pasture for them.

They are like grains of rice.

He wonders if it is possible to shrink something out of existence.

He wonders if the sheep are aware of their tininess, if they have any sense of scale. Perhaps they just think the test tube is a glass barn . . .

He wonders what he should do with them; they certainly have less meat and wool than ordinary sheep. Has he reduced their commercial value?

He wonders if they could be used as a substitute for rice, a sort of woolly rice . . .

He wonders if he just shouldn't rub them into a red paste between his fingers.

He wonders if they're breeding, or if any of them have died.

He puts them under a microscope and falls asleep counting them . . .

RUSSELL EDSON

Sleeping

Though winners are rarely declared this is an arduous contest
similar, some feel, to boxing. This fact can be readily corroborated
by simply looking at people who have just awakened. Look at their
red and puffy eyes, the dishevelled hair, the slow sore movements,
and their generally dazed appearance. Occasionally, as well, there
are those deep scars running across their cheeks. Clearly, if
appearances don't lie, they have been engaged in some damaging
and dangerous activity and furthermore have come out the losers.
If it's not dangerous—and you still have doubts—why do we hear
so often the phrase, *He died in his sleep?*

VERN RUTSALA

1. Would you describe these two works as poems? One more than the other?
   Analyze and explain the ways in which, in your opinion, these works are or
   are not poems.
2. Is form more important or less important than other features in defining what
   is or is not a poem?
3. What would be the difference between a prose poem and poetic prose?

Edson's "Counting Sheep" is broken into rather long lines, but it is
hard to tell whether we are to think of them as long lines or as short paragraphs, because they do not seem especially rhythmic. "He wonders" is
repeated several times. The poem is a series of images with variations. It
is compressed, but it seems more narrative than lyric.

Rutsala's "Sleeping" could be broken into lines easily enough:

Though winners are rarely declared
this is an arduous contest
similar, some feel, to boxing.

Even though there are no end rhymes, there are natural pauses in the
sense, rhythm, and punctuation. But this is not what makes it a prose
poem. The word "poem" applies because of the integration of idea and
structure, and because this structure incorporates evocative associations,

repetitions, and images. This takes us back to the idea that poetry is something that can be said in no other way, whether the way involves rhyme, meter, imagery, or any of the other elements of craft.

Very different from the prose poem, another example of improvised or open form is the following by Kenneth Patchen.

The Murder of Two Men by a Young Kid Wearing Lemon-colored Gloves

Wait.

                                        Wait.

                    Wait.

            Wait. Wait.

    Wait.

                                        Wait.

                    W a i t .

        Wait.

                        Wait.

                            Wait.

            Wait.

                            Wait.

    Wait.

            NOW.

                                KENNETH PATCHEN

---

1. Imagine that this is about a true event and that you are a newspaper reporter writing a story about that event. What would you have to change to turn the poem into a newspaper article? What would be lost in the transformation?
2. Does the spacing of Patchen's poem contribute to the way you would read this poem aloud? Does it add to the mood or feeling of the poem? Explain.

Patchen's title has more different words than all the rest of the poem and is an essential part of the work, not merely decoration. We have talked about titles in earlier chapters and noted how they can add to or change the meaning of a poem. Like closure, titles are a tricky and often important part of the form of a poem. The title sits up front and influences the way the reader approaches a poem. This alone makes some poets eschew titles, wanting to let the poem speak for itself without the interference of a title. Sometimes a title is also the first line of a poem. A poem may have a minimal title, such as "Poem" in the William Carlos Williams poem at the beginning of this chapter. Sometimes a poem in a particular form uses the title to call attention to the form, as in Phyllis McGinley's "Ballade" or Jan Mitchell's "Sestina, Winchell's Donut House," which appears later in this chapter. The title may call attention to an important feature of the poem, as in Stafford's "The Epitaph Ending in And." Often a title indicates some irony or twist in the poem itself, as in Paula Gunn Allen's "Taking a Visitor to See the Ruins." A title may simply announce the subject of the poem, as in "The End of the World" by MacLeish.

A title is not something to get hung up on, but you should remember that it provides an opportunity for shaping the reader's response, for establishing tone, and for giving necessary information. You may start off liking fancy titles and your taste may change to something low-keyed and deliberately self-effacing. If you find yourself struggling with titles, either enjoy the struggle or just use something simple, such as the first words or line of the poem, a simple subject announcement ("The Accident"), or even the time honored "Poem." If you're writing a group of poems on related subjects, come up with one title for the group and then number the various poems instead of giving titles.

On the other hand, if you want to get wild with your titles, do it. If you like the way it sets the mood, don't be afraid to give a poem a perfectly nonsensical, crazy title containing obscure references only you will recognize: "Quartet for Frogs on the Fourteenth Floor of the Library." It's your poem.

Following are several poems, each of them interesting for some different aspect of form.

Jim Harrison explores the **ghazal** form in this account of a son's feelings of self-doubt. A poet coming from a family of "honest farmers," he thinks of how he might vindicate his choice of career by becoming a county agent of poetry.

The ghazal (or Ghasel) was originally an Arabic or Persian poem written in rhymed couplets celebrating love. The ghazal has been so freely adapted to English language poetry that it can be described simply as a poem in unrhymed couplets with a certain passionate spirit or attitude. The number of couplets varies, from five or six to a dozen. The statement-break-statement-break pattern of the ghazal in English lends itself to a kind of emotional declaration.

As you read the following ghazal, notice how the speaker's mind seems to jump around, and yet a unified and complex emotion, blending shame, pride, hope, and despair, finally comes through.

II

I load my own shells and have a suitcase of pressed
cardboard. Naturally I'm poor and picturesque.

My father is dead and doesn't care if his vault leaks,
that his casket is cheap, his son a poet and a liar.

All the honest farmers in my family's past are watching
me through the barn slats, from the corncrib and hogpen.

Ghosts demand more than wives & teachers. I'll make a
"V" of my two books and plow a furrow in the garden.

And I want to judge the poetry table at the County Fair.
A new form, poems stacked in pyramids like prize potatoes.

This county agent of poetry will tell poets "more potash
& nitrogen, the rows are crooked and the field limp, depleted."

JIM HARRISON

---

1. How do the pauses between the couplets affect the reading of the poem? For example, do the pauses imply breaks in thought, changes of feeling, or unspoken implications? What would change if there were no breaks between the couplets?
2. Does the order of the couplets matter? Try mixing them around to see what happens in the poem.

In the following poem, William Butler Yeats uses rhyme and repetition to give his poem a musical quality. Because the poem tells a story about fantastic events in an old-fashioned natural setting, it also has characteristics of a folk **ballad.** The child in the poem is invited to leave the human world with all its beauty and sorrow and go to live in fairyland. The hypnotic repetition of the refrain and the realistic details and place names of the human world take the reader through a complete transformation of feeling.

The Stolen Child

Where dips the rocky highland
Of Sleuth Wood in the lake,
There lies a leafy island
Where flapping herons wake
The drowsy water-rats;
There we've hid our faery vats,
Full of berries
And of reddest stolen cherries.
Come away, O human child!
To the waters and the wild

With a faery, hand in hand,
For the world's more full of weeping than you can understand.

Where the wave of moonlight glosses
The dim grey sands with light,
Far off by furthest Rosses
We foot it all the night,
Weaving olden dances,
Mingling hands and mingling glances
Till the moon has taken flight;
To and fro we leap
And chase the frothy bubbles,
While the world is full of troubles
And is anxious in its sleep.
Come away, O human child!
To the waters and the wild
With a faery, hand in hand,
For the world's more full of weeping than you can understand.

Where the wandering water gushes
From the hills above Glen-Car,
In pools among the rushes
That scarce could bathe a star,
We seek for slumbering trout
And whispering in their ears
Give them unquiet dreams;
Leaning softly out
From ferns that drop their tears
Over the young streams.
Come away, O human child!
To the waters and the wild
With a faery, hand in hand,
For the world's more full of weeping than you can understand.

Away with us he's going,
The solemn-eyed:
He'll hear no more the lowing
Of the calves on the warm hillside
Or the kettle on the hob

Sing peace into his breast,
Or see the brown mice bob
Round and round the oatmeal-chest.
For he comes, the human child,
To the waters and the wild
With a faery, hand in hand,
From a world more full of weeping than he can understand.

WILLIAM BUTLER YEATS

1. Make notations of Yeats's rhyme scheme. Are his end rhymes regular or irregular?
2. You will notice that each stanza begins with alternating rhymes and then shifts to rhyming couplets. Is there a change of pace or feeling that goes with the change in rhyming?
3. Are there any exceptions to the rhyme pattern noted in the preceding question? Are there other irregularities in the form, such as the number of lines in each stanza or the number of stressed syllables in each line?
4. How does our understanding of the repeated lines at the end of each stanza change throughout the poem?

Ballads can be an appealing form for the modern poet who has a story to tell and wants to try an alternative to free verse. Although the traditional ballad stanza is a four-line stanza consisting of alternating four- and three-stress lines, the ballad is flexible enough to include a variety of musical story poems. Rhyme, repetition of a refrain, themes of love and death, images of nature—these are a few of the common characteristics of the ballad. For another example of the ballad in modern form, see Helen Adam's "I Love My Love" in Chapter 9. Classic examples of the anonymous folk ballad are the Scottish border ballads such as "Twa Corbies" and "Lord Randall." Remember also that contemporary popular songs are sometimes called ballads, a definition which particularly fits the storytelling country-and-western or love song.

It's hard to describe exactly the emotional effect of rhyme, though it is usually, certainly, a musical quality. In the following poem, however, Philip Larkin uses consonant rhyme in a way that is not musical at all. In fact, the reader can almost hear the poet spitting out the repeated sounds in disgust. As you read "Toads," consider whether this effect is actually inherent in his choice of repeated sounds or is simply the result of what he says influencing the sound of the poem.

Toads

Why should I let the toad *work*
    Squat on my life?
Can't I use my wit as a pitchfork
    And drive the brute off?

Six days of the week it soils
    With its sickening poison—
Just for paying a few bills!
    That's out of proportion.

Lots of folk live on their wits:
    Lecturers, lispers,
Losels, loblolly-men, louts—
    They don't end as paupers;

Lots of folk live up lanes
    With fires in a bucket,
Eat windfalls and tinned sardines—
    They seem to like it.

Their nippers have got bare feet,
    Their unspeakable wives
Are skinny as whippets—and yet
    No one actually *starves*.

Ah, were I courageous enough
    To shout *Stuff your pension!*
But I know, all too well, that's the stuff
    That dreams are made on;

For something sufficiently toad-like
Squats in me, too;
Its hunkers are heavy as hard luck,
And cold as snow,

And will never allow me to blarney
My way to getting
The fame and the girl and the money
All at one sitting.

I don't say, one bodies the other
One's spiritual truth;
But I do say it's hard to lose either,
When you have both.

PHILIP LARKIN

---

1. What kinds of rhymes does Larkin use at the ends of most or all of his lines? Are they mainly vowel or consonant rhymes or both?
2. Describe the way "Toads" looks on the page. What are some things you notice visually about the way the poem is organized?
3. Notice where the periods and semicolons appear in the poem. Are the lines mainly end-stopped or enjambed?
4. Count the syllables in the lines of the poem. Is there a pattern in numbers of syllables to each line?
5. Try to scan the meter of the lines. Are they metrical? Is there a predominant meter in the lines? If so, what is it? If not, is there a regular number of stressed syllables in each line regardless of the number of unstressed syllables?

A challenging form which adapts itself readily to poetry in English is the **sestina,** a form consisting of seven stanzas. There are six seven-line stanzas with a pattern of repeated words at the end of lines. A seventh three-line stanza includes the repeated words, three of them in the middle of lines and three at the ends. As you look at Jan Clausen's sestina, notice where the words "morning," "grease," "pink," "light," "change," and "alone" reappear in different order in each of the stanzas.

Sestina, Winchell's Donut House

Watching the black hours through to morning,
I'd set out each successive tray of grease-
cooked donuts on the rack, chocolate and pink-
frosted, to harden beneath the fluorescent light,
talk to crazy Harry, count the change,
listen to top-forty radio. Mostly, I was alone.

Every stranger's suspect when you're alone.
A woman was beaten badly early one morning
by a man who sneaked in the back while she made change,
so I'd rehearse scenarios of scooping grease,
flinging it at the assailant's face, cooking the light
or dark flesh to curl away at the impact, angry pink.

The cab drivers came in every night, faces polished pink
and boyish, arriving in pairs or alone.
Their cabs clotted like moths at the building's light.
They were outlaws and brothers, despised men who rise
    in the morning.
They'd swagger, still dapper if fattened on sweets and grease,
call me sugar and honey. I smiled. I kept the change.

Often I was too busy to see the darkness change,
flush from black to blue to early pink.
At four o'clock, my face smeared with grease,
I think I was happiest, although most alone.
The harder hours were those of fullblown morning,
fighting depression, sleeping alone in the light.

Linda came in at six, awash with light,
businesslike, making sure there'd be enough change
to get her through the rigors of the morning.
She had a hundred uniforms; I remember pink.
Sometimes she'd cheat, leave me to work alone,
sneak out to flirt in parked cars, fleeing lifetimes of grease.

I can see her cranking the hopper, measuring grease,
indefatigable, wired on coffee, just stopping to light
her cigarettes. She didn't want to be alone.
It was only my fantasy that she could change,
stop wearing that silly, becoming pink.
burn free of the accidents, husband and children, some morning.

I remember walking home those mornings, smelling of grease,
amazed in summer's most delicate pink early light,
to shower, change, and sleep out the hot day alone.

JAN CLAUSEN

---

1. There is a system for rotating the end words in each stanza of a sestina. Can you determine what the system is from this example? Be sure to find all the repeated words in the last three lines.
2. Although the same words appear at the end of lines, do they always mean the same thing? Look at one of the words throughout the poem, "change" for example. What does it mean in each stanza?

Both Larkin and Clausen use run-on or enjambed lines to provide flow within structured poems. Enjambment is a way of adding counterpoint and flow to a poem. In the following example, notice how Seamus Heaney plays off the regularity of stanzas and meter against the loosely structured and enjambed sentences and unrhymed lines. When he does introduce end rhyme, it has a particularly poignant effect.

Mid-Term Break

I sat all morning in the college sick bay
Counting bells knelling classes to a close.
At two o'clock our neighbours drove me home.

In the porch I met my father crying—
He had always taken funerals in his stride—
And Big Jim Evans saying it was a hard blow.

The baby cooed and laughed and rocked the pram
When I came in, and I was embarrassed
By old men standing up to shake my hand

And tell me they were 'sorry for my trouble'.
Whispers informed strangers I was the eldest,
Away at school, as my mother held my hand

In hers and coughed out angry tearless sighs.
At ten o'clock the ambulance arrived
With the corpse, stanched and bandaged by the nurses.

Next morning I went up into the room. Snowdrops
And candles soothed the bedside; I saw him
For the first time in six weeks. Paler now,

Wearing a poppy bruise on his left temple,
He lay in the four foot box as in his cot.
No gaudy scars, the bumper knocked him clear.

A four foot box, a foot for every year.

SEAMUS HEANEY

---

1. Are more of these lines enjambed or end-stopped? Overall, does this give the poem a flowing or tightly controlled feeling?
2. Are there rhymes at the end of any of the lines? Slant rhymes or half rhymes?
3. Although they are not as pronounced as end rhymes, repeated sounds within lines may work as internal rhymes. Are there any repeated sounds or internal rhymes in the poem? For example, the poem starts with "I." How many times do you hear that sound repeated throughout the poem?
4. Are there other sound repetitions, such as alliteration, occurring throughout the poem?

5. Would you describe the form of "Mid-Term Break" as formal or informal? Explain.
6. How does the rhyme at the end give a sense of closure?

A set form from another culture is the Japanese **haiku**. Although Japanese and English are very different languages, the succinct imagery and form of the haiku have engaged and inspired many English-language poets of the twentieth century. The haiku is an unrhymed **syllabic form,** meaning that it is determined by counting syllables rather than metrical feet. Traditionally the Japanese haiku deals with nature and, by some surprising image or juxtaposition, startles the reader into insight. Western writers have taken liberties with the form and reinterpreted it in various ways. Following are two interesting variations by American poet Sonia Sanchez. In one she addresses "love." Even more unconventionally, in the other she deals with the subject of racial equality and public bathrooms. Though her images are not of nature, she does provoke the reader into a fresh viewpoint while working within the traditional syllabic form.

never may my thirst
for freedom be appeased by
modern urinals.

SONIA SANCHEZ

Haiku

if i had known, if
i had known you, i would have
left my love at home.

SONIA SANCHEZ

---

1. How many syllables are in each line of these two poems?

2. Does your expectation of what "Haiku" is about change in the short space of the three lines?
3. What emotion do you feel from Sanchez's juxtaposition of the words "thirst for freedom" and "urinals"? Does that feeling support the statement she makes?
4. Have you read haiku elsewhere? Were they like these poems or different? Explain.

In terms of form, this last example is more related to the first poem in this chapter, William Carlos Williams's "Poem," than to any of the other poems in this section, although it is much longer and perhaps the relationship between form and content is more difficult to interpret. William Meredith writes about the death of a loved one, a death which he compares to someone taking back a Christmas present. The mood of the poem is both playful and sorrowful, sweet and grim.

Give and Take

(Christmas, after a death in the family)

What are these presents   Look how many
have come unwrapped   & the stockings
tight with tangerines & kisses
& heavy Swiss things   deserved &
undeserved & deserved again
before you can open them   Look
they are stolen by little unwrappers
who whisper at dawn   who
come downstairs in their bed-clothes
to loot & grow older & us

Presence of love in this house
gifts of it   words of it
words for giving assent   about taking too
taking too much   Tell the children not to
Why not   tell ourselves not to
it is more blessed not to   but we take
naturally   we take to one another

wrapped in flesh tinsel & tissue   we are all
gaudy rejoicers in taking   two's   those two
we two   some alone   some alone

It's about time   & about love   both
this impatience to unwrap   to wrap
arms around airy expensive unholdable
things   Swiss chocolate kisses & pine
trees or spruce   one another
Often we're shiny & wanted
Tinsel is cheap   We believe it
It wouldn't glisten without eyes

No one in the whole world was ever bad
we lie   greedy or not   Hurry up   unwrap
this love is for you   where's mine
Hug the world now & thank it

Because over it hangs like our green wreath
a black wreath   a prescience
of days coming to some end
Not all spruce-smell & singing is gay
Some are not here

Boxes gape open   compartments of time
Is it nicely snowing outside this snug room
or do we stand suddenly in an autumn field
Who is the one in the box   Will God unwrap her
gladly & tell her the rest
after we've tied her up grassily
& told her goodnight   Lie still now
we've told her   God will be glad
at what we've thought of to bring him
He who has everything   sooner or later

It's hard giving people   Lucky is our habit
Are we lucky   still clutching here   losing
& trying to give back to the indian-giver
while the dark wreath reminds on the door

Just now in the early twilight
how dark the hemlock wreath
already unchristmassed
& these are not mechanical Swiss things
we are asked to rewrap & return
We do it as well as we can
but we're small thieves by nature　　& keepers

In the autumn field where we left her
stands a distant insatiable relative
waiting to take what is his　　to ease us
or torture us　　which　　into a box
where we'll lie still　　still murmuring
give me　　*love me*　　smaller & smaller
asking in a voice of tiny unwrapping
astonishment　　*mine*　　*is it really for me*

WILLIAM MEREDITH

---

1. Meredith uses no conventional punctuation in the poem. Is it possible to recognize beginnings and endings of sentences? How do we know how to read the poem?
2. What purpose do the spaces within the lines seem to serve?
3. Some of the sentences or statements in the poem seem truncated or incomplete, such as "tell ourselves not to" in the second stanza and "to ease us / or torture us　　which" in the last stanza. What sort of rhythm is Meredith building with these truncated statements, with the line breaks, and with the spaces within the lines? How does that rhythm fit the subject of the poem "Give and Take?
4. Would you call this a formal or informal poem?
5. What sort of closure does Meredith use? Is it very definite, open-ended, soft? Does it change the way we read the rest of the poem? What does closure here do for the poem?

There are so many possibilities of form in poetry, it really doesn't have to come down to a choice between formal or informal, closed or open, or any of the other terms that have been used to describe the dichotomy of differing approaches to form in poetry. Certainly experiments with form should go farther than merely alternating between the sonnet and completely free verse. The recent movement to a **new formalism** shows that poets are always looking for some sort of challenge. The movement asserts both a concern for solid grounding in the craft of poetry and an interest in seeing what new things can be done within the constraints of older forms. However, this does not mean that writers are suddenly going to start writing imitations of fifteenth-century verse. Even though they may use the conventions of the past they are bound to do something to make them new. Moreover, there is no sign of poets' giving up on free verse. Within the improvised and organic form, there is abundant room for experimentation, for music, for tension and complexity and counterpoint.

Some Useful References

There is too little space here to give anything like a full treatment of the subject of form in poetry. There are whole books devoted to the subject. A useful one is Lewis Turco's *The New Book of Forms: A Handbook of Poetics* (Hanover University Press of New England, 1986), which catalogs forms according to the number of their lines. The book includes all the well-known forms, such as the sonnet, the villanelle, the sestina, the Japanese haiku, and also some odd ones such as Welsh forms whose names you may be at a loss to pronounce. There are also notes on *prosody* and a bibliography of contemporary examples. This book will intrigue and challenge anyone inclined to write in forms.

The Longman Dictionary of Poetic Terms by Jack Myers and Michael Simms (Longman, 1989) has excellent, substantial definitions and discussions of various poetry topics including forms. This dictionary makes interesting reading under a wide variety of topics. Appendices in the back list and categorize terms found alphabetically arranged in the main part of the book and provide good browsing.

A Dictionary of Literary Terms and Literary Theory by J. A. Cuddon (Blackwell Reference, 3rd edition 1991) is a nice fat book about literature in general and thus contains many useful definitions and discussions of poetry including questions of form and forms.

Miller William's *Patterns of Poetry, An Encyclopedia of Forms* (Louisiana State University Press, 1986) gives clear illustrations and examples and is all-around good reading with many examples of entire poems. William Packard's *The Poet's Dictionary, A Handbook of Prosody and Poetic Devices* (Harper and Row, 1989) is also useful.

Rhyming dictionaries are not necessary for writing poetry. Still, there's something intriguing about a rhyming dictionary, something that appeals to the writer's playful side. You can use a rhyming dictionary, or any other dictionary for that matter, to collect interesting-sounding words to give you ideas for poems. A rhyming dictionary is also sometimes useful in writing **light verse** when one wants to study an array of options that might not normally come to mind. For anyone who loves words there is something fascinating about seeing the language broken down and categorized by sound. I recommend *The Penguin Rhyming Dictionary,* compiled with the help of a computer from an extensive list of "phonetic transcriptions . . . extracted from a standard dictionary data base." Sound groups are easy to find through the index. Obscure words are briefly defined. It's fun to scan even if you don't want to write rhymed poetry. Another choice that is generally available in libraries is *The Complete Rhyming Dictionary* by Clement Wood. This older rhyming dictionary has recently been republished in a new revised edition (Ronald Bogus and John Duff, Doubleday, 1991). A visit to your library will no doubt turn up others.

Two other references are worth mentioning. The first is a general handbook of literary terms, *A Handbook to Literature,* Hugh Holman and William Harmon (Macmillan 1986). Although the text is not limited to poetry, many of the entries have to do with poetry and provide clear, brief explanations of terms and forms.

The second book is involved with theories of poetry. The *Princeton Encyclopedia of Poetry and Poetics* (Princeton University Press 1974), edited by Alex Preminger, is not a writing book but is rather a scholarly encyclopedia in one volume. It is a full and fascinating reference book for the writer as well as the scholar. Among topics as varied as "Polish Prosody," "Icelandic Poetry," and "Interpretation," the writer will find authoritative essays on various aspects of the craft of poetry.

Remember, there are no absolute laws of poetry. There is, however, a long and abundant tradition, and you are free to use it, build on it, or rebel against it.

Suggestions for Writing

1.   Write a poem about the physical action of an animal in which the form of the poem somehow matches the content.

2.   Write a poem about some other sort of movement, such as by trees in a storm, a person stretching and waking up, a car crash, or a jet

plane taking off. Use one of these subjects or invent your own. Sound elements, line breaks, and rhythms should all work to add to the sense.

3. Write a poem that is a variation on one of the sonnet forms, but change one of the structural elements—either rhyme pattern, meter, or stanza breaks—to create a variant sonnet. Try to make the poem sound modern rather than traditional.

4. Write a poem in a traditional French or Italian form such as the villanelle or the sestina. Here are their definitions:

   Villanelle. Nineteen lines of any length in five three-line stanzas and a final quatrain, with two rhymes and two refrains. Remember, two refrains means that two lines are repeated throughout the poem. Here is the rhyme scheme, with the refrain lines in capitals and designated as 1 and 2: A^1 b A^2, a b A^1, a b A^2, a b A^1, a b A^2, a b A^1 A^2. Start by getting the two refrain lines. Literally write the refrains on the specified lines, mark the required rhymes on the other lines, and try to fill in the spaces. This sounds mechanical, but it eases the construction. (See Dylan Thomas's "Do Not Go Gentle into That Good Night," Chapter 12.)

   Sestina. Thirty-nine lines of any length, divided into six sestets and one triplet. The sestina is not rhymed but instead the six end words of the lines in stanza 1 are repeated as end words in a specific order throughout the poem to give a sense of unity. In the final three-line stanza three of these end words appear at the ends of the lines and the others appear within the lines. Here the letters represent repeated words, not rhymes.
   A B C D E F, F A E B D C, C F D A B E, E C B F A D, D E A C F B, B D F E C A, E C A
   The words *B, D,* and *F* occur within the last three lines, which end with the words *E, C,* and *A.*

5. Write a poem with long lines. Determine the length of the lines by making them one of these:
   a) The longest lines possible sustaining some regular meter
   b) Long, irregular lines broken at a pause for breath

6. Write a poem with an invented hidden structure. For example: the first letter of each line spells out a word or statement (an acrostic); or the last word of each line is the first word of the next line.

7. Write a prose poem that seems very "poetic" to you even though it does not have rhyme or meter.

8. Write a poem that seems like prose except that it is broken into lines.

9. How many rhymes can you work into a free-verse poem without the rhymes becoming too obvious? Try it (with internal rhyme, slant rhyme, beginning rhyme, and consonant rhyme, especially).

10. Write a poem using an *a b a b, c d c d, e f e f* pattern for the stanzas and rhyme, but use consonant rhyme instead of vowel rhyme.

11. Write a sonnet with a conventional rhyme scheme. Then, rearrange the sonnet so that the line breaks occur in unexpected places, rhymes come in the middle of lines, and so on. Can you disguise the fact that it is a sonnet?

12. Write a free-verse poem using repetend. You can improvise as you go along, or try something like this: Run your sentences past line breaks; in each new sentence use a word or image from somewhere near the end of the preceding sentence, to create a pattern of interlocking words or images.

13. Use enjambment. Write a poem that is all one sentence, or a poem that gives a feeling of rushing or excitement. Or use enjambment in a first-person poem to give the speaker's monologue a headlong feeling.

14. Write a poem using a series of discrete couplets, as in the ghazal.

15. Write a poem using three-line stanzas to give the poem a flowing, forward, nonstop feeling. Experiment with both end-stopped and run-on lines and stanzas.

16. Choose a poem you've already written and revise it by giving it different kinds of closure such as: a) a couplet summing up the overall idea; b) an enigmatic off-the-wall last line; c) two or three lines using several words that occur elsewhere in the poem; d) a truncated ending, that is, one in which you cut off some lines which you originally considered necessary to end the poem.

17. Make a list of titles you could give a) poems you haven't written, or b) poems you've written and called something else. Try both fancy and plain titles. Think about how a title makes you feel about your own poems.

7

Configuration and Revision

Sometimes writing poetry is like looking for pictures in inkblots. The inkblot itself is not a specific pictorial representation of anything, but an individual will see two cats fighting, a child eating an ice cream cone, a scary face, and so on.

In finding material for a poem, the inkblot approach might work like this. You burn your toast at breakfast. You are late for an appointment. You read in the paper about someone who has missed an airplane but later learns the plane was involved in a hijack attempt. Your work goes badly all day. Some people invite you to go out with them after work, but you go home instead with a bad headache. There, you find that an old friend from out of town is waiting for you. Finding your friend after work, you feel like the person who missed the airplane, upset at first but later realizing it was the best thing after all. The day's events could inspire a poem about bad timing, the comforts of friendship, and burnt toast as a sacrifice to the gods of chance.

Such a sequence, of course, does not represent everything that happens in a day. There would be much more from which to select, and many different interpretations might arise from the "inkblot" of events. But the fascinating thing about such perceptions is that, as a necessary part of being human, we focus on some details, ignore others, and seek to make meaningful connections between events.

This human capacity to see pattern is at the heart of the creative process. Even when there is no inherent pattern, we look for one. Lewis Carroll's Alice struggles with the riddle: how is a raven like a writing desk? It is a frustrating riddle because it has no answer. But still, we could invent an answer. We are unsatisfied with randomness and incongruity. Just as we trace constellations in the stars and use a camera's lens to put a

131

frame around eternity, we write poems in order to make life memorable, meaningful, and coherent. Is there a pattern to what happens to us in any one day? If we think about it for a while, we start manufacturing one. The question virtually creates the answer. And once a pattern is seen, it will in some real sense exist.

All of the above involves the idea of pattern or *configuration,* a concept of *Gestalt* psychology, which claims that the nature of the parts is determined by, and secondary to, the whole. This is a very powerful idea in the hands of a poet. Recall that in Chapter 2, we dealt with early memory and how it takes on meaning when viewed later in life; Chapter 3 explored how presenting things in sequence gives them a connection.

Working at poetry through the idea of configurations means keeping open to possibilities. The journal or notebook suggested in Chapter 2 is a good place to start. (If you have not been keeping a journal or notebook, perhaps begin one now.) Read through the random notes, reflections, and anecdotes in your journal and look for some pattern or grouping. If you cannot find a pattern, arbitrarily select five different items and write a poem in which you *force* them to make sense, that is, connect the dots. When you finish, you will be surprised. Five arbitrary observations *can* become a coherent statement. It is a matter of emphasis, perception, and arrangement—a perfectly valid way of finding meaning and order.

This means that it can often be a good idea to plunge into a poem without always knowing for certain where you are going. It also means that different writers will pare away and shape material in different ways. it is good to remember that while revision and paring are often necessary, it is also possible to revise the vitality out of a poem. Some poems are decidedly explicit, while others remain ambiguous, and still others seem to have been torn ragged out of the imaginative universe and framed.

Compare the ways in which the poets make the separate parts cohere in the following poems. Robert Bly's "Mourning Pablo Neruda" flows like the water that Bly describes. The title informs the configuration, but the associative quality of the poem lets its meaning expand beyond the title.

Mourning Pablo Neruda

> Water is practical,
> especially

in August, water
fallen
into the buckets
I carry
to the young willow trees
whose leaves
have been eaten off
by grasshoppers.
Or this jar of water
that lies
next to me
on the carseat
as I drive to my shack.
When I look down,
the seat all around the jar
is dark,
for water doesn't intend
to give,
it gives anyway,

and the jar of water
lies there quivering
as I drive
through a countryside
of granite quarries,
stones soon
to be shaped
into blocks for the dead,
the only thing
they have left
that is theirs.

For the dead remain
inside us, as water
remains
in granite—
hardly at all—
for their job is to go away,
and not come back,

even when we ask them.
But water comes
to us,
it doesn't care
about us, it goes
around us, on the way
to the Minnesota River,
to the Mississippi,
to the Gulf,
always closer
to where
it has to be.
No one lays flowers
on the grave
of water,
for it is not
here,
it is gone.

ROBERT BLY

---

1. What are some of the individual images in the poem? That is, what are some of the concrete things the speaker mentions? What are some of the different actions he takes note of?
2. What is one image that comes up again and again in the poem?
3. How does the title inform or change our understanding of the poem? How does the poem expand our understanding of the title?

Both of Lawson Inada's poems, following, show him looking for pattern, meaning, configurations in everyday life. In "Garbage," he moves from literal description to a self-descriptive metaphor to generalizations about disgust, love, and self-love. The doctor in "In These Times" says, "You're laughing too much." As we try to make sense of the jump from this to the declaration of love, the meaning of the poem comes clear as a statement about the speaker's life.

Garbage

I

Something has scattered my garbage—

the can I keep for cans,
bags, bones, wrappings . . .

These are in the driveway—
gnawed on, slimy . . .

It might have been an actual kind of animal,

for in this creeked ravine
the park repeats the watershed,
the flagrant hills above.

One can easily be displaced.

The sun stuns me with its headlight
this frosty Oregon morning,

hunched over garbage in a red
sweatshirt with the numbed,
naked face

and desperate appendages of an orangutan.

II

There is washing to be done:

the apparatus hums with suds in the cellar;
the dishes are stacked . . .

There was slime on my fingers
this morning, scooping up garbage . . .

And if the drains reacted,
spewing back the mucous . . .

Even after an eloquent meal
that faint sensation

hovers over the juice and gristle.

How do we love one another

if even our selves disgust?

LAWSON INADA

---

1. At what points in the poem does Inada move from simply describing a distasteful event to generalizing about the human condition?
2. How are parts I and II of "Garbage" alike and how are they different? Could these two parts of the poem be called variations on a theme? What would be lacking from the poem if either part I or II were deleted?

In These Times

Lately, my front teeth have been aching,
and my lips are always rough.
The doctor says: "You're laughing too much."

And that's how much I love my only son.

LAWSON INADA

---

1. List the things mentioned in this poem. What are the connections between them?
2. How would the poem change if Inada were to say, "Because I love my only son so much / I laugh all the time. / This makes my lips dry / and my teeth hurt"? Is this version clearer or less clear? More interesting or less? More pleasing or less? Explain.
3. How does this poem fit the proposition that unsaid things are as important as the things that are said in poetry?

In *Asian Figures,* W. S. Merwin has adapted aphorisms, riddles, and proverbs from Asian literature. In the introduction to the collection Merwin is careful to explain that he does not know oriental languages but depends on translations and advice from others, which he adapts freely in his own words. By grouping different "figures" together, even though each is complete in itself, Merwin suggests connections or continuity. Sometimes, as in the consonant rhyme of "tiger" and "matter" in the poem "Chinese Figures," below, continuity arises through sound. Some of the discrete statements seem as if they might be read continuously, such as "A liar / an egg in mid-air / Poisons him / and charges him for it." Even the ambiguous statements challenge us for meaning. What, for example, are we to make of the last image: "Write a bad dream / on a south wall / the sun will turn it into a promise"? Does a bad dream disappear when the sun moves so that the wall falls into shadow? Do bad dreams disappear on the following night? Or is something implied about the morning sun? or that bad dreams will come true, or that something bad can be turned into good? Although it is sometimes dangerous for the reader to read too much into poems, the ambiguities involve the reader in the creative act, by this very faculty of configurative perception.

Chinese Figures (Third Series)

Seventh month
sharpens the mosquito's mouth

The little snow stops the plows
the big snow stops the river boats.

Set out in an evening
of mist

Long ago famous for learning
now nothing but a common
god in a village

Old peasant sees statue
asks How
did it grow

Old peasant sees stilt walker
says Half of him
isn't human

Old man's harvest
brought home in one hand

Just because you're cured
don't think you'll live

If it's dirty work
borrow the tools

O locusts
just eat
the neighbor's fields

Tell a man
that you'd thought him much younger
and that his clothes look expensive

Poisons himself
to poison the tiger

In every family
something's the matter

That isn't a man
it's a bean on a straw

A liar
an egg in mid-air

Poisons him
and charges him for it

Don't tease
a nine-tailed fox

Rat falls
into the flour jar
white eyes rolling

Too stingy
to open his eyes

Wheat found for nothing
and the devil the miller

He'll grow up to be a clown
third class

Even the gods lose
when they gamble

Heart like fifteen water-buckets
seven rising
eight going down

Write a bad dream
on a south wall
the sun will turn it into a promise

W. S. MERWIN

---

1. Merwin uses the word "figures" to describe these short poems. Look up the
    word "figure" in a good dictionary and try to decide which of the meanings
    he has in mind.
2. How has Merwin used line breaks to make an impression on the reader? For
    example, is there a change in your understanding of the poem that takes place
    from one line to another? Does the second or third line of a figure turn the
    meaning around somehow?
3. Is it easy or difficult to say what this work is about? Can you enjoy it with-
    out completely understanding it?
4. Can you imagine adding some sort of last line or couplet telling the reader
    the main idea of this poem, a message? How would such an addition change
    the poem?

John Ashbery gives the reader very little help in understanding his poems. Thus "The Couple in the Next Room" may lack denotative sense, and we may be like the naive museumgoer who stands in front of an abstract painting and says, "Looks like a cow to me," when the point of the painting is its form and color. Yet, even here, there does appear to be pattern, configurations: "blue drapes," "an iron-blue chamber"; "a star," "rising behind the stars"; "names from the turn of the century," "great graves," "a slab of business"; "she," "they," "a boy," "hers." "we." Does this poem "mean" or "be"? Even if the poem is like an abstract painting, we will continue to look for an interpretation.

The Couple in the Next Room

She liked the blue drapes. They made a star
At the angle. A boy in leather moved in.
Later they found names from the turn of the century
Coming home one evening. The whole of being
Unknown absorbed into the stalk. A free
Bride on the rails warning to notice other
Hers and the great graves that outwore them
Like faces on a building, the lightning rod
Of a name calibrated all their musing differences.

Another day. Deliberations are recessed
In an iron-blue chamber of that afternoon
On which we wore things and looked well at
A slab of business rising behind the stars.

JOHN ASHBERY

---

1. In what sense is this poem like a *collage?*
2. Try to imagine this poem as a picture. What do you see?
3. Are there any words that stand out as odd, surprising, or puzzling to you? What do they suggest to you? Could they have more than one meaning? Could they have a different meaning for Ashbery than they have for you?
4. Try editing out various lines of the poem. Can you change the poem by such editing and still have what seems like a poem?

You will want to experiment with varying degrees of specificity in your poems. Are you trying to confine the pattern of ideas or images in a poem to a particular meaning, or do you expect the reader to see patterns you might not anticipate? Can you write a poem in which you use words as an abstract painter uses form and color, without denotation?

One of Ashbery's predecessors was Gertrude Stein, who experimented with treating language as abstraction and shaking it loose from its acquired contexts, connotations, and associations. An example of her work from *Tender Buttons* is included in Chapter 1; but try to look up the whole work, if you are not familiar with it. The novelty of her language is startling. Reading it for the first time, one staggers between contradictory impulses: the desire to interpret and the apparent impossibility of doing so.

In working on your own poetry, think about the following. Do you want or intend to control the ambiguities of language? to what extent? Are you trying to jar the reader's imagination into new configurations? Do you create a center from which the poem radiates like spokes or from which it moves outward like circles on a pond?

Revision is an important stage in finding pattern in poetry. Following is "Other Lives," a poem by Vern Rutsala, in drafts ranging from a notebook entry to its sixth and final draft. As you read through the different drafts, notice the various changes and their effect on the poem. Then compare version #1 and version #6 to see how alike or different they are.

#1 Notebook Entry

Idea: Other lives . . .
Overheard . . .
Dream of . . .
(Lives perfect as cliches
where every holiday
is met properly . . .)
In windows, walking . . .
Strangers . . .
In books, magazines . . .
No envy, just mystery
& the regret of never knowing
Lost in their certainty
Swimming in the perfection

of their manners, the exact
way they age—only getting
gray like actors in
a high school play——. . . .

DRAFT #1

1. Read this notebook entry, then look away from the page. What images or
    words stay in your memory?
2. How would you summarize the idea of this passage in a short phrase?

#2 Notebook

You see them from train windows
in little towns, single lights
on the midnight plains, the mysteries   outside cities,
of backyards. They come to life   a single
in gas stations as you're driving   family caught
through, exist in bits, overheard,   looking up.
glimpsed only once, figures
from dreams, memories too far back
to hold. You go out to all those
strange rooms, the airports, motels
fit for suicide, busrides through
dying landscapes. But there are all   Walking in
those drawn shades, the huddled   strange neigh-
taverns on the highway, cars nosed   borhoods you
in close together. Glimpsed this way   sense it out of
other lives grow sleek as daydreams,   the corner of
larger than they are, fed by   your eyes—the
mystery & the regret of never knowing.   amber win-
Some towns blink on like pictures   dows, the secret
from magazines and you feel   lives as un-
the people lost in certainty,   known as the
swimming in the perfection   furniture, the
of their manners, lives exact   unseen cars in
replicas of the calendar (an illustration)   their garages
& everything is believed.   . . .

~~They~~ age with precision, greying   (Such people)
like actors in a high school play
all else remains the same . . .
Lives where chrome is believed,
where questions are always answered.   Fantasy lives—

DRAFT #2

1. What are some new words and images introduced in this version? Has anything from #1 been left out?
2. Where is the speaker in version #2? Do you get a clearer sense of setting in the revision?
3. Try reading a few lines from #1 and #2 aloud. How has the sound of the poem changed in the second draft? Does it sound more like a poem than #1?

#3 Other Lives

You see them from train windows
in little towns, in single lights   ⟨ those
across   ~~on~~ the ~~midnight~~ plains.   Nebraska
the mysteries of backyards speeding by,
in a single ~~face~~ looking up,   figure
blurred and stiff as a ~~snapshot~~—   photograph
They come to life ~~briefly~~—   quickly
in gas stations as you drive through,
overheard, glimpsed only once,
families from dreams like memories
too far back to hold. Then they
snap shut, fall ~~away~~ into the past forever.
Still you go out to all those strange rooms,
You travel,   all those drawn shades, those huddled
sustained by   taverns on the highway, cars nosed in,
by their brev- so close they seem to touch.
ity, the lives All those secret lives in strange neighborhoods
are so short   you walk through . . .
you seem im-   Glimpsed this way other lives grow
mortal—you   sleek, larger than they are, fed by
feed on this. mystery and the regret of never knowing. (So brief)

and on the	Towns blink on like pictures from magazines,
hope that	the people swim in certainty,
somewhere	lost in the perfection of their manners,
people are as	and they age with precision, greying
you were told	like actors in a high school play . . .

DRAFT #3

1. How does Rutsala seem to be using the notes in the margins? Does he make changes from draft to draft which are not marked on an earlier draft?
2. When you revise your work, do you make marginal notes? Do you retype drafts after small changes or wait until you've handwritten most of your revisions on an earlier draft? Think about typing, handwritten notes, pencils and pens, cut and paste. How do you revise? Describe the physical act of revision as you do it.
3. Has anything from draft #2 been deleted in draft #3? If there are deletions, speculate on why Rutsala made them.
4. Is the tone of voice clearer or stronger in #3 than in the earlier drafts or about the same? Explain.

#4 *Other Lives*

You see them from train windows
in little towns, in those solitary lights
across t̶h̶e̶ Nebraska p̶l̶a̶i̶n̶s̶   all
in the mysteries of backyards in cities

a single figure looking up,
blurred and still as a photograph.
They come to life quickly
at gas stations, overheard in diners,

glimpsed only once, families from dreams
like memories too far back to hold.
T̶h̶e̶y̶ ̶t̶h̶e̶y̶ ̶s̶n̶a̶p̶ ̶s̶h̶u̶t̶,̶ ̶f̶a̶l̶l̶ ̶i̶n̶t̶o̶ ̶t̶h̶e̶ ̶p̶a̶s̶t̶
f̶o̶r̶e̶v̶e̶r̶,̶ ̶g̶o̶n̶e̶ ̶f̶o̶r̶ ̶g̶o̶o̶d̶.
Driving by you go out to all those
strange rooms, all those drawn shades,

those huddled taverns on the highway,
cars nosed-in so close they seem to touch.
Then they snap shut, fall into the past
forever, lives ended in an instant.

Such lives are so short you seem immortal.
You feed on this and on that hope
dim as a half-remembered phone number
that somewhere people are as you were

always told they were—people who swim
in certainty, who b̸e̸l̸i̸e̸v̸e̸ believe, who age
with precision, growing gray like actors
in a high school play———.

DRAFT #4

1. Compare draft #4 and draft #3 *line* by line. Pay particular attention to word
   changes. When you see a change, such as the change from "single lights" to
   "those solitary lights," or from "plains" to "Nebraska," try to figure out why
   the author made the change and whether you think the change was a good
   one.
2. Stanza breaks appear for the first time in draft #4. What do the stanza breaks
   add to the poem? Do they make it easier to read, help emphasize ideas, or
   serve some other purpose?

#5 Other Lives

You see them from train windows
in little towns, in those solitary lights
all across Nebraska, in the mysteries
of backyards outside cities—   loom up &
                                                 dwindle

a single face looking up,
blurred and still as a photograph.
They come to life quickly ȷ́
in gas stations, overheard in diners,

glimpsed only once, families from dreams
like memories too far back to hold.
Driving by you go out to all those
strange rooms, all those drawn shades,

Those huddled taverns on the highway,
cars nosed-in so close they seem to touch.
And they always snap shut, fall into the past
forever, vast lives over in a moment.

You feed on this shortness, this mystery
of nearness and regret—such lives are
so brief you seem immortal as you
travel. You ~~carry~~, too, that hope   feed on

dim as a half-remembered phone number
that somewhere people are as you were
~~were~~ always told they were—people who swim
in certainty, who believe, who age

with precision, growing gray like actors   only
in a high school play. . . .

DRAFT #5

1. What does Rutsala delete in this draft?
2. What does he add?
3. Does he make any changes in form, such as line breaks or stanza breaks?
4. One of the things a poet works for in revision is to make the poem *sound* right. How does the poem sound in this draft? Does it read smoothly? Does it sound interesting? Does Rutsala seem to be making revisions based on the sound of the poem?

#6 Other Lives

You see them from train windows
in little towns, in those solitary lights
all across Nebraska, in the mysteries
of backyards outside cities—

a single face looking up,
blurred and still as a photograph.
They come to life quickly
in gas stations, overheard in diners

loom up and dwindle, families
from dreams like memories too
far back to hold. Driving by
you go out to all those strange ~~rooms~~

rooms, all those drawn shades,
those huddled taverns on the highway,
cars nosed-in so close they seem
to touch. And they always snap shut,

fall into the past forever, vast lives
over in an instant. You feed
on this shortness, this mystery
of nearness and regret—such lives

so brief you seem immortal.
You feed, too, on that old hope,
dim as a half-remembered
phone number, that somewhere

people are as you were always
told they were—people who swim
in certainty, who believe, who age
with precision, growing gray like

actors in a high school play.

DRAFT #6

1. Compare draft #1 and draft #6. How are the two drafts alike? How is draft #6 different from draft #1?
2. At what point did the title come into the poem?
3. From studying the revision steps in "Other Lives," list some of the things a poet does in revising a poem. Add any items from your own experience with revision. Can you put the items into any sort of order showing which comes first, or do they all occur more or less at the same time?

It is instructive to see how the final poem has evolved from a certain general idea and the image of actors in a high-school play, the only constants in the various versions. Notice where the stanzas appear—as the poem nears its final form. Notice how the image of "motels / fit for suicide" in draft #2 disappears—it does not fit the idea of "people who swim in certainty." Rutsala also cuts down on discursive passages that explain too much. The idea of seeing others from train windows is not in the original notebook entry. In draft #3 the persona is walking through strange neighborhoods as well as watching from a train, which makes the situation somehow less focused than in the final version, where the point of view is definitely from a train crossing the plains.

There is really only one way to go about this kind of revision. The poet must go over the poem again and again, tinkering, adjusting, looking for what occurs in the language, the imagery, the dynamics of the poem or the idea. Start at the top and work downward, over and over, until it is right.

Vern Rutsala's poem started from a brief note and developed into a longer poem. It can work either way. Sometimes it is a good tactic to begin with a large chunk of material and cut back, as if chiseling a form out of stone, an image particularly appropriate to William Stafford's poem, following. As you read through these drafts, notice how the earliest version sounds more lyrical than later versions. The first draft is more rhythmical. It also seems to have more sound repetitions such as the "eye" sound in "finds" and "line" and the alliteration in "finds," "fate," and "feels." If you are attracted to those elements in poetry, you may find the final version rather stark by comparison. Such choices depend on the impression the poet aims to achieve. In revision we are trying to make a work better, but that's not all. We are also trying to make the poem say the thing we want it to say. The creative act of writing poetry is a process of making choices with many branching paths along the way. In this revision, the poet may be discarding parts of the early draft that could lead to a very different, well-written poem in order to develop the poem that seems to him more interesting or true. The handwritten version is the first draft, with a typed copy for clarity.

29 February 1992

This train won't wait. Come on.
It moves through time and forks
new stations all along the line.

By thinking as you go
you move the track — it feels
like fate but changes ~~shrines~~   or goes back.
~~But~~ wide-eyed and innocent,
this train invents the world
by being ~~there~~ and voicing pain.

Old sound, I'll follow you
or make the tint myself
~~maybe what the world's about myself.~~
maybe I'm what the world's about.

They said come in, I came.
Now I'm here — they said get out.   On another tombstone
  On a tombstone in ~~somess~~   I'm gone.
Got said come in. I came.
Then God said get out.   On another
                                                vini viti abecundi
  yet another,
I never had a clue.   and yet another
                                         I've gone to find my real name.
and I'm   Too hot   short Rope
what's the hurry?   Bad Brakes   my appetite
Sometimes I looked   Black Ice
at the sky.   They called me Smiley

29 February 1992

This train won't wait. Come on.

It moves through time and finds

new stations all along the line.

By thinking as you go

you move the track—it feels

like fate but changes or goes back.

Wide-eyed and innocent,

this train invents the world

by being here and voicing pain.

Old sound, I'll follow you

or make the toot myself

Maybe I'm what the world's about.

They said come in. I came.

Now I'm here—they said get out.

On a tombstone in Kansas   On another tombstone

God said come in. I came.   I'm gone.

Then God said get out.   On Another

Yet another   Vini Vidi Abscondi

I never had a clue

                                    And Yet Another

And On   I've gone to find my real name.

What's the hurry?   Too fast   Short Rope
                              Bad Brakes   My appendix
Sometimes I looked   Black Ice
   at the sky.
                              They called me Smiley

---

1.   What does the poem seem to be about in the first draft?
2.   Which images do you remember after a first reading?

March 92

~~From~~ Tombstones ~~is~~ ✗ Back Home

~~On a tombstone in Kansas:~~ 1.

> God said come in. I came.
>
> Then God said get out.

~~On Another Tombstone:~~ 2.

> Vini Vidi Abscondi.

~~Yet Another:~~ 3.

> I never had a clue.

~~And Again:~~ 4.

> I'm here.

~~And:~~ 5.

> What's the hurry ?

~~Yet More:~~ 6.

> I've gone to find my real name.

~~And On~~ 7.

> Bad brakes.

~~And Last:~~ 8.

> They called me Smiley.

✗ 9.

> Sometimes I looked at the sky.

From Tombstones Back Home

Light April 92 [handwritten]

March 92 [handwritten]

1.

God said come in. I came.
Then God said get out.

2.

Vini Vidi Abscondi.

3.

I never had a clue.

4.

I'm here.

5.

What's the hurry?

6.

I've gone to find my real name.

7.

Bad brakes.

8.

They called me Smiley.

9.   *From tomb D* [handwritten]

Sometimes I looked at the sky.

---

1. Look back at the first draft and pick out the parts that are still in the second draft. What is Stafford saving from the first draft?
2. Make a list of lines from the first draft that Stafford omits in the second. What kind of poem could be made from those lines? How are they different, if at all, from the lines he saves?
3. On the March 92 draft, you will notice that Stafford makes some handwritten changes on the manuscript. How do these changes affect the poem? For example, what is the difference between "Tombstones" as a title and "From

Tombstones Back Home"? How does the omission of transitional phrases and the addition of numbers change the poem?

4. Read the different drafts aloud. How does the sound of the poem change from draft to draft? Try to describe the sounds of the various drafts in terms of rhythm, sound structures, and tone.

You will have noticed the word "Light" on the final poem, which was typed from the changes in the second draft, along with the dates on each draft. These notes are part of Stafford's record-keeping process, the dates recording when the drafts were written. *Light* is the name of the magazine that accepted the final poem for publication, April 2 is the date the poem was accepted, and "from tomb D" refers to the disk on which the poem is filed.

Difficult as it is to give up good lines and images which don't work, remember that one can keep a file of deleted materials. Maybe they can be used somewhere else or will work to help you start a different poem. Or perhaps keeping such a file will give you the psychological freedom to edit freely.

Besides starting small and enlarging on notes or starting large and editing back to something shorter, a third way to work is to collect lots of little pieces that interest you and then figure out a way to connect them into a whole poem. Try all three approaches to see what works for you.

Some people enjoy revision more than others do. If you are such a person, you may often get to a point where you know that it is only a matter of time, ink, sweat, and paper before an idea or a chunk of material turns into a poem. Other writers, however, prefer to think about something until it is perfect in their heads; or they wait for the flash of inspiration that gets put down on paper unchanged. But in any case, give yourself plenty of chances to revise, and do not be too quick to call a poem done. Save your various drafts, and if you do edit out too much you can always put material back in.

Revision Exercises

Revision usually consists of changing words, adding words, and deleting words; it also consists of changing the way the words are organized into lines and stanzas on the page. In making these changes the writer is also involved with the revision of ideas and tone. Changes in word choice, deletions, and organization affect the emphasis of the poem, its meaning, sound, and tone.

These exercises should not take too much time. In workshops they can be done in class or in small groups and read aloud. The important thing is to use them to play with the language in a poem and to notice various ways in which revision changes the poem. Select one or more, depending on available time.

1. Carefully read one of the poems in this or another chapter, prefer-ably a short one. Then put the poem away and try to write down the poem. If you remember parts of it exactly, fine. What you don't re-member, paraphrase or fill in with your own words and ideas. What you end up with should be something that is like the original in some ways but not entirely. Use the original and your version as the basis for discussion on revision: a) *Quality.* Do you think one version is better than the other or are they simply different? Explain. What makes a poem good? b) *Intention.* How does the effect on the reader vary in the two versions? c) *Meaning.* Do the two versions mean ba-sically the same thing? Discuss similarities and variations in meaning and how they are created.

    The point of this exercise is to help you notice the importance of word choice and organization in the total impression of a poem.

2. Choose one of your own poems or a poem by someone else. Rewrite the poem by substituting synonyms for as many of the words in the original as possible while trying to keep the original meaning of the poem. How do the word changes affect the poem?

3. Choose one of your own poems and rewrite it by giving it com-pletely different line breaks. Make no other changes but experiment with wildly different ways of breaking the lines. For example, if you've written a sonnet, break the lines so that the words are scat-tered over the page into at least twenty-eight lines with lots of white space. Try versions with very short lines and very long lines. Break the lines to that they all end in the middle of sentences or on less im-portant words such as "of" and "but." Break the lines so that they all end with periods, colons, or semicolons. How do the different ways of breaking lines affect the poem?

4. Choose one of your own poems and revise it by editing out at least half of the words. How do you like the revision? How has it changed the poem? Try this again with a well-known poem by someone else. Do you think you can make a better poem with half the words?

5. Choose a poem and revise it by doing the opposite of the preceding exercise. That is, without adding any important new ideas, add words so that the revision is at least twice as long as the original.

6. Revise a *free-verse* poem into a *rhymed* and *metered* poem or vice versa.

7. Use all the words in some well-known, fairly short poem to make a completely different poem with the words in a completely different order.

Suggestions for Writing

1. Write or type on one subject by free-associating. Cover a page or two with ideas as they come to you. After a day or so, go back and try to find constellations of meaning in these notes. Choose a general or abstract topic, if you wish, but be sure to keep a lot of concrete material: images, events, things about people and objects.
   In this way, try the following:
   a) Find two different poems in your notes, not duplicating any of the images.
   b) Find two different poems in your notes allowing one, but no more than one, of your images to appear in both poems.
   c) Extract what you consider the *best* possible poem from your notes.

2. Experiment with different kinds of connections, such as ones of theme, chronology, sound, repetition, periodicity, and opposition. For example:
   a) A poem based on the lead story in the newspaper on three consecutive Sundays
   b) A poem about three people you know who have interesting noses
   c) A poem of which the first letter of each line, taken in order, spells out the name of someone about whom you like to think, even though the poem is not about that person

The point here is to start with some relatively arbitrary condition and force meaning.

3. Write a poem which seems to you to fit one of the following descriptions:
   a) A fragment—something ripped out of the world and framed
   b) A constellation of connected dots
   c) An inkblot—something different to everyone and a key to reader's personality
   d) An open field given a focal point

4. Write a poem in two steps:
   a) A draft consisting of mysterious, disconnected images
   b) A second draft, incorporating several different people's paraphrases of your first draft (a sentence or two)

5. Make notes on the next three times that:
   a) Someone tells you about their childhood
   b) Someone calls you on the phone
   c) You wake up and find that it is raining
   d) Someone asks you for something
   Take one set of notes, either a, b, c, or d, and show a connection between the three events.

6. Write a poem in which you make a connection between:
   a) Yourself and some stranger
   b) Yourself and some faraway event
   c) Yourself and some past event in history

7. Dig out one of your old poems. Whether old means two weeks or ten years depends on you, but choose a poem that you rather like but that never seemed to work. Take the poem through at least six complete revisions. Go over it thoroughly and retype it each time; do not just scribble in the margin. See what happens. Surprise yourself.

8

Allusion

The following poem by Daniel Langton is a **found poem.** That is, Langton has taken language from some other source, in this case a report of the San Francisco Society for the Prevention of Cruelty to Animals, and arranged it to create something new. As you read the poem, consider whether you would have read the words differently had you first come upon them in their original context.

What We Did

*(from the January 1967
report of the San
Francisco SPCA)*

22 cases involving
22 large animals
reported to the office
or located by officers:

Horses: sick or injured, 5;
stray, 2;
overridden, 15.

252 cases involving 121
other animals
investigated:

Dogs:
>   without proper care,
>   without shelter
>   not fed
>   improperly tied
>   in need of medical attention
>   between walls
>   suspected poisoned
>   caught in car window
>   behind stove
>   on roof
>   locked in cars
>   caught in fence
>   reported vicious
>   abandoned
>   nuisance (143)
>   locked in buildings

Cats:
>   without proper care
>   without shelter
>   mishandled
>   on roofs
>   on poles
>   on signboards
>   in trees
>   between walls
>   between buildings
>   under floor
>   locked in car
>   locked in building
>   in engine
>   caught in fence
>   in need of medical attention
>   suspected poisoned
>   reported shot
>   in skylight
>   abandoned
>   nuisance

behind furnace
in lightwell
in elevator shaft

Snakes in houses   foxes stray   sea lion in need of
medical attention   skunks trapped   bat in house
white mouse in house
rabbit without shelter
monkeys in store   turtles in need   hamsters in need
gibbon on street   squirrel in building
pigeons
caught in string   in stores   in school   suspected
poisoned   in chimneys   in air vent   in laundry

Parakeet without proper care

seagulls sick or injured   turkeys stray without shelter
ducks sick or injured   woodpecker between walls
sparrowhawk in store   hummingbird in house

Sparrows   in stovepipe one   in market one.

Cockatoo   caught in wire

Blackbird in store

Pelican: injured.

DANIEL LANGTON

1. Can you tell how Daniel Langton feels about this subject? Does he want the reader to feel a particular way? How do you know?
2. This work is not only a found poem but also a catalog or list poem. How does the long list add to the idea of the poem?
3. How is the title important in this found poem?
4. Breaking speech into short lines tends to slow down and emphasize certain words. Words in a long line would therefore be read more quickly. How do the line breaks affect the way this poem is read? Should the poem be read more quickly in the first or second half?

5.   Is it important to know where the words of this poem came from? Does
     knowing that Langton got his material from an SPCA report influence the
     way in which we read "What We Did?"

A found poem, such as this one, is not like any poetry we have considered so far. (Some would say this is not even a poem, since the words are not original.) The term *found* describes a text lifted out of some original context and arranged to give the appearance, form, or sound we associate with poetry. The found material is thrown into a new, possibly amusing or ironic light by this rearrangement.

According to George Hitchcock, editor of the anthology of found poetry *Losers Weepers,* the main criterion of the form is that it "must have been found somewhere amidst the vast sub- or non-literature which surrounds us all." You cannot make a legitimate found poem out of a prose passage from a novel, for instance, or even from some popular sort of literature, such as *The Guinness Book of World Records.* While the use of the materials to make a found poem is usually sophisticated, or at least self-conscious, the materials themselves must be taken from an innocent or naive context.

Whether or not found poetry is art does not concern us here. What is important, however, is that found poetry can help us sharpen our awareness of what might be material for poetry and of how to break a line of free verse. Experiments with found material can also confront the natural rhythms of language. Finally, since found poetry refers to an original source, it is related to the general use of allusion in all poetry.

An **allusion** is a reference to something outside the poem. It may be to something of general knowledge: if a poet refers to someone looking like Washington crossing the Delaware, we imagine a painting, a certain expression, perhaps the historical context. The poet does not need to explain the background of the allusion. Allusions may be more literary, as in the following lines from T. S. Eliot's "The Waste Land," which echo and thus allude to writings by Baudelaire and Dante.

> Unreal City,
> Under the brown fog of a winter dawn,
> A crowd flowed over London Bridge, so many,
> I had not thought death had undone so many.
> Sighs, short and infrequent, were exhaled,
> And each man fixed his eyes before his feet.

The poem also alludes to Tarot cards, Shakespeare, Ovid, St. Augustine's *Confessions,* Buddhism, the account of an antarctic explorer, the *Handbook of Birds of Eastern North America,* and assorted other works and sources. A far cry from a poem taken from an SPCA report, one might say, yet each example makes its point. By invoking something outside the work itself, a poet expands the content and meaning of a poem beyond what is actually stated.

With a found poem the allusion, or reference, is to the original source of the words used. For example, Langton's poem refers to an SPCA report. Without that reference, the poem would have little force. As an allusion to real problems concerning cruelty to animals and their difficulties in a human world, and with the title given it by the "finder," the poem takes on a serious meaning. "We" presumably is the human race; if this is "what we did," Langton seems to ask, what sort of creatures are we?

Generally, one may not add words to, or otherwise unfairly distort, the original of a found poem. The finder may, however, edit the original. He or she can, for example, add a title, as Langton does, or lineate the words on the page for emphasis or for rhythm. Yet if nothing is added to the original, how can the finder claim to have made a creative effort?

For one thing, the found poem illuminates qualities of language or meaning that were in the original in a less emphatic or apparent form.

This next passage is from a book of prose, an old local history. It gives a firsthand account of wildlife on the Oregon coast in the early part of this century. The passage lends itself to rearrangement of lines to emphasize the rhythms of the storyteller's words. The rearranged version, which follows the prose passage, brings out a melancholy, nostalgic feeling for the lost frontier and the abundance of its creatures. You might want to try rearranging the prose into lines of poetry yourself, before you look at the second version.

The Long Billed Curlew

This bird is fast becoming extinct throughout America and it has been many years since one has been seen along our coastline. At one time they were fairly numerous. As a kid, I remember my Dad bagging two of the big birds upon the sandy beach in the vicinity of Charleston, Coos County. The birds were lined up and killed by one bullet from his rifle.

The Curlew stands upon long stilted legs and has a very long curved bill. Its call is an eerie whistle and once heard is never forgotten.

LANS LENEVE
From *A Century of Coos and Curry*

Here's the rearranged version:

The Long Billed Curlew

"Once heard ... never forgotten"

This bird is fast becoming extinct
throughout America
and it has been many years
since one has been seen
along our coastline.
At one time
they were fairly numerous.
As a kid,
I remember my Dad
bagging two of the big birds
upon the sandy beach
in the vicinity of Charleston,
Coos County.
The birds were lined up
and killed by one bullet
from his rifle.

The Curlew stands upon long
stilted legs
and has a very long curved bill.
Its call is an eerie whistle
and once heard
is never forgotten.

Other than the line breaks, the only adjustments to the original are a citation of the source and the addition after the title of the quote from the end of the passage used. Juxtaposed against the grotesque and pathetic features of this account of man's effect on nature, this quote takes on an ambiguous and sinister quality. Thus even though it might be argued that local histories are quasi-literary, and perhaps even written by nonamateurs such as professional journalists, over the years such writings may accrue unforeseen associations.

Found poetry is often based on highly ephemeral sources that are part of our popular culture, our contemporary folklore. And found poetry itself purports to invoke a sophisticated, ironic, or humorous vision of that popular culture. But will an allusion to a current movie star, an ad for stomach medicine, a television situation comedy, or a popular toy, mean anything to a reader ten years from now? Whether you are working with such ephemera in found poetry or as allusions in other poetry, this is something you will want to think about.

Finding poetry obviously requires a certain kind of vision—double vision no doubt, for one has to be able to see the original intention of the text and its potential as a poem. Some people, probably the same ones who assert that the pun is the lowest form of humor, will see no point in found poetry. But, properly handled, it can be more than just a way of playing with words or an intellectual game.

A similar strategy is more central to poetry in general: the use of found material in otherwise original poems. Thus the material from some outside source is excerpted for its own appeal; or whole clouds of associations may appear in the poem as the result of a single word or phrase.

Marianne Moore is a poet who has made frequent use of allusions in the form of quotations. Her tone is deliberately flat, proselike, and her rhythms mimic those we associate with precise, logical argument. The secondary source materials contribute to this quality.

Poetry

(Original version)

I, too, dislike it: there are things that are important beyond all
            this fiddle.

Reading it, however, with a perfect contempt for it, one
                                        discovers in
    it after all, a place for the genuine.
        Hands that can grasp, eyes
        that can dilate, hair that can rise
            if it must, these things are important not because a

high-sounding interpretation can be put upon them but because
                                            they are
    useful. When they become so derivative as to become
                                        unintelligible,
    the same thing may be said for all of us, that we
        do not admire what
        we cannot understand: the bat   .
            holding on upside down or in quest of something to

eat, elephants pushing, a wild horse taking a roll, a tireless
                                            wolf under
    a tree, the immovable critic twitching his skin like a horse that
                                        feels a flea, the base-
    ball fan, the statistician—
        nor is it valid
            to discriminate against "business documents and
        school books"; all these phenomena are important. One must
                                        make a distinction
                however: when dragged into prominence by half poets,
                                the result is not poetry,
            nor till the poets among us can be
                "literalists of
                the imagination"—above
                    insolence and triviality and can present

for inspection, "imaginary gardens with real toads in them,"
                                    shall we have
    it. In the meantime, if you demand on the one hand,
    the raw material of poetry in
        all its rawness and

that which is on the other hand
genuine, you are interested in poetry.

Diary of Tolstoy, p. 84: "Where the boundary between prose and poetry lies, I shall never be able to understand. The question is raised in manuals of style, yet the answer to its lies beyond me. Poetry is verse: prose is not verse. Or else poetry is everything with the exception of business documents and school books."

"Literalists of the imagination." Yeats, *Ideas of Good and Evil* (A. H. Bullen, 1903), p. 182. "The limitation of his view was from the very intensity of his vision; he was a too literal realist of imagination, as others are of nature; and because he believed that the figures seen by the mind's eye, when exalted by inspiration, were 'eternal existences,' symbols of divine essences, he hated every grace of style that might obscure their lineaments."

MARIANNE MOORE

---

1. What do the quotations add to Moore's poem?
2. Is it important that Marianne Moore gives us sources for her allusions? Is it enough that she merely puts quotation marks around the words about "real toads"?

Moore provides a reference for some but not all of her quotations. "Imaginary gardens with real toads in them," for example, is not explained, and we do not know whether it is, in fact, a quote or whether she is instead emphasizing her own words with quotation marks. In Eliot's "The Waste Land" one must know the sources of allusions to understand the poem fully. In Moore's poem this seems less true. Her quotations are used for tone and style, rather than to convey Eliot's type of historical irony. The effect is sometimes one of a **collage** in which blocks of words are layed in for their verbal coloration and because the poet perhaps liked their sound and sense.

Allen Ginsberg's "Sunflower Sutra," although it does not make use of quotations, does use unexplained allusions to people and places in order to create texture. Here are the first lines of the poem:

I walked on the banks of the tincan banana dock and sat down under
the huge shade of a Southern Pacific locomotive to look at the
sunset over the box house hills and cry.

Jack Kerouac sat beside me on a busted rusty iron pole, companion,
  we thought the same thoughts of the soul, bleak and blue and sad
  eyed, surrounded by the gnarled steel roots of trees of machinery.
The oily water on the river mirrored the red sky, sun sank on top of
  final Frisco peaks, no fish in that stream, no hermit in those
  mounts, just ourselves rheumy-eyed and hungover like old bums
  on the riverbank, tired and wily.
Look at the Sunflower, he said, there was a dead gray shadow against
  the sky, big as a man, sitting dry on top of a pile of ancient
  sawdust—
—I rushed up enchanted—it was my first sunflower, memories of
  Blake—my visions—Harlem

ALLEN GINSBERG

Notice how the specific allusions make the poem more concrete,
more particularly of a certain time and place. You need to know that a
sutra is a part of Buddhist scriptures; that Jack Kerouac was a beat poet
and novelist, author of *On the Road,* friend of Ginsberg, and part of the
"San Francisco Renaissance"; and that Blake was a mystical poet who
lived in England between 1757 and 1827. "Southern Pacific," "Frisco,"
and "Harlem" suggest the cross-country landscape of America, and imply
that traveling the country was considered akin to a mystical experience by
the beats. But it is not just this knowledge that makes the allusions work.
Ginsberg could have said "locomotive" instead of "Southern Pacific locomotive," and "a friend" instead of "Jack Kerouac." But even before we
understand exactly what they imply, these concrete allusions convey a flavor that is part of the meaning of the poem.

In the following example of allusion, "Poem for Aretha," a tribute
to the singer Aretha Franklin, specific songs, situations, and individuals
give the poem an interestingly dense texture. The poet acknowledges
Franklin's power and influence among black people and at the same time
criticizes her fans and others for making her "a freak." This is a poem
about sharing responsibility and not destroying those who have talent. Is
there some field that means a lot to you? Try to write a poem about it,
a poem in which you air your feelings and inform your readers at the
same time.

Poem for Aretha

cause nobody deals with aretha—a mother with four children—
   having to hit the road
they always say "after she comes
home" but nobody ever says what it's like
to get on a plane for a three week tour
the elation of the first couple of audiences the good
feeling of exchange the running on the high
you get from singing good
and loud and long telling the world
what's on your mind

then comes the eighth show on the sixth day the beginning
to smell like the plane or bus the if-you-forget-your toothbrush
in-one-spot-you-can't-brush-until-the-second-show the strangers
pulling at you cause they love you but you having no love to give
   back
the singing the same songs night after night day after day
and if you read the gossip columns the rumors that your husband
is only after your fame

the wondering if your children will be glad to see you and
   maybe
the not caring if they are the scheming to get out
of just one show and go just one place where some doe-doe-
   dupaduke
won't say "just sing one song, please"

nobody mentions how it feels to become a freak
because you have talent and how
no one gives a damn how you feel
but only cares that aretha franklin is here like maybe that'll
stop:
        chickens from frying
        eggs from being laid
        crackers from hating

and if you say you're lonely or scared or tired how they always
just say "oh come off it" or "did you see
how much they loved you did you see huh did you?"
which most likely has nothing to do with you anyway
and i'm not saying aretha shouldn't have talent and i'm certainly
not saying she should quit
singing but as much as i love her i'd vote "yes" to her
doing four concerts a year and staying home or doing whatever
she wants and making records cause it's a shame
the way we are killing her
we eat up artists like there's going to be a famine at the end
of those three minutes when there are in fact an abundance
of talents just waiting let's put some
of the giants away for a while and deal with them like they have
a life to lead
aretha doesn't have to relive billie holiday's life doesn't have
to relive dinah washington's death but who will
stop the pattern

she's more important than her music—if they must be separated
and they should be separated when she has to pass out before
anyone recognizes she needs
a rest and i say i need
aretha's music
she is undoubtedly the one person who put everyone on
notice
she revived johnny ace and remembered lil green aretha sings
"i say a little prayer" and dionne doesn't
want to hear it anymore
aretha sings "money won't change you"
but james can't sing "respect" the advent
of aretha pulled ray charles from marlboro country
and back into
the blues made nancy wilson
try one more time forced
dionne to make a choice (she opted for the movies)
and diana ross had to get an afro wig pushed every
Black singer into Blackness and negro entertainers

into negroness you couldn't jive
when she said "you make me/feel" the blazers
had to reply "gotta let a man be/a man"
aretha said "when my show was in the lost and found/ you came
along to claim it" and joplin said "maybe"
there has been no musician whom her very presence hasn't
affected when humphrey wanted her to campaign she said
"woeman's only hueman"
and he pressured james brown
they removed otis cause the combination was too strong
the impressions had to say "lord have mercy/ we're moving
on up"
the Black songs started coming from the singers on stage and the
    dancers
in the streets
aretha was the riot was the leader if she had said "come
let's do it" it would have been done
temptations say why don't we think about it
                    think about it
                    think about it

NIKKI GIOVANNI

---

1. Do you recognize any allusions to songs in this poem? Are there words and
    phrases you don't recognize but suspect are quoted from songs?
2. Who are some of the people Giovanni mentions in the poem? What does it
    add to the poem to mention them?

In the following poem, Ingrid Wendt writes about her daughter's
anxiety in connection with a famous painting by Breughel. Wendt describes the painting vividly so that even if we have not seen it, we can
imagine it and understand why her child is troubled by what the painting depicts.

Remembering Breughel's
"Massacre of the Innocents"

for my daughter, Erin

I'd known it hung there, in Vienna. But home
was the place for warnings of strangeness, of not
taking rides, or candy. With me now
even wieners from butcher shop owners were safe.
Together now we were climbing palatial
marble steps, the guidebook having said
nothing of archways twice
as high as our house, completely studded
with color, real gold-covered crossbeams,
a ceiling of painted-on seasons of glory: each hair
on each head (as my father would say) so precise
you could see it, assuming you could get close
as the artists had, hanging there day after day
for months, their dangers of falling so far removed
from our journey past sculptures on landings
to canvas in far-off rooms.

I would have stared upward longer but you
were obsessed with the head of Medusa in What's-
his-name's hand, my memory not
so needed as saying it's really all make-believe.
No one could ever have snakes for hair, no one
cut off her head although maybe
he would have, had she been real.
What's true is I didn't avoid when I could have
that room with fifteen original Breughels, the first
I had ever seen not in a book.
"The Tower of Babel." "Peasant Dance." The other
I couldn't draw you away from, could only
respond: those soldiers lived too far back
to remember, they must have been following orders,
their leaders must have been mean. More
I could have said and still not enough.

So much you already knew of betrayals and still
you returned again and again from rooms of Rembrandt
   and Reubens,
Cranach's Adam and Eve and hundreds of Christs on the cross
you returned to take in details no one could
forget: the mothers pleading, the children
lying in blood, in snow, in a huge commotion of lances,
hooves, dogs, the wails of the children, the mothers
helpless with blood on their laps, on their hands,
their eyes turned back from Heaven.

Erin, no one forgives such things.
Nor do I know why we stayed until closing, hurrying out
with our postcards and parcels into the late May drizzle.
Why I sat on a park bench while you tried finding
pleasure in dancing like pigeons, hiding from me
again and again behind the base of Maria Theresa's statue,
knowing I knew where you were, insisting
I couldn't find you, anywhere.

INGRID WENDT

---

1. Imagine a poem Wendt might have written about her daughter's childhood fears of death without reference to this painting. How would it have been like, and how different, from this poem?
2. Have you ever seen a painting or a reproduction of a painting by Brueghel? If you know what a Breughel painting looks like, does that help you to understand the poem?
3. Besides the allusion to Breughel's paintings, there are other allusions, such as the name of the city, "Medusa in What's- / his-name's hand," "Maria Theresa's statue," and Cranach. What do these allusions add to the poem?

In "grandma, we are poets," Lucille Clifton alludes to definitions from a dictionary and an encyclopedia. The allusions provide a structure and add another dimension to a poem about an autistic child.

grandma, we are poets

for anpeyo brown

autism: from Webster's New Universal Dictionary
    and the Random House Encyclopedia

in psychology a state of mind
characterized by daydreaming

say rather
i imagined myself
in the place before
language imprisoned itself
in words

by failure to use language normally

say rather that labels
and names rearranged themselves
into description
so that what i saw
i wanted to say

by hallucinations, and ritualistic and repetitive
patterns of behavior
such as excessive rocking and spinning

say rather circling and
circling my mind i am sure i imagined
children without small rooms
imagined young men black and
filled with holes imagined
girls imagined old men penned
imagined actual humans
howling their animal fear

by failure to relate to others

say rather they began
to recede to run back

ward as it were
into a world of words
apartheid   hunger   war
i could not follow

by disregard of external reality,
withdrawing into a private world

say rather i withdrew
to seek within myself
some small reassurance
that tragedy while vast
is bearable

LUCILLE CLIFTON

---

1. The italicized passages are taken from the reference books. How are these parts different from the other parts? Is tone different? Vocabulary? Content?
2. A dedication in a poem is a different kind of allusion that helps us understand the object of or inspiration for the poem. How do the dedication and the title work together here to clarify the poem? Who is the "we" in the title?
3. The poem is structured as a dialogue. One voice is that of the reference books. The other is that of the autistic child. Which voice seems most convincing here? Most interesting? If you feel they are equally convincing and interesting, explain.

There are many more possibilities for using material from other sources to create new work. Without actually quoting from a source, you might write a poem incorporating information about plant life or the habits of some distant culture or the most recent theory on the origins of black holes. You might use quotations from someone you admire and build a poem of tribute around them. Fragments of language from popular culture, from advertising, from signs along a freeway, or any other source whose language interests you can be used to enrich the language and imagery of a poem, even when the poem is finally about the poet's own experience.

Suggestions for Writing

1. Choose a newspaper or magazine article. Look especially for one in which there is a sentence or a phrase that catches your ear. Use that as inspiration for a poem. You can address someone or simply describe: "Reading the paper, today / I saw that Mr. Smith was divorcing Mrs. Smith / because she insisted / on keeping a pet snake with her at all times."

    Such a poem need not be humorous or satirical, although absurdity may be the easiest thing to find in the news. But obviously, many sources exist for poems that explore serious, universal questions.

2. Use a typographical error as inspiration for a poem, especially an error that suggests something fantastic or imaginary.

3. Think of your favorite poem by your favorite poet. Write a poem in which you include a phrase or a line from that poem, worked into some different but related context. Think of this as a tribute to the original. You may put the borrowed phrase in quotes, as Marianne Moore does, or subtly work it in so that someone might find it and recognize your intention.

4. Experiment with found poetry. Look for a passage in a newspaper article or an advertisement, or in an old textbook, history, or medical manual. Arrange the words in lines to bring out some non-evident quality. Remember, by taking the words out of their original context, you change the way we see them. Think about whether you want your found poem to have a humorous or a serious effect.

5. Write a poem including allusions to one or more of the following:
    a) The personal: names of friends; an event relating to your birth; habits; life history; your deep, dark secrets
    b) Popular culture: advertising, movies, comics, fads, fashions, music
    c) Style: a parody of a well-known poem; a serious imitation of a well-known poem for the purpose of showing a variation; an imitation of the speech patterns of some well-known person; an imitation of a type of person, such as a sports commentator or first-grade teacher or political activist
    d) Esoteric knowledge: learned references to science, the humanities, religious beliefs, historical figures or events

6. Select some field, for example, music, Bogart movies, astrology, stamp collecting, the history of airplanes, or sports. Draw on your memory or do some research. Make notes on names, events, and dates. Find some quotations on the subject. Work this material into a long poem. Pay attention to the style of language in the secondary source material. Try to use it to play off your own voice in the poem, or to create a collage of mixed voices.

7. Go to a particular environment—for example, a large department store, a grocery store, or a shopping mall. Walk around. Make a list of signs or write down things you overhear—conversations, bits of songs, loudspeaker announcements. Work these notes into a poem suggesting the atmosphere of the place or your feelings about the place.

9

Surrealism and Romanticism

"Be realistic," we say, cautioning a friend to be prudent and constructive. "Be rational," we add, advising someone to calm down and bring emotions under control. Being realistic and rational is frequently considered healthy, and yet too much of these down-to-earth qualities can lead to writer's block. Sometimes it is good to listen to different advice: "Be fantastic. Be unreal." Even, "Be surrealistic."

In an earlier chapter we talked about seeing connections between unrelated things, forcing connection if need be, in order to make coherence out of formlessness. In this chapter let us allow the connections to take care of themselves, as in the following:

The Autopsy

In a back room a man is performing an autopsy on an old raincoat.

His wife appears in the doorway with a candle and asks, how does it go?

Not now, not now, I'm just getting to the lining, he murmurs with impatience.

I just wanted to know if you found any blood clots?

Blood clots?!

For my necklace. . . .

RUSSELL EDSON

---

1. What are some of the unexpected or odd things that appear in the poem?
2. Do you get any particular feelings from the odd or unexpected things in the poem?

3. What things in the poem seem normal or common?
4. How would you describe the mood in this poem? How does the mood fit or contrast with the events and images in the poem?

We might try to explicate this prose poem, to describe the feelings of confusion, revulsion, and curiosity it arouses. We could try to explain just why we might feel like laughing at the surprising, absurd ending. The poem is both convincing and unreal. But what does it *mean?* Here, certainly, poetry seems to be fulfilling the definition that says a poem is something that can be said in no other way. Its total effect on us is greater than the literal meaning of any of its parts.

Edson's prose poem is in the surrealist tradition. Surrealism is a modern art movement, influenced by Freudian psychology, that seeks to explore and communicate the reality of the psyche through images like those presented by dreams and fantasies. Freud showed that dreams can tell us things about our feelings which our conscious mind has denied or forgotten. The surrealist assumes that the sensible and rational are only the surface of things, a surface which masks a deeper and more complicated reality.

The word **surrealism** (or super-realism) was first used early in the twentieth century by poet Guillaume Apollinaire. A few years later, another French writer, André Breton, founded the surrealist movement with the publication of his *Manifeste de Surrealism (Surrealist Manifesto)* during the 1920s. The following excerpt from Breton's long poem "L'Union Libre" ("Free Union") is representative of the way in which the surrealists used *free association* to create a dreamlike progression of strange and appealing images. Notice how the central realistic image of the wife provides a pivotal center for the surrealistic associations. Syntactical repetition also provides structure, as in Anne Waldman's poem in Chapter 3.

From "Free Union"

My wife whose hair is a brush fire
Whose thoughts are summer lightning
Whose waist is an hourglass

Whose waist is the waist of an otter caught in the teeth of a tiger
Whose mouth is a bright cockade with the fragrance of a star of the
    first magnitude
Whose teeth leave prints like the tracks of white mice over snow
Whose tongue is made out of amber and polished glass
Whose tongue is a stabbed wafer
The tongue of a doll with eyes that open and shut
Whose tongue is incredible stone
My wife whose eyelashes are strokes in the handwriting of a child
Whose eyebrows are nests of swallows

ANDRÉ BRETON
translated by David Antin

---

1. What images stay in your mind after reading this excerpt from the poem?
   Why do you remember them?
2. Throughout the poem, Breton compares his wife's body to different things.
   Do the various comparisons make sense? Do they seem "right"? Are they
   strange or surprising?
3. Are any of the images in this poem *symbols?* Why or why not?
4. What if anything does this poem tell you about the poet's feelings for his
   wife? What if anything does it tell about his wife in a realistic way?
5. Given these three choices, would you describe this poem as being about:
   a) emotion, b) information, c) language?

    Although surrealism refers specifically to a French movement in literature and other arts during the early twentieth century, the term is sometimes used more generally to describe qualities in later art influenced by or reminiscent of that movement. For example, in the introduction to a collection of her work *Trilogy,* Diane Wakoski says of one section: "In *Coins & Coffins,* the poems could often be called surrealist in style, though their purposes are very different from a Surrealist Manifesto concern for poetry." And in the introduction to Crowell's *Handbook of Contemporary American Poetry,* Karl Malkoff writes about Robert Bly's "Waking from Sleep" and says that the central image of the poem, "which quite literally unites inner and outer realities, which breaks down barriers between conscious and unconscious perception, between imagination and 'objective' reality, could justifiably be described as surreal."

An important surrealistic quality in poetry is that however irrational the content, it *feels* real. Like a dream, it has emotional, if not literal, truth. This indicates the absorbing and convincing "reality" of surrealistic fantasy.

"The Autopsy" may remind you of the paintings of Spanish surrealist Salvador Dali. One of Dali's best-known paintings is "The Persistence of Memory"—an arid landscape of sand and rock, with a sea in the distance and large, melting pocket watches draped across various forms in the foreground. Although the content is fantastic, the style is realistic. That is, if giant pocket watches could melt, they would probably look just as they do in the picture—never mind what they are doing there. Dali supposedly said that the melting watches were inspired by his love of Camembert cheese. Not all surrealists have Dali's sense of humor, but often surrealism does convey a dark or grotesque sense of absurdity, and humor and horror can coexist in surrealistic art.

Surrealism, however, is not the whole story of fantasy and the irrational in poetry. There are different degrees of, and different means of access to, the logic of the subconscious. This chapter deals with a number of such degrees and means, from simple free association and automatic writing, to fantastic stories and the conscious juxtaposition of odd or unsettling images to jar awareness into the supra-ordinary.

What these approaches to poetry have in common is an emphasis on the cultivation of emotion rather than of intellect. The idea from popular modern psychology that it is good to "get in touch with your feelings" expresses a related concept. Some reasons for experimenting with surrealism, fantasy, and unpremeditated writing, if we need reasons, are (1) to develop richer, more imaginative writing, (2) perhaps to gain deeper self-knowledge, (3) to play, and (4) to learn techniques from the tradition of romantic literature.

The techniques, attitudes, and examples in this chapter could be called romantic. The word **romantic,** in referring to literature, does not mean having to do with love—though love could be written about romantically—but implies the emotional or subjective experiencing of the world. For example, the following poem, by Helen Adam, is a modern work in the romantic tradition. It is not the love story of the poem that determines this, but that the poem appeals more to the emotional than to the rational.

I Love My Love

> *"In the dark of the moon the hair rules."*—Robert Duncan

There was a man who married a maid. She laughed as he led
her home.
The living fleece of her long bright hair she combed with a
golden comb.

He led her home through his barley fields where the saffron
poppies grew.
She combed, and whispered, "I love my love." Her voice like a
plaintive coo.
Ha! Ha!
Her voice like a plaintive coo.

He lived alone with his chosen bride, at first their life was sweet.
Sweet was the touch of her playful hair binding his hands and feet.

When first she murmured adoring words her words did not appall.
"I love my love with a capital A. To my love I give my All.
Ah, Ha!
To my love I give my All."

She circled him with the secret web she wove as her strong
hair grew.
Like a golden spider she wove and sang, "My love is tender
and true."
She combed her hair with a golden comb and shackled him to
a tree.
She shackled him close to the Tree of Life. "My love I'll never
set free.
No, No.
My love I'll never set free."

Whenever he broke her golden bonds he was held with bonds
of gold.

"Oh! cannot a man escape from love, from Love's hot smothering
hold?"
He roared with fury. He broke her bonds. He ran in the light of
the sun.
Her soft hair rippled and trapped his feet, as fast as his feet could
run,
Ha! Ha!
As fast as his feet could run.

He dug a grave, and he dug it wide. He strangled her in her sleep.
He strangled his love with a strand of hair, and then he buried
her deep.
He buried her deep when the sun was hid by a purple thunder
cloud.
Her helpless hair sprawled over the corpse in a pale resplendent
shroud.
Ha! Ha!
A pale resplendent shroud.

Morning and night of thunder rain, and then it came to pass
That the hair sprang up through the earth of the grave, and it grew
like golden grass.
It grew and glittered along her grave alive in the light of the sun.
Every hair had a plaintive voice, the voice of his lovely one.

"I love my love with a capital T. My love is Tender and True.
I'll love my love in the barley fields when the thunder cloud
is blue.
My body crumbles beneath the ground but the hairs of my head
will grow.
I'll love my love with the hairs of my head. I'll never, never
let go.
Ha! Ha!
I'll never, never let go."

The hair sang soft, and the hair sang high, singing of loves that
drown,
Till he took his scythe by the light of the moon, and he scythed
that singing hair down.

Every hair laughed a lilting laugh, and shrilled as his scythe swept
  through.
"I love my love with a capital T. My love is Tender and True.

Ha! Ha!
Tender, Tender, and True."

All through the night he wept and prayed, but before the first
  bird woke
Around the house in the barley fields blew the hair like billowing
  smoke.
Her hair blew over the barley fields where the slothful poppies
  gape.
All day long all its voices cooed, "My love can never escape,
No, No!
My love can never escape."

"Be still, be still, you devilish hair. Glide back to the grave
  and sleep.
Glide back to the grave and wrap her bones down where I buried
  her deep.
I am the man who escaped from love, though love was my fate
  and doom.
Can no man ever escape from love who breaks from a woman's
  womb?"

Over his house, when the sun stood high, her hair was a dazzling
  storm,
Rolling, lashing o'er walls and roof, heavy, and soft, and warm.
It thumped on the roof, it hissed and glowed over every window
  pane.
The smell of the hair was in the house. It smelled like a
  lion's mane,
Ha! Ha!
It smelled like a lion's mane.

Three times round the bed of their love, and his heart lurched
  with despair.
In through the keyhole, elvish bright, came creeping a single hair.

Softly, softly, it stroked his lips, on his eyelids traced a sign.
"I love my love with a capital Z. I mark him Zero and mine.
Ha! Ha!
I mark him Zero and mine."

The hair rushed in. He struggled and tore, but whenever he tore
    a tress,
"I love my love with a capital Z," sang the hair of the sorceress.
It swarmed upon him, it swaddled him fast, it muffled his every
    groan.
Like a golden monster it seized his flesh, and then it sought
    the bone,
Ha! Ha!
And then it sought the bone.

It smothered his flesh and sought the bones. Until his bones
    were bare
There was no sound but the joyful hiss of the sweet insatiable hair.
"I love my love," it laughed as it ran back to the grave, its home.
Then the living fleece of her long bright hair, she combed with a
    golden comb.

HELEN ADAM

1. How does Adam use sound to appeal to your emotions in this poem? For
    example, how do the rhyme and rhythm of the poem make you feel?
2. Does the story in this poem seem to take place in the present or at some time
    in the past? What period in history does the poem remind you of?
3. Do the events and images in this poem seem strange or common?
4. Does the poem deal with strong emotions or evoke strong emotions in the
    reader? Explain.

Adam's poem exemplifies romantic literature in other ways as well.
We have come to the meaning of "romantic" through a long evolution
from Old French, a language derived from Latin, the language of Rome,
thus romance. Popular medieval stories of knights and heroes, written in

Old French, became known as romances. (The word "roman" still means "novel" in French.) These romances tended to be fanciful, imaginary, and adventurous, evoking strong emotions with strange or otherwise moving events. Other ideas associated with "romantic" include mysticism, a turning away to the past, an interest in arcane lore, a sympathetic relationship with nature, and a belief in the natural goodness of persons and in the importance of individual as opposed to societal norms (that is, in instincts as opposed to learned behavior). Although this is a very fragmentary history of the term, it does indicate why we now call a love story a romance, since it involves emotions, even though "romantic" includes much more.

"I Love My Love" demonstrates a number of these qualities. Helen Adam is unusual as a modern poet in that she works in a style from folk literature, the ballad. But even though she borrows material from an earlier period, her rendering is freshly original and contemporary, and her use of rhyme and regular meter with traditional motifs is anything but restricted. Rhyme and meter carry the poem naturally to its conclusion, and the fantastic story of love, death, and revenge demands a strong emotional response. Her images, especially those of the hair—the woman's long hair, the lion's mane, the single devilish hair coming through the keyhole, the dead woman's hair growing up out of the ground like wheat—are psychologically convincing, like the events in a dream.

As a means of tapping such subconscious material, you should now try automatic writing. **Automatic writing** is this: One takes pen in hand or poises fingers on the typewriter or keyboard and, without consciously ordering one's thoughts, attempts to sustain a stream of words. The point is not to censor, anticipate, or consciously organize. In addition, you should experiment with automatic writing in a particular rhyme and meter. Start with a line you provide yourself or that someone else makes up for you. Push yourself to go rapidly, without pauses. Let yourself get involved in some strange story or in a dreamlike series of events and images.

The following example uses traditional iambic pentameter—Shakespeare's meter—somewhat irregularly, with one end rhyme and without preconception of content.

> I walked upon the beach to be alone.
> I stubbed my toe upon a dark green stone.
> I hopped along and made an awful moan
> until I found a horse, it was a roan.
> I stole the horse—it really was a loan,
> but the man who owned it didn't have a phone.

I rode along the way the wind had blown
until I came upon an ancient crone
who muttered in an unintelligible drone,
then further on her twin—was she a clone?
The twin was sitting on a seaweed throne
her face the color of a sea-swept bone

And so on.

We have already encountered another way to free up the associative imagination, namely, the chant or litany. (See Anne Waldman's "Fast Speaking Woman," excerpted in Chapter 3). Try repeating a simple phrase such as, "I have lost . . ." or "I have found. . . ."

I have lost my shoes
I have lost my socks
I have lost the way I was going in my shoes and socks
I have lost the game and you have won the game
I have lost my three best marbles
I have lost all my marbles

Try not to worry too much about the results of these exercises, and do not play psychiatrist or Freudian critic. Think of it as an exercise in movement or a test hole dug into the imagination. You can drill a well later.

If you are sufficiently warmed up now, you might try automatic writing or free association in its purest sense. That is, for a few minutes, simply write a flow of unpremeditated words. Incorporate rhymes or metrical patterns if it helps, but do not concentrate on that. If you want a starting point, take a cliché or an advertising slogan or, if these seem dull, take the first thing someone says to you when that person comes into the room or a nonsense statement you make up yourself. Write for a long enough time to get into the spirit of the exercise. The less conscious attention you give to what you are writing, the better.

The idea of giving way to the imaginative flow is an ancient one. It appears in such literary conventions as the fool or madman who speaks wisdom without knowing it, or in the romantic image of the poet as one possessed. It has also been a convention of literature to invoke a muse who inspires the poet or, in fact, speaks through the poet, as if the poet were merely a vehicle through which creative powers express themselves. Milton's elegy "Lycidas" invites the goddess of poetry to inspire the poet:

Begin then, sisters of the sacred well
That from beneath the seat of Jove doth spring.
Begin, and somewhat loudly sweep the string

Milton's muse was definitely classical. What sort of muse would you invoke? Perhaps a good start toward unleashing your hidden imaginative power would be to write an **invocation** to your muse, ancient or modern, romantic or ironic, straight-faced or silly, whoever he or she or it may be. The sense of surrendering one's censorious, commonsense self is important here, and if it takes an invocation to the muse of running water, to the muse of the wheel, to the muse of the Statue of Liberty, or to whatever other muse you care to invoke, then do it.

A writer who looked for freedom of expression in something like automatic writing was Jack Kerouac, a novelist and poet. Instead of using sheets of typing paper, Kerouac used rolls of paper on his typewriter to facilitate a continuous flow of words without having to interrupt at the end of the page. He worked at writing nonstop, letting the words flow at high speed onto the page. Appropriately enough, he is best known for his novel *On The Road,* whose characters are possessed by speed and travel. His method of writing seems as metaphorical as his subject: life as the transcendent journey, life as an endless roll of blank paper waiting to be filled.

At about the same time but at the other end of the country, Charles Olson, teaching at Black Mountain College in North Carolina, also urged poets to push themselves. In Olson's essay "Projective Verse," he insists:

in any given poem always, always one
perception must must must MOVE, INSTANTER, ON ANOTHER!
So there we are, fast, there's the dogma.

The point is to loosen up and overcome the inhibitions, preconceptions, and habits that prevent us from being more imaginative, insightful, and genuinely ourselves. Even if we later revise stringently, the brainstorming process that precedes revision must be open and receptive. As Robert Duncan, another Black Mountain poet, once said, the poet must "live in the swarm of human speech."

Automatic writing and **stream of consciousness** have been associated with the whole area of **avant-garde** and romantic literature of the late-nineteenth and early twentieth centuries. This includes schools or movements such as *symbolism,* **dadaism,** and *surrealism.*

Writing about symbolism in *Axel's Castle,* Edmund Wilson speaks of "images unrelated by logic." As a literary movement, *symbolism* meant writing in which the difficult, personal, basically incommunicable experience of an individual is rendered by symbols. A *symbol* is a concrete object which represents some abstract quality. In other words, a symbolist might write a poem including a black rose, a wound that has been sutured with gold thread, various cat characters with human qualities, an elm tree with its roots wrapped around an ancient stone, and a face with no mouth. You can picture these things, but their larger meaning would be in the feeling each symbol provokes. You might not even be able to articulate the intellectual content of the symbol, yet the symbol telegraphs an emotional intensity. These images may be "unrelated by logic" but they are not unrelated by feeling; they add up to a definite atmosphere.

Perhaps you could create a system of symbols that represents the concerns of your emotional life. It need not be logical, but you should feel strongly that, for you at least, its symbols evoke a certain state of feeling.

One source for such a system of symbols is dreams. Long before Freud, artists acknowledged the power of dreams. Like the speaker in John Keats's "Ode to a Nightingale," which ends, "Fled is that music:— Do I wake or sleep?" all of us have experienced waking from a dream and being unable to shake off its mood. If someone treats us badly in a dream, we may wake up angry at that person. Let the person protest and disclaim all responsibility—we *feel* angry, therefore we *are* angry. Remember, this chapter is about the priority of emotions over reason, so we need not apologize. The rational mind fastidiously distinguishes between imagination and reality, but the emotions recognize a connection, invisible but real, like an underground stream.

In one sense, dream images are the poetry we make when we sleep. If we find ourselves flying, or having recurrent dreams about a being who is half human and half swan, or if a hand turns into a pomegranate, so much the better—these indicate rich interior life.

Simply to say, "I dreamed . . ." and tell your dream as a poem is one way of using dream material. Here is Robert Lowell's poignant poem about his dead friend, poet Randall Jarrell:

Randall Jarrell

The dream went like a rake of sliced bamboo,
slats of dust distracted by downdraw;
I woke and knew I held a cigarette;
I looked, there was none, could have been none;
I slept the years now, and I woke again,
palming the floor, shaking the sheets. I found
nothing smoking. I am awake, I see
the cigarette burn safely in my fingers . . .
They come this path, old friends, old buffs of death.
Tonight it's Randall, the spark of fire though humbled,
his gnawed wrist cradled like his *Kitten*. "What kept you so long,
racing your cooling grindstone to ambition?
Surely this life was fast enough . . . But tell me,
Cal, why did we live? Why do we die?"

ROBERT LOWELL

---

1. The poem begins with a difficult image of a bamboo rake and a movement in the dusty air. How do you picture this image?
2. In his dream Lowell imagines a visit from Randall Jarrell, an old friend and poet who is now dead. What does this visitation say to him?
3. Does this poem seem to be more about an idea or a feeling?
4. Have you ever had the experience of imagining something in a half-waking state and then being unable to say exactly what it was? In what way does this poem recreate an emotion that is difficult to express in any other way?

"Randall Jarrell" is not a surrealist poem in the manner of Edson's "The Autopsy," for the events here are definitely of the real world rather than of a world with its own rules. But by conveying the strangeness and confusion of the dream state, Lowell creates a mood of sadness and regret, as if life itself were a dream.

The transition from waking to dreaming and back again has fascinated writers from Shakespeare to Lewis Carroll, no doubt because it entails crossing the boundary from one kind of consciousness into another—a mysterious event, no matter how many times we experience it.

It is said that we all dream, though some people seem to forget their dreams as soon as they awaken. If you are such a person, try to ask yourself, immediately upon awakening, what you were dreaming—you may find that the dream has not yet vanished. By consciously applying yourself in this way, you will probably find yourself the possessor of many dreams.

One of the qualities we think of as dreamlike is the odd juxtaposition of things and events. You open the mailbox and a pair of lobster claws reach out. Next, you are walking down the street and suddenly your feet are stuck in large bowls of chocolate pudding. Then a voice says, "I'm sorry, you'll have to move to the next parking ramp. This one is for small cars only." The effect is reminiscent of a visual collage where bits and scraps from various sources are incorporated into one work, sometimes for surrealistic effect. Imagine a face, for example, with a cutout of city skyscrapers pasted in the place teeth ought to be; or a picture of wings pasted onto a picture of a telephone, the whole image made to appear as if it is flying out of the top of a man's head. Would the equivalent gesture in poetry be things such as: sounds heard from the street mingled with a person's thoughts and excerpts from television advertisements? Clashing or bizarre images? Russell Edson's prose poems?

Robert Bly, whose poem appeared in Chapter 7, is a contemporary poet, translator, and editor. He recommends what he calls wild association in writing poetry. This is a useful term because it has a feeling of giving permission. Don't worry about things—go wild! Bly frequently counsels writers to get out of the head and into the physical and emotional. For Bly, the head is not imagination but rather overly refined, critical intellect without sensitivity or feeling. Another phrase Bly uses is "leaping poetry," which may be even better than "wild association" because a leap implies a space between the point of takeoff and the point of landing. If the points are images, how do we get across that incomprehensible space? Leap! Bly does not want poets to get bogged down in:

> that slow plodding association that pesters
> us in so many poetry magazines, and in our own work when it is
> no good, association that takes half an hour to compare a child-
> hood accident to a crucifixion, or a leaf to the I Ching.

You will recognize Bly's stance as a romantic one and his recommendation as a variation of "images unrelated by logic."

How can the imagination learn to "leap" if it has gotten in the habit of "plodding"? The romantic would say that it originally comes naturally to children but that society or the wrong kind of education, or fear, or lack of practice make the imagination decrepit. The associative, rambling, imaginative speech of small children goes underground and becomes the interior monologue we all have going in our heads, or going even further underground, becomes the life we lead only in dreams.

I would like to complete this chapter with a group of poems that cross into that area of consciousness conveyed by dreams, surrealist art, and intuitive, deeply felt imagination.

"The Drive Home" is convincingly dreamlike; Merwin's atmosphere is not dangerous—every one is having such a good time—but strange things do happen.

The Drive Home

I was always afraid
of the time when I would arrive home
and be met by a special car
but this wasn't like that
they were so nice the young couple
and I was relieved not to be driving
so I could see the autumn leaves on the farms

I sat in the front to see better
they sat in the back
having a good time
and they laughed with their collars up
they said we could take turns driving
but when I looked
none of us was driving

then we all laughed
we wondered if anyone would notice
we talked of getting an inflatable
driver
to drive us for nothing through the autumn leaves

W. S. MERWIN

1. Here is another poem somewhat like Russell Edson's "The Autopsy" in that ordinary events are mixed with strange ones. Identify the ordinary and strange parts.
2. Is "The Drive Home" more like "The Autopsy" or more like "Randall Jarrell"? Explain.
3. Merwin uses certain ambiguous words and phrases, such as "a special car" and "the young couple." How does the ambiguity contribute to or detract from this poem? What feeling do you get from the ambiguity of the poem?

Swenson's "The Surface" is actually a realistic poem, but it is about something seen so closely that it seems surreal and strange. May Swenson has a great gift for looking at the ordinary in an extraordinary way.

The Surface

First I saw the surface,
then I saw it flow,
then I saw the underneath.

In gradual light below
I saw a kind of room,
the ceiling was a veil,

a shape swam there
slow, opaque and pale.
I saw enter by a shifting corridor

other blunt bodies
that sank toward the floor.
I tried to follow deeper

with my avid eye.
Something changed the focus:
I saw the sky,

a glass between inverted trees.
Then I saw my face.
I looked until a cloud

flowed over that place.
Now I saw the surface
broad to its rim,

here gleaming, there opaque,
far out, flat and dim.
Then I saw it was an Eye:

I saw the Wink that slid
from underneath the rushes
before it closed its lid.

MAY SWENSON

---

1. Is this poem more or less realistic than the other examples in this chapter?
2. How does Swenson use strange images to give a mood to the poem? Do the images seem less strange after you have read the poem a couple of times?

William Stafford's "The Farm on the Great Plains" is a good example of the way in which this poet can turn common, even folksy subjects into the extraordinary. Here, when the persona calls, or imagines calling, the farm where he grew up, no one exists to answer the phone. With the strange image, "an eye tapered for braille," a transition is made to a ghostly tenant who finally answers that no one is home. Finally, the speaker realizes that the past is no longer alive except as he contains it—a difficult perception conveyed by the last six lines.

The Farm on the Great Plains

A telephone line goes cold;
birds tread it wherever it goes.
A farm back of a great plain
tugs an end of the line.

I call that farm every year,
ringing it, listening, still;
no one is home at the farm,
the line gives only a hum.

Some year I will ring the line
on a night at last the right one,
and with an eye tapered for braille
from the phone on the wall

I will see the tenant who waits—
the last one left at the place;
through the dark my braille eye
will lovingly touch his face.

"Hello, is Mother at home?"
No one is home today.
"But Father—he should be there."
No one—no one is here.

"But you—are you the one . . . ?"
Then the line will be gone
because both ends will be home:
no space, no birds, no farm.

My self will be the plain,
wise as winter is gray,
pure as cold posts go
pacing toward what I know.

WILLIAM STAFFORD

---

1.   What are some of the words in this poem that give it a strange, eerie feeling?
2.   What does the telephone dialogue add to the poem? Who is speaking in the italicized lines?
3.   What is the mood at the end of the poem? How has that mood been created?

Gregory Orr's "Gathering the Bones Together" is an excellent example of a dreamlike poem that handles a realistic subject. "Leaves shaped like mouths" and "Snails glide / there, little death-swans," for example, are images that work both as real description and as surreal interpretation of the landscape, establishing atmosphere and tapping into the subconscious.

Gathering the Bones Together

one

A Night in the Barn

The deer carcass hangs from a rafter.
Wrapped in blankets, a boy keeps watch
from a pile of loose hay. Then he sleeps

and dreams about a death that is coming:
Inside him, there are small bones
scattered in a field
among burdocks and dead grass.
He will spend his life walking there,
gathering the bones together.

Pigeons rustle in the eaves.
At his feet, the German shepherd
snaps its jaws in its sleep.

two

A father and his four sons
run down a slope toward
a deer they just killed.
The father and two sons carry
rifles. They laugh, jostle
and chatter together.
A gun goes off,
and the youngest brother

falls to the ground,
A boy with a rifle
stands beside him, screaming.

three

I crouch in the corner of my room,
staring into the glass well
of my hands; far down
I see him drowning in the air.

Outside, leaves shaped like mouths
make a black pool
under a tree. Snails glide
there, little death-swans.

four

Smoke

Something has covered the chimney
and the whole house fills with smoke.
I go outside and look up at the roof,
but I can't see anything.
I go back inside. Everyone weeps,
walking from room to room.
Their eyes ache. This smoke
turns people into shadows.
Even after it is gone, and the tears are gone,
we will smell it in pillows
when we lie down to sleep.

five

He lives in a house of black glass.
Sometimes I visit him, and we talk.
My father says he is dead,
but what does that mean?

Last night I found a child
sleeping on a nest of bones.
He had a red, leaf-shaped
scar on his cheek. I lifted him up
and carried him with me, even though
I didn't know where I was going.

six

The Journey

Each night, I knelt on a marble slab
and scrubbed at the blood.
I scrubbed for years and still it was there.
But tonight the bones in my feet
begin to burn. I stand up
and start walking, and the slab
appears under my feet with each step,
a white road only as long as your body.

seven

The Distance

The winter I was eight, a horse
slipped on the ice, breaking its leg.
Father took a rifle, a can of gasoline.
I stood by the road at dusk and watched
the carcass burning in the far pasture.

I was twelve when I killed him;
I felt my own bones wrench from my body.
Now I am twenty-seven and walk
beside this river, looking for them.
They have become a bridge
that arches toward the other shore.

GREGORY ORR

1. In a few words, what information do you get in each of the sections of Gregory Orr's poem?

2. After reading the poem, what are some of the images that particularly stay in your mind? Why do you remember these images?

Suggestions for Writing

1. The feeling of dissociation is common in dreams. One might suggest this feeling in writing by speaking of oneself as "you" or by using the present tense for immediacy and to emphasize that one does not know what is coming next. Using these or other devices, write a poem about an experience of dissociation, the split self.

2. In the manner of Edson, tell a short, fantastic story which feels emotionally real because people act in normal, recognizable ways, but in which strange or grotesque events occur. The mood should be: frogs fall out of the sky, but business goes on as usual.

3. Write about a true, painful experience—your own or someone else's. Think about the way in which terrible things sometimes seem unreal because they are too much to bear. This is a hard exercise to do because, if you do it seriously, it can be very uncomfortable. You may feel like Flaubert, who became violently ill after writing the death of the character he created, Madame Bovary. The point, however, is not to make yourself sick, but to try to understand the experience. Write so that reality and unreality come together.

4. Listen to a piece of music without words. What emotions and images do you get from it? Write a poem that is the equivalent in words of the music.

5. Practice automatic writing:
    a) To music
    b) In a darkened room so you cannot see what you are writing
    c) In some regular pattern of rhyme and meter

6. Write a poem based on surrealist painting, such as a work by Dali or Magritte. The poem can be about the work itself, or about your own feelings evoked from the work.

7. Choreograph a poem—drawing from the traditions of dadaism, surrealism, the happening, or the theater of the absurd*—that is an absurdist performance. Remember, one thing such a performance does is to surprise, shock, or bewilder the audience in order to move people into reconsidering the question, what is art?

8. Write a poem beginning with the title "In a Dream."

9. Invent or draw from your memory three symbols that represent three themes in your life. For example, if you remember liking to play under a certain tree when you were a child, perhaps a tree of that kind would be a symbol of innocence, of imagination, or of the lost past. Work out an iconography of symbols for yourself. Try using these symbols, or some of them, in more than one poem. Think of them as a key to emotional states difficult to express in any other way.

Happenings are performances associated with the pop art movement of the 1960s, which originated, like dadaism, during a period of protest against war. The happening might combine music, street theater, and poetry, all juxtaposed to produce an emotional rather than an intellectual response. Similarly, *theater of the absurd,* of which the plays of Samuel Beckett or Eugene Ionesco would be examples, rejects a more rational-seeming theater in favor of apparently illogical or absurd statements and actions, in order to say something about the absurdity of the human condition.

10

Voice

Voice is the medium and instrument of poetry, whether that poetry is spoken aloud or read silently. Voice is also the mark of the individual poet. To have developed one's own voice means to have matured as a poet, to be in control of technique and content and to have demonstrated personal style and a grasp of one's subject.

Tone is an aspect of that voice, an expression of the poet's attitude toward the poem's subject: an angry tone, an ironic tone, a frightened tone. In related meanings, tone is also the verbal coloration and musical quality. A poem in which we cannot determine the tone is apt to be unsuccessful. We do not know whether the poet is being sarcastic, reverent, angry, or loving—meaning is obscured, and we wonder whether the poet knows what he or she feels about the subject.

Still, tone need not give itself up with complete ease. A fine ironic tone may turn us two ways at once. Tone may convey ambiguity and multiple meanings. Sometimes our understanding of an author's tone changes midway in a work, as in satire.

What constitutes tone? Words and all the choices we make in using them affect tone. For example, the same event may be called a date, a meeting, a rendezvous, a get-together, or an assignation. Persona and point of view are also part of tone—who is speaking? Rhythm, sound, sentence pattern, literal content, and a certain resonance traditionally associated with various forms—such as the lyricism of the sonnet, the playfulness of the villanelle, or the absurdity of the limerick—all these contribute to the tone of a poem.

Consider the differences of tone in the following three poems.

Upon Julia's Clothes

Whenas in silks my Julia goes,
Then, then, methinks, how sweetly flows
That liquefaction of her clothes.

Next, when I cast mine eyes and see
That brave vibration each way free,
O how that glittering taketh me!

ROBERT HERRICK

1.   A word may seem "fancy" or elaborate because it is long and polysyllabic or because it is uncommon. Which words stand out in the poem as particularly fancy or elaborate? What do they mean?
2.   Substitute plainer synonyms for the fancy words. How does this change the poem?

I Knew a Woman

I knew a woman, lovely in her bones,
When small birds sighed, she would sigh back at them;
Ah, when she moved, she moved more ways than one:
The shapes a bright container can contain!
Of her choice virtues only gods should speak,
Or English poets who grew up on Greek
(I'd have them sing in chorus, cheek to cheek).

How well her wishes went! She stroked my chin,
She taught me Turn, and Counter-turn, and Stand;
She taught me Touch, that undulant white skin;
I nibbled meekly from her proffered hand;
She was the sickle; I, poor I, the rake,
Coming behind her for her pretty sake
(But what prodigious mowing we did make).

Love likes a gander, and adores a goose:
Her full lips pursed, the errant note to seize;
She played it quick, she played it light and loose;
My eyes, they dazzled at her flowing knees;
Her several parts could keep a pure repose,
Or one hip quiver with a mobile nose
(She moved in circles, and those circles moved).

Let seed be grass, and grass turn into hay:
I'm martyr to a motion not my own;
What's freedom for? To know eternity.
I swear she cast a shadow white as stone.
But who would count eternity in days?
These old bones live to learn her wanton ways:
(I measure time by how a body sways).

THEODORE ROETHKE

---

1. Is Roethke's language elegant, plain, fanciful—or a mixture? For example, what is the tone or flavor of such words as "lovely," "undulant," "repose," and "prodigious"? What about "cheek to cheek," "gander," "goose," and "old bones"?
2. Is the language of Roethke's poem similar to the language in Herrick's or different? Explain and pick out examples.
3. Sometimes writers use exaggeration to establish tone or to make a point. What are some examples of exaggeration in "I Knew a Woman"? How do such examples affect the tone of the poem?
4. How do rhyme and rhythm influence the tone in "I Knew a Woman" and "Upon Julia's Clothes"?

Epitaph for a Darling Lady

All her hours were yellow sands,
Blown in foolish whorls and tassels;
Slipping warmly through her hands;
Patted into little castles.

Shiny day on shiny day
Tumbled in a rainbow clutter,
As she flipped them all away,
Sent them spinning down the gutter.

Leave for her a red young rose,
Go your way, and save your pity;
She is happy, for she knows
That her dust is very pretty.

DOROTHY PARKER

1. Compare and contrast the speaker's attitude toward the subject in this poem to that in the two preceding poems. Does Parker feel as warmly toward the "Darling Lady" as Herrick and Roethke seem to feel toward their subjects?
2. How do you know how Parker feels toward her subject? Is it determined by the literal meaning of her words or something else?

Herrick's tribute has a more formal, antique flavor than Roethke's, which in part comes from the language: "liquefaction," "vibration," "whenas," and "taketh." Herrick also maintains a greater distance between the speaker and "Julia" than exists between Roethke's speaker and the "woman, lovely in her bones," in that Herrick focuses on the clothes rather than on the woman herself. Yet therein lies much of the subtle sensuousness of the poem. There is a tension between tone and subject.

Roethke's tone is colored by humor and extravagance of imagery, as when he suggests that only gods or a chorus of classically educated English poets could sing the praises of his beloved, or that "she casts a shadow white as stone." Still, there is much that is similar in these poems. Herrick's "how sweetly flows / That liquefaction of her clothes" is very similar to "when she moved, she moved more ways than one" and to "her flowing knees." A writer could use slang to express the same thought, but how different the tone would be.

In contrast, Parker's tone is sarcastic, mocking. What determines this final tone? The first eleven lines concentrate on images of pretty things, though the word "clutter" paired with "rainbow" and "gutter" hint at something else. But it all gets to be too much, like decorative frosting on a tasteless cake, and we realize the sarcasm in the writer's voice, that she has been mocking the trivial vanity of the "darling lady." Parker is intentionally excessive—she invokes sentimental language and cliché, then brings the poem up short with the image of the lady's dust, her worthlessness. This is not a nice poem, and Parker is very good at being not nice.

It is easy to recognize that Herrick and Roethke are sincere in their admiration while Parker is satirical. It is often difficult, however, for a writer to predict how much is too much, where the fine line is between delightful extravagance and cloying sentimentality or satire. If you are trying to be serious and lofty and find your audience laughing, or if your best wit provokes only puzzled frowns, you may have a failure of tone. Roethke's *hyperbole,* or overstatement for rhetorical effect, pushes his poem close to sentimentality, yet we understand that his feeling is edged by wit and a sharp self-awareness. Herrick's excessive formality is offset by the sensuousness of his subject, while Parker's satire is humorous but malicious.

Achieving the right tone is not like mixing paint in a hardware store—there is no set formula, so many drops of this and so many of that. You can become more adept by practice and by noticing how various poets manipulate and convey tone.

Tone in a poem sometimes involves the character of the speaker. You can explore or exaggerate your own character by using a certain tone, which is an aspect of your personal voice. You can also go beyond that and create a completely different identity; that too influences the tone or attitude expressed toward the subject. The term for such an identity, a term we have used earlier, is **persona.** In general, the persona, or speaker, may be some version of yourself—you and yet not you—or it may be a specific identity or mask, such as Ulysses or Isadora Duncan or a butcher or a lost child or an animal. The title of a poem may indicate who is speaking, although that is not always necessary.

Following are several examples of poems in which the poet adopts a persona specifically different from the personal voice of the poet.

A poem that identifies the persona in the title is Mary Oliver's "The Lamb." Does the voice of the poem seem in keeping with the persona? Whether it does or not, think about how our interpretation of the tone is influenced not only by word choice and rhythm, but also by our sense of the speaker, or persona.

The Lamb

I did not know that in the world there lurked
Various death:
Fangs and fruits and falling trees,
Mushrooms and a writhing mud.
I did not know that in the world
Grew sinister berries and dubious roots.
I was young and quick, I was wary of none of these.
I drank black water and clattered through caves.
I was a creature of the shepherd, and this was my game.

All day long
I sipped and I nibbled: shoots from glistening trees;
Tart berries, for the sake of their shining husks; garlands
That fostered a bane under their bright petals; pools
With fevers in their dark mirrors I found, and drank from
    every one.

And not till I lay
Swelled and cracked on the grass did I guess what I had eaten.
Not till I lay
With crumbling hooves kicking the grass
Did I guess what I had done.
My shepherd and my flock
Called for me down the dusky fields; but childhood
Had no potion that could lave over this fever,
And they called and they called in vain.

MARY OLIVER

---

1. How would this poem have changed had Oliver written about the lamb in the third person instead of from the lamb's point of view?
2. Does the voice of the poem seem believable as the voice of a lamb? Explain and give examples.
3. What is the overall tone of the poem? How does that tone emphasize or contrast with the subject of the poem?

Imagine how different Mary Oliver's poem might sound had she adopted a different persona, "The Lamb" might have been written from the viewpoint of the shepherd, or of a child who is revolted by the dead animal and is then spoken to by the lamb itself. For that matter, as long as we can speak in the personae of animals, the poem could be in the voice of the lamb's mother or of the grass, the earth, the stones; an insect might talk to the dead lamb. Really, the possibilities are endless. In each of the above cases, think of how tone might have altered correspondingly, and how a change of tone and persona would have altered the sense of the poem.

Whatever the tone of this poem, it is not like anything you would expect from a lamb, even if lambs could talk. The language is formal and ornamental, "Tart berries, for the sake of their shining husks; garlands / That fostered a bane under their bright petals." You might compare this to Diane Wakoski's "Wind Secrets," which appears in Chapter 1 and deals with the subject of loss of innocence through the voice of a persona. There is a gothic and horrific quality about "The Lamb." Whether we read this poem as a parable of growing up or of a child's learning about death or as some other variation on the loss-of-innocence theme, Oliver has rendered a nightmarish and grotesque fantasy—not only is this poem in the voice of the lamb, the lamb is dead. Her attitude toward the subject is grim.

Following is another poem in which the tone seems somewhat at odds with the content. Like her poem in Chapter 1, "Not Waving but Drowning," this Stevie Smith poem uses images of drowning presented in a strangely buoyant tone of voice.

The River God

(Of the River Mimram in Hertfordshire)

I may be smelly and I may be old,
Rough in my pebbles, reedy in my pools,
But where my fish float by I bless their swimming
And I like the people to bathe in me, especially women.
But I can drown the fools
Who bathe too close to the weir, contrary to rules.
And they take a long time drowning
As I throw them up now and then in a spirit of clowning.

Hi yih, yippity-yap, merrily I flow,
O I may be an old foul river but I have plenty of go.
Once there was a lady who was too bold
She bathed in me by the tall black cliff where the water runs cold,
So I brought her down here
To be my beautiful dear.
Oh will she stay with me will she stay
This beautiful lady, or will she go away?
She lies in my beautiful deep river bed with many a weed
To hold her, and many a waving reed.
Oh who would guess what a beautiful white face lies there
Waiting for me to smoothe and wash away the fear
She looks at me with.   Hi yih, do not let her
Go.   There is no one on earth who does not forget her
Now.   They say I am a foolish old smelly river
But they do not know of my wide original bed
Where the lady waits, with her golden sleepy head.
If she wishes to go I will not forgive her.

STEVIE SMITH

---

1. Who is speaking in the poem? How does the poem describe the speaker?
2. Is this a believable or convincing voice for a river?
3. What is the overall tone of the poem? How does that tone emphasize or contrast with the subject of the poem?

"Alphonse Imagines what the People's Thoughts will be when he is Gone" uses a persona Paul Zimmer has developed in a number of poems, a persona who may be the poet's *antiheroic alter ego.* Such a figure may be an extension of the poet's personality, a hidden self, or a puppet to act out the poet's imagination; this tactic has been used by other writers, such as John Berryman, in his "Henry" poems, and the German writer Christian Morgenstern, who created Korf and Palmstroem. By creating a character who has a personality and a history, and who reappears in various situations in different poems, the poet can externalize feelings and make them

more dramatic and concrete than he or she might by using the personal
I. (This subject is further discussed in Chapter 12 as personal mythology.)

Not only is Alphonse removed from Zimmer, but Alphonse thinks
of himself in the third person, imagining what others will say about him.
Here the hyperbolic tone becomes humorous and is sustained by words
such as "gaseous" and "custardy," and by the fact that these others repri-
mand themselves for not appreciating Alphonse, even while we are aware
that Alphonse is indirectly reprimanding them. The scene is like Twain's
portrait of Tom Sawyer moved to pathos at his own funeral. Zimmer's
handling of a bombastic and inflated tone makes the poem successful.

Alphonse Imagines what the People's Thoughts will be when he is Gone

Where is that gaseous Alphonse
Whose round head used to rise
Upon a string above ours,
Whose bat wing eyebrows
Lofted him above our heads?
Where is he, whose words
Between his custardy teeth,
Dropped to us like stale bread
To the geese? Ah sadness!
He is gone like ancient light waves,
Like fingerprints on icicles.
Invisible and unloved he slipped
Through our blockish fingers.
Ah sin, our obtundity, our sin!
Now we would give him all
Our love, if only he returned.

PAUL ZIMMER

1. How does Zimmer feel about Alphonse? About the speaker or speakers in
   the poem? How do you know?
2. Is the author's feeling the same as the persona's? Explain.

3.   Paul Zimmer creates a contrast between the elegiac, lofty sentiments of the persona and the words used to describe Alphonse, such as "bat wing eyebrows" and "custardy teeth." How would you describe the effect of this contrast?

The next two poems are older ones. Thomas Hardy's "Ah, Are You Digging on My Grave?" and Robert Browning's "My Last Duchess" are classic examples of irony conveyed by tone and persona. The first is a dialogue and the second a monologue. Each poem depends on nuances of voice to unfold a particular drama.

Ah, Are You Digging on My Grave?

'Ah, are you digging on my grave,
    My loved one?—planting rue?'
—'No: yesterday he went to wed
One of the brightest wealth has bred.
"It cannot hurt her now," he said,
    "That I should not be true."'

'Then who is digging on my grave?
    My nearest dearest kin?'
—'Ah, no: they sit and think, "What use!
What good will planting flowers produce?
No tendance of her mound can loose
    Her spirit from Death's gin."'

'But some one digs upon my grave?
    My enemy?—prodding sly?'
—'Nay: when she heard you had passed the Gate
That shuts on all flesh soon or late,
She thought you no more worth her hate,
    And cares not where you lie.'

'Then, who is digging on my grave?
    Say—since I have not guessed!'

—'O it is I, my mistress dear,
Your little dog, who still lives near,
And much I hope my movements here
    Have not disturbed your rest?'

'Ah, yes! *You* dig upon my grave. . . .
    Why flashed it not on me
That one true heart was left behind!
What feeling do we ever find
To equal among human kind
    A dog's fidelity!'

'Mistress, I dug upon your grave
    To bury a bone, in case
I should be hungry near this spot
When passing on my daily trot.
I am sorry, but I quite forgot
    It was your resting-place.'

THOMAS HARDY

---

1. The poem consists of two voices. Who are the speakers in the poem and how do you know?
2. One way to get a feeling for the tone of a poem is to read it aloud in a dramatic way. How would you read the two voices differently?
3. Speaking in the voice of a dead person may seem like an odd choice of persona, but it gives the poet a certain freedom and dramatic intensity. How would the poem have changed had the dead woman not had a chance to speak?
4. How would you describe the similarities and differences in voice and tone between this poem and Stevie Smith's "Not Waving but Drowning" in Chapter 2? Between this poem and "The River God"?

Browning's "My Last Duchess" is a **dramatic monologue,** that is, a speech in the voice of one character which implies dramatic action and the presence of a listener. "My Last Duchess" is taught in literature classes mainly as an example of irony and to show how the writer conveys things that are not explicitly stated. This is certainly important from a student writer's point of view, but also note how effectively Browning gets inside a thoroughly rotten character. If you were to construct an evil persona, who would you be and what effect would you want? Would you be a sophisticated, wealthy character like Browning's duke; an uneducated criminal who is as much a victim as not; or someone who shows a powerful exterior and a cowardly interior?

My Last Duchess

Ferrara

That's my last duchess painted on the wall,
Looking as if she were alive. I call
That piece a wonder, now: Frà Pandolf's hands
Worked busily a day, and there she stands.
Will't please you sit and look at her? I said
"Frà Pandolf" by design, for never read
Strangers like you that pictured countenance,
The depth and passion of its earnest glance,
But to myself they turned (since none puts by
The curtain I have drawn for you, but I)
And seemed as they would ask me, if they durst,
How such a glance came there; so, not the first
Are you to turn and ask thus. Sir, 'twas not

Her husband's presence only, called that spot
Of joy into the Duchess' cheek: perhaps
Frà Pandolf chanced to say "Her mantle laps
"Over my lady's wrist too much," or "Paint
"Must never hope to reproduce the faint
"Half-flush that dies along her throat": such stuff
Was courtesy, she thought, and cause enough
For calling up that spot of joy. She had
A heart—how shall I say?—too soon made glad,
Too easily impressed; she liked whate'er
She looked on, and her looks went everywhere.
Sir, 'twas all one! My favor at her breast,

The dropping of the daylight in the West,
The bough of cherries some officious fool
Broke in the orchard for her, the white mule
She rode with round the terrace—all and each
Would draw from her alike the approving speech,
Or blush, at least. She thanked men—good! but thanked
Somehow—I know not how—as if she ranked
My gift of a nine-hundred-years-old name
With anybody's gift. Who'd stoop to blame
This sort of trifling? Even had you skill
In speech—which I have not—to make your will
Quite clear to such an one, and say, "Just this
"Or that in you disgusts me; here you miss,
"Or there exceed the mark"—and if she let
Herself be lessoned so, nor plainly set
Her wits to yours, forsooth, and made excuse,
—E'en then would be some stooping; and I choose
Never to stoop. Oh sir, she smiled, no doubt,
Whene'er I passed her; but who passed without
Much the same smile? This grew; I gave commands;
Then all smiles stopped together. There she stands
As if alive. Will 't please you rise? We'll meet
The company below, then. I repeat,
The Count your master's known munificence
Is ample warrant that no just pretense
Of mine for dowry will be disallowed;
Though his fair daughter's self, as I avowed

At starting, is my object. Nay, we'll go
Together down, sir. Notice Neptune, though,
Taming a sea-horse, thought a rarity,
Which Claus of Innsbruck cast in bronze for me!

ROBERT BROWNING

1. Who is speaking in Browning's poem? How does the poet use one person's voice to create a sense of action involving more than that one person?
2. Summarize the story told in the poem. How does Browning let us know about certain unstated things, such as what happened to his former wife, without coming right out and telling us?
3. How would you describe the mood and character of the speaker? When you read the poem aloud, what expressions would you use to convey the tone of the words? How do you know how the poem should be read?

Although it is true that one has numerous choices in manipulating the voice, and thereby the effect, of any one poem, we also use the word "voice" to describe the more or less consistent style of a mature poet. To speak of the poetic voice might bring to mind such formally heightened lines as Tennyson's "Break, break, break, / On thy cold gray stones, O Sea!" But the poetic voice is apt to be as varied as the human voice, and most modern poets create highly individualized voices out of the common language.

A mature writer, even when experimenting with different approaches, usually shows consistency of style. However, such consistency should not unduly obsess a beginning writer. If your work is honest, technically sound, and true to your own intellect and imagination, sooner or later it will show your individual stamp. In the meantime, feel free to experiment, change voice, or try on different attitudes to see what feels right.

Does every poem have qualities of tone and voice? We might look at Kenneth Patchen's "The Murder of Two Men by a Young Kid Wearing Lemon-colored Gloves" in Chapter 6 or Gertrude Stein's "A Petticoat" in Chapter 1 and ask this question. Yet, even in a concrete poem like Mary Ellen Solt's "Lilac" (Chapter 1), built from one word, and where there would seem to be little room for expression of attitude, there is a tinge of something we could call *atmosphere;* even when it is as elusive as a whiff of perfume on a city street, atmosphere is a part of tone. Texture, associations, and vocal qualities exist even for a single word.

By now, it is probably evident that the most influential element in establishing the tone of a poem is word choice. Our language is rich in words to render nuances of meaning in related or similar things. For example, under "courtesy," *Roget's Thesaurus* gives the related, but not necessarily synonymous, "civility, gallantry, good manners, polite deportment, savoir-faire, breeding, mealymouthedness, gentility, smoothness," and so on. Would you rather entertain a mealymouth or a courteous person?

English is a double language, in that it derives in large measure from Latin and Anglo-Saxon (or Old English). **Latinate** words are generally the polysyllabic ones of the romance languages. They are often musical or fluid: "delectable," "abstraction," "equestrian," "exhilaration"; and indirect, as "seduction": "the leading aside of." They tend to be formal, allusive, circuitous, built syllable by syllable, sometimes euphemistic, such as "expectorate." **Anglo-Saxon** words, on the other hand, from the northern European and Germanic invaders of early England, are considered to be less polite, more direct. "Four-letter" words and other short, earth-bound words are usually Anglo-Saxon derived, "spit," for example, or "wise," which feels more basic perhaps than the Latinate "judicious," with its implied legalistic weight. "He expectorated on terra firma" seems pretentious, too fancy, and indirect compared to "He spit on the ground." Paul Zimmer used "obtundity" in his Alphonse poem to create a feeling of bombast and inflated rhetoric for comic effect.

Words from other languages have found their way into English, too, of course, and can be used for particular effects. Besides these root-language distinctions, we have colloquial language or slang. Usually today, plain, direct language is considered most effective, a form-follows-function view of art and communication that eliminates frills. But while it is good not to be affected, sometimes a polysyllabic or fancy word can musically accent the tone, as in Herrick's "liquefaction of her clothes." If we know that the root meaning of this word is "makes liquid," then the sound of the word itself seems liquid, flowing.

Skim through a dictionary, noticing the roots of various words. Do Latin or Anglo-Saxon words predominate? What words do you notice from other languages? Choose any poem and see which class of words dominates, the polysyllabic and indirect or the short and direct. How does this affect tone? It would be instructive to choose any well-known poem and rewrite it using synonyms or words with similar meanings. For that matter, you might try this with one of your own poems. Go from Anglo-Saxon derived words to Latinate ones or from formal language to slang, for example.

Connotation of a word is not solely a matter of Latin or Anglo-Saxon, of course. Connotation, and thereby tone, may be formed by association. Many words were originally metaphorical, though we may have forgotten such beginnings. Describing hunger, the user of "ravenous" should notice the black birds of carrion, the ravens, nesting in it. One should recall a scene of famine, burnt fields, or winter hardship, if "famished" is written. The Anglo-Saxon derived "hungry" has more to do with having an appetite, though if one is hungry one may even be "starving," which possibly goes back to a word meaning "rigid," like a corpse. If you are going to be a poet, when you arrive for a meal you ought to know whether you are ravenous, famished, hungry, or starving.

The problems of word choice in getting the right tone and *meaning* in a poem are demonstrated clearly when we look at translations of the same work by different people. Federico García Lorca's "Romance Sonámbulo" has been translated numerous times. Here, for example, are lines 10, 11, and 12 of the original, and four different translations of those lines.

Bajo la luna gitana,
las cosas la están mirando
y ella no puede mirarlas.

While the gypsy moon beam plays
Things at her are gazing keenly
But she cannot meet their gaze.

Translated by Roy and Mary Campbell

Under the gypsy moon,
Things are watching her,
Things she cannot see.

Translated by Rolfe Humphries

Beneath the gypsy moon,
all things look at her
but she cannot see them.

Translated by Steven Spender and J. J. Gile

Beneath the gipsy moon, things are looking at her, but she cannot look back at them.

Prose translated from *Penguin Book of Spanish Verse,*
edited by J. M. Cohen

---

1. Which of the translations seems most poetic?
2. Choose one word and its four translations, such as "gazing," "watching," "look," and "are looking" as translations of *mirando*. Try to describe the difference each choice makes in the translation.

3. Besides word choice, sound patterns and rhythms also influence the mood or tone of a poem. How do different sound patterns and rhythms influence these translations?
4. Whether or not you know Spanish, you could look up the words in the original and write your own translation. Try to write a fair translation that is somewhat different from these four.

Different word choices create striking differences in meaning. "She" either feels guilty and won't look up, is blind and cannot see, is under some sort of enchantment and unable to see, or exists under some other interpretation that is finally the translator's. Any translation depends on the translator's aims as well as skill. Is it desirable to give the most literal translation, or to try to convey the spirit and tone of the original even if that means altering the meaning? Is it possible or even desirable to imitate the rhyme and meter of the original if that means using less accurate translations of individual words? Should translation be colloquial or scholarly? Even if these questions are resolved, there will be debates over which English words actually represent the Spanish most accurately, because tone, including connotation and actual word sound, is part of the meaning of the poem, and even if translation is as literal as possible, how is one to translate tone?

Rhyme and meter and other sound structures are also influential in altering voice and tone. The use of certain rhymes and meters is associated with a certain attitude toward the subject. A Shakespearean sonnet, for example, cues the sensitive reader to listen for a certain progression of ideas, variations leading to a turn in thought, and a sense of surprise or changing view at the end. Circular French forms, such as the **villanelle,** lend themselves to a light, musical tone, although Dylan Thomas's villanelle "Do Not Go Gentle into That Good Night" treats the subject of death seriously. One can work with the customary tone of a form or work against it, but in any case, one should be aware of its effect. An obvious example of a form with an associated tone is the limerick. Is it possible to write a serious poem using the rhyme and meter of a limerick? Try it if you dare.

The following poem is not a limerick nor is it an example of *light verse.* It does, however, use rhyme in a formal way, which gives the poem a musical, light quality. The contrast in tone between the rhymed, regular stanzas, the incongruous images of the woodchucks dying with darkly comic gestures, and the ultimately grim subject surprises the reader into laughter and then into serious recognition. Notice how Maxine Kumin uses ordinary speech within a tight, rhyming form for ironic effect.

Woodchucks

Gassing the woodchucks didn't turn out right.
The knockout bomb from the Feed and Grain Exchange
was featured as merciful, quick at the bone
and the case we had against them was airtight,
both exits shoehorned shut with puddingstone,
but they had a sub-sub-basement out of range.

Next morning they turned up again, no worse
for the cyanide than we for our cigarettes
and state-store Scotch, all of us up to scratch.
They brought down the marigolds as a matter of course
and then took over the vegetable patch
nipping the broccoli shoots, beheading the carrots.

The food from our mouths, I said, righteously thrilling
to the feel of the .22, the bullets' neat noses.
I, a lapsed pacifist fallen from grace
puffed with Darwinian pieties for killing,
now drew a bead on the littlest woodchuck's face.
He died down in the everbearing roses.

Ten minutes later I dropped the mother. She
flipflopped in the air and fell, her needle teeth
still hooked in a leaf of early Swiss chard.
Another baby next. O one-two-three
the murderer inside me rose up hard,
the hawkeye killer came on stage forthwith.

There's one chuck left. Old wily fellow, he keeps
me cocked and ready day after day after day.
All night I hunt his humped-up form. I dream

I sight along the barrel in my sleep.
If only they'd all consented to die unseen
gassed underground the quiet Nazi way.

MAXINE KUMIN

---

1. Kumin begins the poem with an almost petulant sounding complaint against no one in particular. Does the tone she uses in this first line prepare you for her mood at the ending of the poem?
2. In part, tone is a matter of word choice. Are there any words that stand out as particularly important in establishing the tone of the poem? For example, "knockout bomb," "case," "airtight," "up to scratch," "marigolds," "righteously thrilling," "Darwinian pieties," "mother," "baby," and "Nazi." How do these and other words determine the way in which we read the poem? Try substituting synonyms for some of these words and noticing whether the tone changes.
3. Kumin makes a startling connection between "our cigarettes / and state-store Scotch" and the cyanide she uses in trying to poison the woodchucks. At another point she describes the mother woodchuck dying with her teeth "still hooked in a leaf of early Swiss chard." Can you find other such incongruously linked images? Are these incongruous images more grim or comical?
4. How does rhyme influence the tone of the poem?
5. How does Kumin use humor to draw the reader into her uncomfortable feelings aroused by events described in the poem? How do we feel when we laugh at things that turn out to be serious?

Modern poetry is often described as using patterns of common speech. Maxine Kumin, for example, used a colloquial, conversational style in "Woodchucks," as in the line, "Ten minutes later I dropped the mother." Of course, common speech is often repetitious, trivial, disorganized, and inefficient. Poetry that is said to adopt the style of common speech, however, is not actually like real, incidental speech in this way. It is like common speech in that it uses simple, direct language and natural speech pauses—for breath or emphasis—as line breaks. Here are two excerpts from what might be called a natural-speech poem, Walt Whitman's "Song of Myself."

1

I celebrate myself, and sing myself,
And what I assume you shall assume,
For every atom belonging to me as good belongs to you.

I loafe and invite my soul,
I lean and loafe at my ease observing a spear of summer grass.

My tongue, every atom of my blood, form'd from this soil, this air,
Born here of parents born here from parents the same, and their
    parents the same,
I, now thirty-seven years old in perfect health begin,
Hoping to cease not till death.

Creeds and schools in abeyance,
Retiring back a while sufficed at what they are, but never forgotten,
I harbor for good or bad, I permit to speak at every hazard,
Nature without check with original energy.

6

A child said *What is the grass?* fetching it to me with full hands,
How could I answer the child? I do not know what it is any more
    than he.

I guess it must be the flag of my disposition, out of hopeful green
    stuff woven

Or I guess it is the handkerchief of the Lord.
A scented gift and remembrancer designedly dropt.
Bearing the owner's name someway in the corners, that we may see
    and remark, and say *Whose?*

Or I guess the grass is itself a child, the produced babe of the
    vegetation.

Or I guess it is a uniform hieroglyphic;
And it means, Sprouting alike in broad zones and narrow zones,
Growing among black folks as among white,
Kanuck, Tuckahoe, Congressman, Cuff, I give them the same, I
    receive them the same.

WALT WHITMAN

Whitman's tone is exuberant, excited, like common speech in measuring the line by breath. That is, he tends to pause for a line break at a point where a speaker might pause to take a breath, although lines are rather long. Out of context, a line such as "How could I answer the child? I do not know what it is any more than he" sounds like prose. The rhythm lacks the regular ups and downs of any recognizable metrical cadence. Phrases such as "I guess it must be" and "Or I guess" are casual, conversational, and "nonpoetic," until they are placed in the context of the repetition and the sweeping rhythm of the long lines. Some images, such as "the flag of my disposition" or "the produced babe of the vegetation" sound metaphorical, but their freshness and power come from the way they occur as notes in the larger context.

Remember that tone is not just one thing. When we speak of the voice, tone is a vocal quality that expresses the tension of the poet's relationship to the subject. Recall that the word "tone" is also used to speak of the body's muscles, their definition and flexibility. A poem with an ill-defined tone lacks muscle, lacks definition. Moreover, whether words are spoken aloud or read silently, the voice and its tone create a muscle response in the body, sympathetic memories in our own vocal cords or tongues or throats or lips, sense impressions that have to do with the actual movement required to form the sounds.

Words vibrate on the ear drums when they are spoken aloud, and their meanings evoke sensory memories. Think of how tone is related to the physical experience of language. A shrill tone, hurting the ears. An angry tone, like a blow to the body, threatening. An ironic tone, suggesting the tension of opposites. A joyful tone, making us want to dance or breathe deeply.

By association, tone can also suggest dramatic postures: declamatory, musing, pensive, and so on. What kind of pose would you strike to get into the character of any of the preceding poems? Surely the tone of Roethke's poem would require some different posture or stance than Oliver's; try some poses. When you are working on a poem, imagine, or actually try out, the gesture or pose that goes with the tone you wish to create.

Tone as sound is the opposite of noise. That is, tone is definable, recognizable, of a special quality; noise has no special quality. It is just noise. One of the joys of reading poetry is to recognize the finesse with which a poet achieves exactly the right tone and sustains it.

The following poem by Chilean poet Pablo Neruda and translated by William O'Daly is different from the other examples in this chapter in that it speaks in a simple, direct way, apparently in the voice of the poet, without irony and with just a few fairly general images.

VI

Pardon me, if when I want
to tell the story of my life
it's the land I talk about.
This is the land.
It grows in your blood
and you grow.
If it dies in your blood
you die out.

PABLO NERUDA
translated by
William O'Daly

1. How does the address, "Pardon me," with which Neruda begins the poem, establish the tone of the poem?
2. If you were to make a short list of words that would describe the emotions of this poem, what would they be?
3. Although the poem seems fairly direct and simple, Neruda makes a passionate and extreme statement. What is that statement? How does the tone of the poem work to allow him to make such a large statement?

The next example uses still another sort of voice, an anonymous one that is so subdued we scarcely notice the presence of the speaker here at all. Instead, the voice gives itself over to the creation of mood and landscape. Garrett Hongo is an American poet of Japanese ancestry, born in Hawaii in 1951 and raised in Southern California, and acutely aware of ethnicity in the American landscape. In a dreamy, filmlike narrative, he describes a woman in Los Angeles coming home to her neighborhood with an armload of groceries. The poem is timeless, Hongo gives no specific clues as to exactly when this is taking place, and yet there is a feeling that all of these things take place in a very particular past with particular meaning for the speaker.

Yellow Light

One arm hooked around the frayed strap
of a tar-black patent-leather purse,
the other cradling something for dinner:
fresh bunches of spinach from a J-Town *yaoya,*
sides of split Spanish mackerel from Alviso's,
maybe a loaf of Langendorf; she steps
off the hissing bus at Olympic and Fig,
begins the three-block climb up the hill,
passing gangs of schoolboys playing war,
Japs against Japs, Chicanas chalking sidewalks
with the holy double-yoked crosses of hopscotch,
and the Korean grocer's wife out for a stroll
around this neighborhood of Hawaiian apartments
just starting to steam with cooking
and the anger of young couples coming home
from work, yelling at kids, flicking on
TV sets for the Wednesday Night Fights.

If it were May, hydrangeas and jacaranda
flowers in the streetside trees would be
blooming through the smog of late spring.
Wisteria in Masuda's front yard would be
shaking out the long tresses of its purple hair.
Maybe mosquitoes, moths, a few orange butterflies
settling on the lattice of monkey flowers
tangled in chain-link fences by the trash.

But this is October, and Los Angeles
seethes like a billboard under twilight.
From used-car lots and the movie houses uptown,
long silver sticks of light probe the sky.
From the Miracle Mile, whole freeways away,

a brilliant fluorescence breaks out
and makes war with the dim squares
of yellow kitchen light winking on
in all the side streets of the Barrio.

She climbs up the two flights of flagstone
stairs to 201-B, the spikes of her high heels
clicking like kitchen knives on a cutting board,
props the groceries against the door,
fishes through memo pads, a compact,
empty packs of chewing gum, and finds her keys.

The moon then, cruising from behind
a screen of eucalyptus across the street,
covers everything, everything in sight,
in a heavy light like yellow onions.

GARRETT HONGO

---

1. How would the poem change if the writer had chosen to speak in the voice
    of the young woman? In the first person plural "we"?
2. What are some of the images that stay in your mind after you read the poem?
    Why do you remember these images and how do they influence the mood
    of the poem?
3. What words in particular contribute to the overall feeling or tone of the
    poem?
4. What is the tone of the voice in this poem? What general feeling does that
    voice convey?

Garrett Hongo's poem is written in the third person, present tense,
so as to emphasize the scene rather than a speaker. Other poems in this
chapter use both present and past tenses and a range of viewpoints, including the author speaking through a character in monologue, through
more than one character in dialogue, and the author speaking in his or
her own voice. Point of view and tense are both important in poetry.
Sometimes it's hard to imagine how a poem written from one view might

have been written some other way. Most commonly we write in the first person (I) or in the third person (he or she). "I" naturally feels intimate, even when the poem is clearly in persona. "He" or "she" distances the focus. Making the person plural, "we" or "they" generalizes the effect but can also give it a sort of choral resonance and strangeness that's interesting, as in parts of T. S. Eliot's "The Hollow Men." Writing in the second person (you) is a somewhat more artificial choice than first or third but one which is useful in coloring the tone of the writing. "You" can be used for intentional ambiguity, perhaps meaning "I" but moving the attention away from the speaker rhetorically by displacing the point of view. Use of "you" can also draw the reader into the experience and create a mood that is slightly paranoid or edgy sounding.

Verb tenses can also be changed and the first choice may not always be the most effective one. A poem in the present tense has a feeling of immediacy, but past and even future tenses can be used to color the tone of a poem and alter meaning.

Suggestions for Writing

1. Write a love poem using an unexpected emotional tone, such as:
   a) Indignant
   b) Self-pitying
   c) Mocking
   d) Businesslike
   Can you sustain the tone and somehow make it work to create a sincere statement of love or affection?

2. Choose a poem you have already written and decide whether the language is predominately Anglo-Saxon derived or Latinate. Then rewrite the poem reversing the words. That is, if you use the word "hard," substitute difficult, and so on. How does this change the tone of your poem?

   An alternative to this exercise is to rewrite a poem by a well-known author and reverse the diction. How would a poem by William Carlos Williams sound in polysyllabic and indirect language, for example?

3. Write a poem in which the language is ostentatiously fancy.

4. Start with a subject for a poem, something that has recently happened to you or someone you know, something you have read in the newspaper, or something you have observed. Mentally strike an extreme emotional pose such as outrage, bewilderment, or pity. You can even get in the spirit of the pose by acting it out—sitting at your typewriter, waving your fists or plunging your face in your hands. Make this a method-acting piece. Then write out that feeling; let the feeling create the rhythms of the poem and choose the words for you. Tell about the subject, the faster the better.

5. Write a poem in which the tone seems to go along seriously until the end but ultimately becomes satirical or simply funny.

6. Write a poem in the persona of:
   a) An historical personage
   b) Someone you know, addressing you
   c) An animal or inanimate object
   d) An innocent character who does not realize the significance of what he or she is saying
   e) A part of your body (your nose talks to your feet, for example)
   f) Someone who is your complete opposite in some way, such as a member of the opposite sex, or a completely unsympathetic character whom you would not like

7. Write a poem in the persona of a group. For examples refer to the frequently anthologized "We Real Cool," by Gwendolyn Brooks or "The Hollow Men" by T. S. Eliot.

8. Write a dramatic monologue in an ironic tone, such as Browning's "My Last Duchess."

9. Try rewriting a free-verse poem that you have already done into the form of a sonnet, a villanelle, or some other set form. Does this change the tone, and thereby the sense, of the original?

10. Translate a poem from another language into English.

11. Write a poem in which you imitate the tone of voice of someone in a trivial, common incident, such as talking to the cashier in a grocery store, trying to place a long-distance call, or speaking with a stranger on a bus.

12. Write a poem in which there are two distinctly different voices.

13. Choose a line or a short sequence of lines from one of your own poems. Rewrite the line or lines at least six times, changing point of view and tense in this way.

    Rewrite 1: first person singular, present tense (I am)
    Rewrite 2: second person singular, past tense (you were)
    Rewrite 3: third person singular, present tense (he, she, it is)
    Rewrite 4: first person plural, future tense (we will or will be)
    Rewrite 5: second person plural, present tense (you are)
    Rewrite 6: third person, past tense (they were)

11

Genres

Just as awareness of voice, tone, and persona may help sharpen a poem, thinking about intention can clarify and strengthen your work. What do you intend to do with any given poem? Or what do you intend for the poem to do for the reader? Do you want to change the world, to express the inexpressible, to satirize, or to confront? Should the reader do anything or be changed in some way after reading your poem?

This chapter deals with such intentions and the idea of **genres,** meaning types or kinds, of poetry. Thinking about genres may suggest alternatives for shaping material. Is it best rendered as a narrative, in chronological order? Or does a subject lend itself to dramatic treatment, as art imitating life?

The two genres of poetry posited by Aristotle were **dramatic** and **narrative.** Dramatic has to do with the idea of **mimesis,** imitation of reality. In drama we see reality re-created, acted out. Some modern writers, T. S. Eliot and Federico Garcia Lorca for example, have written poetic drama, but they are exceptions. What was once a dominant form is now practically nonexistent. As an experiment you might incorporate techniques of early drama, such as the use of masks and a chorus, into **performance poetry,** or you might adapt techniques of other kinds of drama, such as the masque, to a performance poem or to your poem's structure. (Since this seems more in the realm of theater than of poetry, it would be difficult to deal with here.) Dramatic monologues, such as Browning's "My Last Duchess" (Chapter 10), Eliot's "Lovesong of J. Alfred Prufrock," or James Dickey's long poems in persona such as "The Lifeguard" and "The Firebombing," though not necessarily intended for performance, work by simulating reality in the voice of a single speaker.

Narrative poetry, on the other hand, is in the poet's own voice. This does not mean that narrative poetry is a personal statement, but rather that it is the poet's own voice telling us about something. An **epic,** such as the *Odyssey,* is classic narrative poetry. In our culture, epic poems seem to have been replaced by epic novels and epic movies. Stories told in poetry today are apt to be remarkably shorter than epics; they are shorter, even, than nineteenth-century narrative poems, such as "The Rime of the Ancient Mariner" by Coleridge and "Sohrab and Rustum" by Matthew Arnold. For our purposes we can think of a **narrative poem** as a story told in the poet's voice and organized chronologically.

Aristotle did not even consider the lyric; that came later. The ancient **lyric** was a song intended to be performed and accompanied by the lyre; the same meaning is still implied when we speak of the words of a song as lyrics. The lyric derived from oral literature and evolved into a poem intended to be read from the printed page rather than to be sung. Rhythmic patterns, rhymes, and melodious language are musical elements that continue to be important in lyric poetry; but even in poems in which these may be negligible, the dominant characteristic of the lyric is the joining of feeling with the sound of words. It is not just what is said that makes lyric poetry, but how it is said. Of course, this is more or less true of all poetry, but the lyric is often difficult or impossible to paraphrase. And yet meanings are communicated through word combinations, sounds, rhythms, repetitions, images, associations, **figures of speech,** and so on. In the twentieth century, lyric poetry predominates. It is usually taken to be:

1. Personal or individualistic.

2. Emotional; concerned with feeling.

3. Musical; not necessarily metrical, but sound elements—such as rhythm and rhyme—are an integral part of sense. Consequently, paraphrasing and translating are difficult.

4. Organized by association rather than by chronology.

5. Compressed, so that figurative speech, allusion, and so forth suggest rather than state explicitly. (The lyric tends to be short, but length is not definitive per se—a long poem may be lyrical or a short poem narrative.)

Because **didactic** poetry has been associated with narrow moral lessons and badly written exemplary verse, it has a bad reputation. But much good poetry has a didactic element. Modern confessional poetry could be said to teach by example; even if the writer is presenting the worst side of himself or herself, there is the idea that truth is instructive. Satirical poetry is surely didactic; and modern social reform movements have encouraged a didactic element. The 1960s fostered a poetry that was critical of the Vietnam War and of social injustice generally. Poetry that is about the art of poetry, such as the work of Wallace Stevens, is somewhat didactic, teaching *aesthetic* principles.

Ours is much broader than the view of didactic poetry as "Thirty days hath September," but clearly there *is* a difference between a poem in which the writer wants to teach us that war is evil and one aimed at expressing an ecstatic experience. In an age when poetry seems to be so much the expression of the individual viewpoint, it is reasonable to ask whether a writer is trying to teach or influence the reader.

Thus, to sum up, if we think of poetic genres in terms of purpose we can say that the dramatic poet wants to imitate (or simulate) reality, the narrative poet wants to tell a story, the lyric poet wants to express emotion, and the didactic poet wants to teach a lesson.

Of course, once a writer completes a satisfactory poem, what difference does it make whether we identify it as a lyric, a narrative, or some entirely new creature? None, really, from the writer's point of view. Critics and scholars analyze and categorize in order to better understand what writers do, but living writers themselves are continually pushing the established genres beyond their limits and into new incarnations.

There is also no need to quarantine one genre from the others. A small story can be set into a lyric poem that predominantly deals with emotions rather than events. Passages of dialogue, as in a verse play, can be combined with lyric or narrative elements. Moreover, although stodgy, didactic verse, such as Victorian poems advising children to be seen and not heard, is happily out of fashion, the tradition of instructing through poetry is alive in contemporary works, and didactic elements appear in both lyric and narrative poems. The reason for studying genres is not to keep ourselves awake nights worrying whether we are writing lyrics or narratives, but merely to point to the existence of genres and their aims, the better to see various possibilities.

Let us apply these categories by asking what the poet seems to be doing in the following examples. You can also consider genre in other poems in this book.

"Oh No" by Robert Creeley seems to tell a sort of story, though the details are not clear; but as the title indicates, it is also about feeling. Is it possible to categorize this short work as lyric, narrative, or didactic?

Oh No

If you wander far enough
you will come to it
and when you get there
they will give you a place to sit

for yourself only, in a nice chair,
and all your friends will be there
with smiles on their faces
and they will likewise all have places.

ROBERT CREELEY

---

1. In your own words, describe the events in this poem.
2. What does the title add to Creeley's poem?
3. Does the sound of the words play an important part in this poem?
4. If Creeley is communicating a feeling, how would you describe the feeling? What causes that feeling?
5. Is this poem didactic in any way?

In "Your Dog Dies," Raymond Carver writes in the present tense about the way writers exploit their own (and others') experience.

Your Dog Dies

it gets run over by a van.
you find it at the side of the road
and bury it.
you feel bad about it.
you feel bad personally,
but you feel bad for your daughter
because it was her pet,
and she loved it so.

she used to croon to it
and let it sleep in her bed.
you write a poem about it.
you call it a poem for your daughter,
about the dog getting run over by a van
and how you looked after the dog afterwards,
took it out into the woods
and buried it, deep, deep,
and that poem turns out so good
you're almost glad the little dog
was run over, or else you'd never
have written that good poem.
then you sit down to write
a poem about writing a poem
about the death of that dog,
but while you're writing you
suddenly hear a woman scream
your name, your first name,
both syllables,
and your heart stops.
after a minute, you continue writing.
she screams again.
you wonder how long this can go on.

RAYMOND CARVER

---

1. "Your Dog Dies" is clearly about feelings, but a case could also be made that it tells a chronological story and is thus a narrative poem. How would you define the poem in terms of genre?
2. In the preceding chapter we addressed the idea that changing voice or person changes the feeling of a poem. Both "Your Dog Dies" and "Oh No" are written in the second person, "you." In your opinion, why did Carver and Creeley choose to use "you" instead of either "I" or the third person?

In "The Apprentice Gravedigger" notice how Herbert Scott reconstructs the experience of working as a gravedigger by telling a series of small stories.

The Apprentice Gravedigger

"You'll always have a job."

1

There is a place for every body.
The Rich have frontage on the road;
the Masons sleep together in neat rows;
the Black lean back in weeds,
beyond the grass, where spotted
ground squirrels burrow in their holes.

2

Three feet of dirt,
two of clay,
the last, gray slate
that's hard to chip away.

We dig them clean and straight
as if our lives depended on it.

3

Two buddies
roared their bikes
beneath a cement mixer
and mixed their bodies.

No telling who
was where or what.
They dug out.
I dug them in.

4

The mourners come,
a fluttering of clothes,
in loose formations
through the stones

like birds that search
for scattered seed
on wintered fields.

5

Six months and three hard rains
the boxes go,
the earth caves in.

Wood rots as good
as man, I think.

The ground now knows
its tenant, not by
reputation.

We truck dirt in
and fill the graves again.

6

T.C., Red, and Boomer
pushed me in a grave
and cranked the casket down
till I was flat, laid out,
my hands above my chest.

"White Boy's learning
how to die,"
they laughed and cried,
then pulled me out
and washed my head.

7

We dug one up instead of down.
The widow came to supervise
the moving to a larger plot.

We winched him high. The vault,
expensive moisture-proof cement,
had split. He tipped
and poured himself a drink.

She knew him right enough.
He rained a putrefaction
you could keep.

8

Each time
the same sad words
for stranger bodies,

women cold with fear,
children weeding noses,

husbands wheezing
rumors of death.

9

I killed a king snake sunning
in the branches of a cedar,
cut him with a spade
until he spilled
his breakfast on the grass.

Five sparrow babies,
slick and sweet,
poured out like heavy jam,
the fruit still warm.

I nudged them in the grave
The snake, the birds, the man,
together in the ground.

10

When it rains
we bury ourselves
in piles of plastic grass,

in the shed,
with straps and shovels,
and visions of the dead.

11

I don't like to dig
the children's graves.
They cramp you in,
not room enough
to swing your axe
or work a sweat.

I'd like to climb in,
brace my back,
and push them longer.
If I was stronger.

12

"What do you do?"
I build holes in the ground.

HERBERT SCOTT

1. Scott divides his poem into several parts. Is this chiefly a lyric, narrative, or didactic device? For what reasons might he have divided his poem in this way?
2. Is the feeling the same in each section of "The Apprentice Gravedigger" or are there changes from stanza to stanza?
3. What genre does this poem represent most clearly? Why?

Because William Stafford's "The Animal that Drank Up Sound" is like a myth or fable, we might expect a lesson of some sort. The poem also tells a story. We wonder, what will happen? Will the world come back to life? How will it happen? We read on to find out and the story is mysterious and compelling, full of strange, beautiful imagery. Notice the blending of elements.

The Animal That Drank Up Sound

1

One day across the lake where echoes come now
an animal that needed sound came down. He gazed
enormously, and instead of making any, he took
away from, sound: the lake and all the land
went dumb. A fish that jumped went back like a knife,
and the water died. In all the wilderness around he
drained the rustle from the leaves into the mountainside
and folded a quilt over the rocks, getting ready
to store everything the place had known; he buried—
thousands of autumns deep—the noise that used to come there.

Then that animal wandered on and began to drink
the sound out of all the valleys—the croak of toads,
and all the little shiny noise grass blades make.
He drank till winter, and then looked out one night
at the stilled places guaranteed around by frozen
peaks and held in the shallow pools of starlight.
It was finally tall and still, and he stopped on the highest
ridge, just where the cold sky fell away
like a perpetual curve, and from there he walked on silently,
and began to starve.

When the moon drifted over that night the whole world lay
just like the moon, shining back that still
silver, and the moon saw its own animal dead
on the snow, its dark absorbent paws and quiet
muzzle, and thick, velvet, deep fur.

2

After the animal that drank sound died, the world
lay still and cold for months, and the moon yearned
and explored, letting its dead light float down
the west walls of canyons and then climb its delighted
soundless way up the east side. The moon
owned the earth its animal had faithfully explored.
The sun disregarded the life it used to warm.

But on the north side of a mountain, deep in some rocks,
a cricket slept. It had been hiding when that animal
passed, and as spring came again this cricket waited,
afraid to crawl out into the heavy stillness.
Think how deep the cricket felt, lost there
in such a silence—the grass, the leaves, the water,
the stilled animals all depending on such a little
thing. But softly it tried—"Cricket!"—and back like a river
from that one act flowed the kind of world we know,
first whisperings, then moves in the grass and leaves;
the water splashed, and a big night bird screamed.

It all returned, our precious world with its life and sound,
where sometimes loud over the hill the moon,
wild again, looks for its animal to roam, still,
down out of the hills, any time.
But somewhere a cricket waits.

It listens now, and practices at night.

WILLIAM STAFFORD

---

1. How would you describe this poem in terms of genre? Explain.
2. Why does the poet divide the poem into two parts? What goes on in the two different parts?
3. In the first two lines, what do you learn that contributes to the story the poem tells?
4. Setting (time and place), action, character, and conflict are all important in fiction writing. Are they important in this poem?

Lucille Clifton writes here about refusing to be defined in other people's terms. She uses the title, "note to my self," and two quotations, an anonymous line from a T-shirt and a statement by another author, to establish a thesis, an opening for the poem, and a point of view regarding racial identity.

note to my self

it's a black thing you wouldn't understand
                              (t-shirt)
amira baraka—*i refuse to be judged by white men.*

or defined. and i see
that even the best believe
they have that right,
believe that
what they say i mean
is what i mean
as if words only matter in the world they know,
as if when i choose words
i must choose those
that they can live with
even if something inside me
cannot live,
as if my story is
so trivial
we can forget together,
as if i am not scarred,
as if my family enemy
does not look like them,
as if i have not reached
across our history to touch,
to soothe on more than one
occasion
and will again,
although the merely human
is denied me still
and i am now no longer beast
but saint.

                              LUCILLE CLIFTON

---

1.   Notice that this is a poem of address. Although Clifton calls this a note to
herself, who else might she be addressing?

2. How would you describe the complex tone Clifton uses here?
3. Is this poem primarily lyric, narrative, or didactic? Explain.

Diane Wakoski's "Sour Milk" uses a convincing metaphor to argue for the appreciation of age and experience.

Sour Milk

You can't make it
turn sweet
again.
        Once
it was an innocent color
like the flowers of wild strawberries,
and its texture was simple
would pass through a clean cheese cloth,
its taste was fresh.
And now
with nothing more guilty than the passage of time
to chide it with,
the same substance
has turned sour and lumpy.

The sour milk
makes interesting & delicious doughs,
can be carried to a further state of bacterial action
to create new foods,
can in its own right
be considered complicated and more interesting in texture
to one who studies it closely,
like a map of all the world.

But
to most of us:
it is spoiled.
Sour.

We throw it out,
down the drain—not in the back yard—
careful not to spill any
because the smell is strong.
A good cook
would be shocked
with the waste.
But we do not live in a world of good cooks.

I am the milk.
Time passes.
You cannot make it
turn sweet
again.
I sit guiltily on the refrigerator shelf
trembling with hope for a cook
who dreams of waffles,
biscuits, dumplings
and other delicious breads
fearing the modern housewife
who will lift me off the shelf and with one deft twist
of a wrist . . .
you know the rest.

You are the milk.
When it is your turn
remember,
there is nothing more than the passage of time
we can chide you with.

DIANE WAKOSKI

---

1. Does "Sour Milk" tell a story? Does it have a chronological organization?
2. Does the poem communicate an emotion that is difficult to express in other words? If so, what it that emotion?
3. How would you describe the sound of this poem? Does it sound lyrical or musical? Is sound important in the poem?

4. Does the author have a point she wants to make? (Why does she say, "When it is your turn/remember . . ."?) Explain.
5. How would you describe "Sour Milk" in terms of genre? Explain.

Kenneth Koch's "Fresh Air" satirizes certain attitudes toward poetry, especially the stuffy and academic; hence the search for fresh air. For a poem attacking just about everybody and everything connected with poetry, by someone who is well known as a writer and teacher of poetry, the satire is remarkably good-humored—more farcical than mean, and extremely funny. This is a poem from the mid-1950s, when many contemporary poets were struggling to throw off the influence of the traditional and the academic in favor of more open forms and indigenous poetry. Koch's satire reflects these concerns, but it is not always easy to see whose side he takes; perhaps no one's, he is having too good a time. It seems aimed at deflating bombast wherever it occurs. If you like wit, high spirits, and excitement in poetry, look up more of Koch's work.

Fresh Air

1

At the Poem Society a black-haired man stands up to say
"You make me sick with all your talk about restraint and mature
     talent!
Haven't you ever looked out the window at a painting by Matisse.
Or did you always stay in hotels where there were too many
     spiders crawling on your visages?
Did you ever glance inside a bottle of sparkling pop,
Or see a citizen split in two by the lightning?
I am afraid you have never smiled at the hibernation
Of bear cubs except that you saw in it some deep relation
To human suffering and wishes, oh what a bunch of crackpots!"
The black-haired man sits down, and the others shoot arrows
     at him.
A blond man stands up and says,
"He is right! Why should we be organized to defend the kingdom

Of dullness? There are so many slimy people connected with
 poetry,
Too, and people who know nothing about it!
I am not recommending that poets like each other and organize to
 fight them,
But simply that lightning should strike them."
Then the assembled mediocrities shot arrows at the blond-haired
 man.
The chairman stood up on the platform, oh he was physically ugly!
He was small-limbed and -boned and thought he was quite
 seductive,
But he was bald with certain hideous black hairs,
And his voice had the sound of water leaving a vaseline bathtub,
And he said, "The subject for this evening's discussion is poetry
On the subject of love between swans." And everyone threw
 candy hearts
At the disgusting man, and they stuck to his bib and tucker,
And he danced up and down on the platform in terrific glee
And recited the poetry of his little friends—but the blond man
 stuck his head
Out of a cloud and recited poems about the east and thunder,
And the black-haired man moved through the stratosphere
 chanting
Poems of the relationships between terrific prehistoric charcoal
 whales,
And the slimy man with candy hearts sticking all over him
Wilted away like a cigarette paper on which the bumblebees have
 urinated,
And all the professors left the room to go back to their duty,
And all that were left in the room were five or six poets
And together they sang the new poem of the twentieth century
Which, though influenced by Mallarmé, Shelley, Byron,
 and Whitman,
Plus a million other poets, is still entirely original
And is so exciting that it cannot be here repeated.
You must go to the Poem Society and wait for it to happen.
Once you have heard this poem you will not love any other,
Once you have dreamed this dream you will be inconsolable,
Once you have loved this dream you will be as one dead,
Once you have visited the passages of this time's great art!

2

"Oh, to be seventeen years old
Once again," sang the red-haired man, "and not know that poetry
Is ruled with the sceptre of the dumb, the deaf, and the creepy!"
And the shouting persons battered his immortal body with stones
And threw his primitive comedy into the sea
From which it sang forth poems irrevocably blue.

Who are the great poets of our time, and what are their names?
Yeats of the baleful influence, Auden of the baleful influence, Eliot
   of the baleful influence
(Is Eliot a great poet? no one knows), Hardy, Stevens, Williams (is
   Hardy of our time?),
Hopkins (is Hopkins of our time?), Rilke (is Rilke of our time?),
   Lorca (is Lorca of our time?), who is still of our time?
Mallarmé, Valéry, Apollinaire, Eluard, Reverdy, French poets are
   still of our time,
Pasternak and Mayakovsky, is Jouve of our time?

Where are young poets in America, they are trembling in
   publishing houses and universities,
Above all they are trembling in universities, they are bathing the
   library steps with their spit.
They are gargling out innocuous (to whom?) poems about maple
   trees and their children,
Sometimes they brave a subject like the Villa d'Este or a lighthouse
   in Rhode Island,
Oh what worms they are! they wish to perfect their form.

Yet could not these young men, put in another profession,
Succeed admirably, say at sailing a ship? I do not doubt it, Sir,
   and I wish we could try them.
(A plane flies over the ship holding a bomb but perhaps it will not
   drop the bomb,
The young poets from the universities are staring anxiously at
   the skies,
Oh they are remembering their days on the campus when they
   looked up to watch birds excrete,
They are remembering the days they spent making their elegant
   poems.)

Is there no voice to cry out from the wind and say what it is like
   to be the wind,
To be roughed up by the trees and to bring music from the
   scattered houses
And the stones, and to be in such intimate relationship with the sea
That you cannot understand it? Is there no one who feels like a
   pair of pants?

3

Summer in the trees! "It is time to strangle several bad poets."
The yellow hobbyhorse rocks to and fro, and from the chimney
Drops the Strangler! The white and pink roses are slightly agitated
   by the struggle,
But afterwards beside the dead "poet" they cuddle up comfortingly
   against their vase. They are safer now, no one will compare
   them to the sea.

Here on the railroad train, one more time, is the Strangler.
He is going to get that one there, who is on his way to a poetry
   reading.
Agh! Biff! A body falls to the moving floor.

In the football stadium I also see him,
He leaps through the frosty air at the maker of comparisons
Between football and life and silently, silently strangles him!

Here is the Strangler dressed in a cowboy suit
Leaping from his horse to annihilate the students of myth!

The Strangler's ear is alert for the names of Orpheus,
Cuchulain, Gawain, and Odysseus,
And for poems addressed to Jane Austen, F. Scott Fitzgerald,
To Ezra Pound, and to personages no longer living
Even in anyone's thoughts—O Strangler the Strangler!

He lies on his back in the waves of the Pacific Ocean.

4

Supposing that one walks out into the air
On a fresh spring day and has the misfortune
To encounter an article on modern poetry

In *New World Writing,* or has the misfortune
To see some examples of some of the poetry
Written by the men with their eyes on the myth
And the Missus and the midterms, in the *Hudson Review,*
Or, if one is abroad, in *Botteghe Oscure,*
Or indeed in *Encounter,* what is one to do
With the rest of one's day that lies blasted to ruins
All bluely about one, what is one to do?
O surely one cannot complain to the President,
Nor even to the deans of Columbia College,
Nor to T.S. Eliot, nor to Ezra Pound,
And supposing one writes to the Princess Caetani,
"Your poets are awful!" what good would it do?
And supposing one goes to the *Hudson Review*
With a package of matches and sets fire to the building?
One ends up in prison with trial subscriptions
To the *Partisan, Sewanee,* and *Kenyon Review!*

5

Sun out! perhaps there is a reason for the lack of poetry
In these ill-contented souls, perhaps they need air!

Blue air, fresh air, come in, I welcome you, you are an art
    student,
Take off your cap and gown and sit down on the chair.
Together we shall paint the poets—but no, air! perhaps you should
    go to them, quickly,
Give them a little inspiration, they need it, perhaps they are out
    of breath,
Give them a little inhuman company before they freeze the English
    language to death!
(And rust their typewriters a little, be sea air! be noxious! kill them,
    if you must, but stop their poetry!
I remember I saw you dancing on the surf on the Côte d'Azur,
And I stopped, taking my hat off, but you did not remember me,
Then afterwards you came to my room bearing a handful of orange
    flowers
And we were together all through the summer night!)

That we might go away together, it is so beautiful on the sea, there
    are a few white clouds in the sky!

But no, air! you must go . . . Ah, stay!

But she has departed and . . . Ugh! what poisonous fumes
  and clouds! what a suffocating atmosphere!
Cough! whose are these hideous faces I see, what is this rigor
Infecting the mind? where are the green Azores,
Fond memories of childhood, and the pleasant orange trolleys,
A girl's face, red-white, and her breasts and calves, blue eyes,
  brown eyes, green eyes, fahrenheit
Temperatures, dandelions, and trains, O blue?!
Wind, wind, what is happening? Wind! I can't see any bird but the
  gull, and I feel it should symbolize . . .
Oh, pardon me, there's a swan, one two three swans, a great white
  swan, hahaha how pretty they are! Smack!
Oh! stop! help! yes, I see—disrespect of my superiors—forgive me,
  dear Zeus, nice Zeus, parabolic bird, O feathered excellence!
  white!
There is Achilles too, and there's Ulysses, I've always wanted to see
  them, hahaha!
And there is Helen of Troy, I suppose she is Zeus too, she's so
  terribly pretty—hello, Zeus, my you are beautiful, Bang!
One more mistake and I get thrown out of the Modern Poetry
  Association, help! Why aren't there any adjectives around?
Oh there are, there's practically nothing else—look, here's *grey,*
  utter, agonized, total, phenomenal, gracile, invidious, sundered,
  and *fused,*
Elegant, absolute, pyramidal, and . . . Scream! but what can I describe
  with these words? States!
States symbolized and divided by two, complex states, magic states.
  states of consciousness governed by an aroused sincerity,
  cockadoodle doo!
Another bird! is it morning? Help! where am I? am I in the
  barnyard? oink oink, scratch, moo! Splash!
My first lesson. "Look around you. What do you think and feel?"
  Uhhh . . . "Quickly!" *This Connecticut landscape would have pleased*
  Vermeer. Wham! A-Plus. "Congratulations!" I am promoted.

OOOhhhhh I wish I were dead, what a headache! My second
lesson: "Rewrite your first lesson line six hundred times. Try to
make it into a magnetic field." I can do it too. But my poor
line! What a nightmare! Here comes a tremendous horse.
Trojan, I presume. No, it's my third lesson. "Look, look! Watch
him, see what he's doing? That's what we want you to do. Of
course it won't be the same as his at first, but . . ." I demur. Is
there no other way to fertilize minds?
Bang! I give in . . . Already I see my name in two or three
anthologies, a serving girl comes into the barn bringing me the
anthologies,
She is very pretty and I smile at her a little sadly, perhaps it is my
last smile! Perhaps she will hit me! But no, she smiles in return,
and she takes my hand.
My hand, my hand! what is this strange thing I feel in my hand, on
my arm, on my chest, my face—can it be . . . ? it is! AIR!
Air, air you've come back! Did you have any success? "What do
you think?" I don't know, air. You are so strong, air.
And she breaks my chains of straw, and we walk down the road,
behind us the hideous fumes!
Soon we reach the seaside, she is a young art student who places
her head on my shoulder,
I kiss her warm red lips, and here is the Strangler, reading the
Kenyon Review! Good luck to you, Strangler!
Goodbye, Helen! goodbye fumes! goodbye abstracted dried-up
boys! goodbye, dead trees! goodbye, skunks!
Goodbye, manure! goodbye, critical manicure! goodbye, you big
fat men standing on the east coast as well as the west giving
poems the test! farewell, Valéry's stern dictum!
Until tomorrow, then, scum floating on the surface of poetry!
goodbye for a moment, refuse that happens to land in poetry's
boundaries! adieu, stale eggs teaching imbeciles poetry to bolster
up your egos! adios, boring anomalies of these same stale eggs!
Ah, but the scum is deep! Come, let me help you! and soon we
pass into the clear blue water. Oh GOODBYE, castrati of
poetry! farewell, stale pale skunky pentameters (the only honest
English meter, gloop gloop!) until tomorrow, horrors! oh,
farewell!

Hello, sea! good morning, sea! hello, clarity and excitement, you
   great expanse of green—

O green, beneath which all of them shall drown!

KENNETH KOCH

---

1. Look at the first few lines of the poem. Do you get a good sense of what sort of poem it's going to be from the first lines?
2. Does the poem tell a story? What is it?
3. Is "Fresh Air" more lyrical, didactic, or narrative?
4. Look at the length of this poem and the others in this chapter. Is length important in achieving a particular effect in a poem? How does the length of "Fresh Air" influence how you read it and how you feel after you've read it? Does breaking a poem into several parts change the feeling of the poem?

In a relatively flat voice, Wing Tek Lum describes a ritual leave-taking at the graves of ancestors, Chinese immigrants who died and were buried in Hawaii. Although he admits that he no longer believes in the power of this time-honored ceremony, in which he asks his ancestors to protect him in his travels, he continues to practice the ritual out of respect for his family and to soften the loss he feels at being estranged from tradition and the past. Notice how the poem becomes a working out of personal conflict.

It's Something Our Family Has Always Done

On every trip away from these islands
on the day of departure and on the day of return
we go to the graves, all seven of them,
but for one sum total of all of our ancestors
who died in this place we call home.

The drive to the cemetery is only five minutes long.
Stopping by a florist adds maybe ten minutes more.

Yet my wife and I on the day of our flight
are so rushed with packing and last minute chores.
Why do we still make the time to go?

The concrete road is one lane wide.
We turn around at the circle up at the top,
always to park just to the side of the large banyan tree
as the road begins its slope back down.
I turn the wheels; we now lock our car.

As if by rote, we bring anthuriums,
at least two flowers for each of our dead.
On our way we stop to pay our respects to the "Old Man"
—that first one lain here, all wind and water before him—
who watches over this graveyard, and our island home.

Approaching my grandparents, we divide up our offering,
placing their long stems into the holes filled with sand.
Squatting in front of each marble tablet,
I make it a point to read off their names in Chinese.
My hands pull out crabgrass running over stone.

I stand erect, clutching palm around fist,
swinging the air three times up and down.
My wife from the waist bows once, arms at her sides.
I manage to whisper a few phrases out loud,
conversing like my father would, as if all could hear.

We do Grandfather, Grandmother, and my parents below them.
Following the same path we always take,
we make our way through the tombstones and mounds,
skirting their concrete borders, to the other two Lums
and to our Granduncle on the Chang side.

Back up the hill, we spend a few moments by the curb
picking off black, thin burrs from our cuffs and socks.
We talk about what errands we must do next.
I glance around us at these man-made gardens,
thrust upon a slope of earth, spirit houses rising to the sky.

As I get into our car, and look out at the sea,
I am struck with the same thought as always.
We spend so little time in front of these graves
asking each in turn to protect us when we are far away.
I question them all: what good does it really do?

I have read ancient poets who parted with sorrow
from family and friends, fearing never to return.
Our oral histories celebrate brave peasants
daring oceans and the lonely beds: they looked even more
to blessings at long distance from their spirit dead.

My father superstitious, even to the jet age,
still averred: but every little bit helps.
These sentiments I know, but I confess I do not feel.
Maybe it's for this loss that I still come here.
They are family, and I respect them so.

WING TEK LUM

---

1. If this is a narrative poem, what is the story? Tell the story in your own words.
2. Does the author seem to be trying to teach the reader something? Is there a lesson here or is the poem simply a slice of life?
3. Is the sound of the poem important? How would you describe the sound of the poem? Are there rhymes or other repeated sounds? Is there noticeable rhythm?
4. Compare Wing Tek Lum's poem with William Stafford's "The Animal That Drank Up Sound." Are setting, action, character, and conflict more or less important in this poem than in Stafford's poem?
5. Describe the poem in terms of genre.

Reading nineteenth-century narrative poetry, such as John Keats's "The Eve of St. Agnes," Samuel Taylor Coleridge's "The Rime of the Ancient Mariner," Matthew Arnold's narratives, or popular works usually considered children's literature, such as Robert Browning's "The Pied

Piper of Hamelin," we notice that the subject matter and atmosphere are often based on an earlier time, a characteristic of romantic writing. Would we want that quality in poetry of our time? There is always the danger that in attempting narrative poetry, poets who are otherwise flexible in their language and conscious of modern innovations may adopt a stilted, antique diction or meter in unconscious imitation of earlier narrative poetry.

Looking at the examples of modern poetry in this chapter, it becomes clear that there is far less difference between a modern lyric and a modern narrative than between, for example, the *Aeneid* and *Antigone*. Perhaps this is so much an age of the lyric that the old distinctions are irrelevant. But could we do the sort of thing in our time that was once done with narrative verse? What subject would be a satisfactory modern equivalent of the hero: a long narrative poem about John F. Kennedy or Martin Luther King? These are relatively recent heroes. King Arthur? But King Arthur has been revived so many times in fiction, musical plays, and the movies; furthermore, what is the relevance of King Arthur to our time? What would be the right tone for a long narrative poem of the twentieth century?

The point is not to discourage anyone from writing a modern narrative poem, either long or short, dealing with the past or present. One should, however, be cautious of this tendency toward the artificial, inflated rhetoric of a period piece. Faced with the dominance of the lyric, it might be a challenge to experiment with narrative in poetry, and doubtless instructive to think of how your present poetry might be changed by developing its narrative or dramatic qualities. Other questions also arise: should your poetry imitate life? should lyric poetry become more musical, more abstract, more associative? is poetry an effective medium for social criticism or the exploration of aesthetics or psychology? Set yourself a problem in one of these areas and experiment with the idea of genre.

Suggestions for Writing

1. Write a poem including three unconnected events. All three events should represent a single emotion. For example, a child's empty tricycle rolls off the sidewalk into the street, a butcher's knife hacks off the wing of a chicken, and a radio plays in an empty house. Might you feel vulnerability? loss? boredom?

2.   When you have finished suggestion 1, write a simple narrative in free verse about an event which gave you a similar feeling, but now emphasize the chronology.

3.   Research and retell the story of a historical character, such as a family member, someone from the past, or someone from the recent history of your hometown (perhaps from a local scandal or a newspaper story) in a short ballad.

4.   Write a poem consisting of dialogue. Develop one of the following structures:

   a)   Make the poem like a short scene in a play, with character designations.

   b)   Two people, one in regular typescript and the other in italics (underlined), speak to each other. Let stanzas indicate when speakers change, but otherwise do not identify them explicitly—let their words identify them. They can be two distinct characters, or some variation on the old body-and-soul theme, such as life talks to death, dog talks to cat, person talks to conscience.

   c)   Use overheard dialogue to make a poem or a capsule drama or a prose poem. Use the designations "He said," "she said," "the driver said," or whatever is appropriate. This will be a poem based on mimesis, imitation of life.

5.   Write a lyric poem with a narrative in it.

6.   Create a persona (see Chapter 8) and tell a first person narrative. In effect, speed up the whole life of that character in order to fit into a single poem.

7.   Write a lyric poem on the subject of:

   a)   Love
   b)   Time
   c)   The seasons
   d)   Death

   Make it concrete and use figurative language.

8.   Write a poem in which you express your views on a moral or ethical issue in an oblique way. Find a subject about which you feel strongly.

9. Write a light verse* that will help you remember some sort of information, such as the parts of an insect's wing, the names of the state capitals, or parts of a carburetor.

10. Write a poem that teaches the history of your family to those who come after you.

11. Write three poems about something that happened to you and about which you later gave much thought:
    a) A lyric that conveys the emotion of the event
    b) A straightforward narrative that dramatizes the event
    c) A didactic poem that draws a lesson from the event

12. Write your own narrative poem of family experience, one that could be given Wing Tek Lum's title, "It's Something Our Family Has Always Done."

---

*Light verse is playful, witty, sometimes satirical, and usually, though not always, formal in its use of rhyme and meter to underscore mood.

12

Myth Making

One of the desolate thoughts bound to strike a writer sometimes is that everything has already been written about by someone else. Moreover, since so many subjects are probably refinements of a few major subjects—love, death, the power of nature, and, after these, art itself—how are we ever to say anything new, fresh, or original? Yet it is both exciting and comforting to discover that repetition in literature does not exhaust the great themes that are, after all, our human obsessions. The best poetry taps into something that is renewed and not depleted in the process.

It is important to distinguish between the creative use of universal themes and images and the failure of imagination which results in stereotypes or clichés. Great poetry seems to possess two paradoxical elements: on the one hand, its recognizable material evokes some common response, and, on the other hand, its qualities of uniqueness and individualism introduce us to another's point of view. Think, for example, of Theodore Roethke's "I Knew a Woman" (Chapter 10) and Ezra Pound's translation of "The River-Merchant's Wife" (Chapter 5)—two extraordinary and very different approaches to the subject of love.

The struggle to write well may be identical to the struggle to meld the two gestures of the universal and the original. And while a formula for originality cannot be given—that would be a logical impossibility—it is good for a beginning writer, still developing a grasp of fundamentals, to keep an eye on the heights, those poems where personal themes and obsessions have intersected with the universal to produce the elusive entity that is excellent poetry. This chapter will deal with some ways of attempting that difficult thing.

Related to the subject of recurrent themes in literature is psychologist **Carl Jung's** idea of archetypes. **Archetype** means "ancient pattern." Reading about archetypes, we see that these patterns are not merely old but of the first order, or *primordial*—from a word meaning "to begin to weave." The archetypal image takes us back to the first patterns, the origins of things, and is evidenced in dreams, in religious ritual, in madness, in ecstasy, in art, and in literature. Thus, an image like the sea is representative of the archetype of the eternal, and other images—such as stairways, tunnels, mazes, hidden rooms, falling, flying, drowning, the wise elder, the monster, paradise, and the promised land—have an immediate archetypal flavor. These archetypes might be engraved in our very being. This concept sounds similar to the mysterious lines from William Butler Yeats's poem "Before the World Was Made,"

> I'm looking for the face I had
> Before the world was made

The power of archetypes connects us with patterns in existence long before we were even born. Not only do such images float up out of the unconscious unbidden; witnessed, they also provoke deep emotional responses which make them immeasurably useful to the poet. Jung called this universal reservoir of images the *collective unconscious.*

One Jungian archetype is the mandala, a symbol of perfection and integrity. Its simplest form is a plain circle, but like the fractured, repetitive pattern seen in a kaleidoscope, it may also be a circular figure of great complexity. The mandala is a common figure in Eastern religious art, but we also recognize it in such representations as the great rose windows of gothic cathedrals of western Europe, in the ancient circle of Stonehenge, in the Aztec calendar or sunstone, or in a geometric drawing demonstrating the proportions of the human body as an intersected circle. In Yeats's "The Second Coming," the image of the falcon spiraling up, up, and outward, away from the controls of the falconer, and the line, "Things fall apart; the centre cannot hold," both evoke a mandala, or wheel, which appears to be disintegrating and spinning out of control.

Yeats uses the spiral gyre figure to represent social disintegration in the cycles of history, a sign of psychosis and nonhealth. Is it necessary to tie the meaning of these images to Irish politics, as Yeats does? Or to Yeats's private cosmogony? Perhaps, to get a full sense of the poem's meaning, but not to feel its emotional weight.

The Second Coming

Turning and turning in the widening gyre
The falcon cannot hear the falconer;
Things fall apart; the centre cannot hold;
Mere anarchy is loosed upon the world,
The blood-dimmed tide is loosed, and everywhere
The ceremony of innocence is drowned;
The best lack all conviction, while the worst
Are full of passionate intensity.

Surely some revelation is at hand;
Surely the Second Coming is at hand.
The Second Coming! Hardly are those words out
When a vast image out of *Spiritus Mundi*
Troubles my sight: somewhere in sands of the desert
A shape with lion body and the head of a man,
A gaze blank and pitiless as the sun,
Is moving its slow thighs, while all about it
Reel shadows of the indignant desert birds.
The darkness drops again; but now I know
That twenty centuries of stony sleep
Were vexed to nightmare by a rocking cradle,
And what rough beast, its hour come round at last,
Slouches towards Bethlehem to be born?

WILLIAM BUTLER YEATS

---

1. Which images in the poem seem most powerful?
2. Which images seem familiar? Are they the same images you mentioned in the first question? Are they taken from myths, popular culture, religion, or other sources?
3. List all of the circular or, by association, cyclical images in the poem. What feelings does Yeats associate with these images?

Whatever the source of the recurrent pattern symbolized by the circle—whether we associate it with the earth, the circular motions of the planets, the sun, the appearance of the sky, the cycle of seasons, the fetal position, the iris of the eye, or even the original cell, the primordial egg— we seem to recognize it naturally as a powerful, meaningful image. As an exercise, try to write a poem that uses a square tire as a symbol of life's journey or an unequal-sided building to express unity. No doubt it could be done, but we would still have to play these odd figures against an imagined archetypal circle.

An earlier representation of the mandala pattern in poetry is in Dante's *Divine Comedy.* Hell, in *The Inferno,* consists of descending, concentric levels, like an inverted solar system, with Satan frozen at the center.

In "The Twelve-Spoked Wheel Flashing," Marge Piercy writes:

> I have tried to forge my life whole,
> round, integral as the earth spinning.

And later, in the same poem:

> A turn of the wheel: nothing
> stays. The redwinged blackbirds implode
> into a tree above the salt marsh one
> March day piping and chittering
> every year, but the banded pet
> does not return.

The image is Yeatsian, but the poems are clearly different in tone and content. Piercy reworks old patterns, but the poem is her own.

Others have expressed something about poetry that seems related to Jung's concept of the archetype. T. S. Eliot, for example, in an essay on Hamlet, has attempted to describe the way in which images in poetry provoke deep feelings that are otherwise difficult to communicate. Eliot says that "the only way of expressing emotion in the form of art" is by the use of "a set of objects, a situation, a chain of events which shall be the formula of that particular emotion, such that when the external facts, which must terminate in sensory experience, are given, the emotion is immediately evoked." Eliot calls this principle the **objective correlative.** It is certainly an argument for concreteness in poetry.

In discussions of contemporary poetry, another term, **deep image,** relates to archetypal patterns in poetry and to the idea of the objective correlative.

A deep image is emotional and intuitive and fires the imagination into comprehension that is supra-logical, what Robert Bly calls an imaginative leap (see Chapter 9). If this seems too abstract, think of it as a surprising association that leads to a new perception. In one sense, this is simply metaphor, like the implied comparison between pale faces and flower petals. What is implied by deep image is that the poet is able to let the subconscious produce these associations: hence they are more powerful, real, and deeply felt than associations produced intellectually.

Of course, archetype, objective correlative, and deep image are not interchangeable terms. Deep image relates to the effect of an image and to the trend toward intuition and feeling in poetry, reacting against so-called objective poetry. Eliot's objective correlative describes a conscious, deliberately intellectual process of working for emotional effect. Archetype is a term from Jungian psychology that refers to the primordial patterns in human consciousness that give rise to various emotionally charged images. And remember, though, that even if it were possible to make a dictionary of archetypes, deep images, and objective correlatives, one could not make deeply felt poetry on order simply by saying, "Life goes round like a wheel," "Blood and bones and seawater," or "Monsters are going to eat you up." One must see old visions through new eyes—one's own.

We have to recognize that imagery calculated for deep emotional effect may be misused, or used badly. "The gull soared high above, lonely and proud." "The poor waif pushed back a lock of golden hair." "The dark and brooding forest was all around." These are not enough to stir deep emotions. They sound clichéd and wordy. Still, images of a bird in flight, an innocent child, or a sinister wood could be used with archetypal force. Dante begins his *Divine Comedy* (in John Ciardi's translation):

> Midway in our life's journey, I went astray
>   from the straight road and woke to find myself
> alone in a dark wood. How shall I say
> what wood that was! I never saw so drear,
>   so rank, so arduous a wilderness!
>   Its very memory gives a shape to fear.
> Death could scarce be more bitter than that place!

Even before we have followed him in his descent through hell, we begin to respond. The reader knows the archetypal fear of passing through that "dark wood."

A poem touching on archetypal material does not have to be strained or elaborate to be original. Often the simplest language and imagery go to the heart of feeling. Consider this excerpt from Burton Raffel's translation of the anonymous eighth-century Anglo-Saxon poem "The Wanderer," in which universals are shaped by the voice of the individual:

> "I've drunk too many lonely dawns,
> Grey with mourning. Once there were men
> To whom my heart could hurry, hot
> With open longing. They're long since dead.
> My heart has closed on itself, quietly
> Learning that silence is noble and sorrow
> Nothing that speech can cure.

The central archetype of "The Wanderer" is the journey—here life is a journey—and the journey in its forms such as quest, exile, adventure must surely be one of the most often invoked of archetypes. For we find it throughout the history of literature, from Moses in the desert and Odysseus trying to get home to Penelope, to the Arthurian quest for the Holy Grail, Demeter's search for her daughter, and the travels of Huckleberry Finn.

Myth and **mythopoeia** are two other terms to consider here. A myth employs archetypes and universal themes and also provides a unifying framework or continuity for a more general set of ideas and perceptions. One basic definition of myth is that it is an explanation of how something came about, how the world began, how man got fire, how the elephant got its trunk, and so on. In this definition, a myth concerns itself with the beginnings of things, and its origins are unknown or forgotten. In discussing poetry, we may extend this meaning.

Mythopoeia is the process of consciously inventing myths, as opposed to folkloric and anonymous myths which have grown out of the collective culture. A writer may turn the materials of his or her own life into a personal mythology, a sort of "how I came to be," so that the poet's perceptions take on a larger or more universal resonance. Or he or she may employ myths and literature from the past in order to create a mythology of the present. Eliot in his long poem "The Waste Land" and James Joyce in his novel *Ulysses,* for example, construct a mythology of a degraded and spiritually diminished world.

In the following three examples, figures or stories from myths give a framework to modern ideas or situations.

Louise Bogan uses the image of Medusa, the snake-haired monster-woman who turned to stone all those who looked at her. Bogan is perhaps saying something about events that come upon us awfully and finally, bringing our daily lives and expectations to a halt, like "the tipped bell [that will] make no sound." Whether we can tie the poem to some specific event in the poet's life, some psychic blow that metaphorically turned her to stone, is another matter. But even without that, we can see how using the mythical figure of Medusa may have allowed Bogan to concretize some trauma. It might be instructive to try to imagine the appearance of such a creature as the Medusa.

Medusa

I had come to the house, in a cave of trees,
Facing a sheer sky.
Everything moved,—a bell hung ready to strike,
Sun and reflection wheeled by.

When the bare eyes were before me
And the hissing hair,
Held up at a window, seen through a door.
The stiff bald eyes, the serpents on the forehead
Formed in the air.

This is a dead scene forever now.
Nothing will ever stir.
The end will never brighten it more than this,
Nor the rain blur.

The water will always fall, and will not fall,
And the tipped bell make no sound.
The grass will always be growing for hay
Deep on the ground.

And I shall stand here like a shadow
Under the great balanced day,
My eyes on the yellow dust, that was lifting in the wind,
And does not drift away.

LOUISE BOGAN

1. What feelings are associated with Medusa and what do you know about her?
2. Without knowing what experience might have caused Bogan to write this poem, describe some hypothetical traumatic experiences that could give rise to the feelings evoked by reading "Medusa." Have you ever had an emotional experience that could be described as "turned to stone"?
3. We can't know for sure who is speaking in the poem, but who do you think the speaker might be? A mythical character? A persona having some difficult experience? Bogan herself?

Robert Creeley's "Kore" is a lyrical, mysterious account of a meeting with Kore, daughter of the earth mother, who was spirited away to hell and kept there half the year by the god of the underworld. Her mother's seasonal mourning over her daughter's absence gives us fall and winter. Although this is a small poem, it engages myth by the use of the journey motif and the allusion to love and fertility rites. Like Bogan's poem, it employs the motif of strange encounters—on life's journey, one occasionally loses the way and finds the unexpected. In the last lines, Creeley gives the poem a universal application—the modern counterpart of Kore, or anyone affected by love, might well ask the same thing.

Kore

As I was walking
    I came upon
chance walking
    the same road upon.

As I sat down
    by chance to move
later
    if and as I might,

light the wood was,
    light and green,
and what I saw
    before I had not seen.

It was a lady
   accompanied
by goat men
   leading her.

Her hair held earth.
   Her eyes were dark.
A double flute
   made her move.

"O love,
   where are you
leading
   me now?"

              ROBERT CREELEY

---

1. What feelings might be associated with Kore? (If you don't recognize the name, perhaps you will recognize one of her other, more familiar designations: Persephone.)
2. Who do you think is telling the story? Who is speaking in the final question?
3. In your own words, what is this poem about? What is it about in terms of concrete events and images, and what is it about in terms of abstract ideas?

Denise Levertov's "The Goddess" is a difficult but elemental poem with an archetypal feeling of both violence and birth. The goddess is a fertility figure, more suggestive of one of the terrifying ancient earth mothers than of a later figure such as Demeter, mother of Kore. In the poem, the goddess violently hurls the poet, or persona, out of the allegorical Lie Castle into contact with the real world of mud, seeds, seasons, and stars. This poem is a particularly excellent example of how archetypal imagery can influence and move us even prior to intellectual analysis.

The Goddess

She in whose lipservice
I passed my time,
whose name I knew, but not her face,
came upon me where I lay in Lie Castle!

Flung me across the room, and
room after room (hitting the walls, re-
bounding—to the last
sticky wall—wrenching away from it
pulled hair out!)
till I lay
outside the outer walls!

There in cold air
lying still where her hand had thrown me,
I tasted the mud that splattered my lips:
the seeds of a forest were in it,
asleep and growing! I tasted
her power!

The silence was answering my silence,
a forest was pushing itself
out of sleep between my submerged fingers.

I bit on a seed and it spoke on my tongue
of day that shone already among stars
in the water-mirror of low ground,
and a wind rising ruffled the lights:
she passed near me returning from the encounter,
she who plucked me from the close rooms,

without whom nothing
flowers, fruits, sleeps in season,
without whom nothing
speaks in its own tongue, but returns
lie for lie!

DENISE LEVERTOV

1. How does "The Goddess" behave in this poem? Describe her in emotional terms.
2. What do we know about the persona speaking in this poem? For example, what do we learn from the words "lipservice" and "passed my time"?
3. What happens? What change takes place in the poem?
4. Although we can't really know what experience caused Levertov to write "The Goddess," what sort of emotion or experience is evoked by the actions and images in this poem?
5. Based on these three poems by Bogan, Creeley, and Levertov, would you say that images from early mythologies adapt well to modern poems? Are there any drawbacks to using mythological figures in modern poems?

The mythical figures of Kore and Medusa and the archetypal goddess have allowed the poets to concretize an emotional event and to convey its quality. A nineteenth-century poem that uses mythic figures is Alfred Lord Tennyson's "Ulysses," itself suggested by an image of Ulysses from Dante's *Inferno,* which was in turn based on the *Odyssey* of Homer; even Homer himself borrowed from orally told tales. It was in this tradition that the novelist James Joyce created his modern *Ulysses.* Perhaps you will want to write a Ulysses poem for the late twentieth century—you will be in good company.

Tennyson's Ulysses faces the problem, is there life after retirement? Never mind that Ulysses spent much of his adult life trying to get back home from the Trojan wars, back to his wife, Penelope. Here Ulysses asks the question, is it the destination or the journey that makes life worth living?

I am a part of all that I have met;
Yet all experience is an arch wherethrough
Gleams that untraveled world whose margin fades
For ever and for ever when I move.
How dull it is to pause, to make an end,
To rust unburnished, not to shine in use!
. . . .
And this gray spirit yearning in desire
To follow knowledge like a sinking star,
Beyond the utmost bound of human thought.

In *A Literary History of England,* Samuel C. Chew writes: "The determination to follow knowledge wherever it may lead is characteristic of the period which was becoming aware of the perilous seas of scientific speculation. Thus Tennyson poured the new wine of modern thought into the old wine-skins of mythology." And so Tennyson gave form and resonance to current ideas by reinterpreting Ulysses for his own time relative to the larger tradition and by borrowing some of the power of that tradition through association.

Of course we do not want to dress every banker and taxi driver in classical disguise and clutter every poem with borrowed mythology, but new variations on old themes are a powerful poetic possibility. And Greek mythology is only one example; another is Native American mythology.

Gary Snyder is a poet who has studied both Native American and oriental cultures, and whose poetry has been influenced by these cultures. Admirably, his involvement is not a matter of merely borrowing images, but is rather one of sincere appreciation and respect, which reflects a continuing part of his life and work. When he alludes to Zen Buddhism or Native American culture, Snyder is putting us in touch with his personal passions and views. Rather than despairing of the present, Snyder strives to learn how to live in it by reestablishing important connections with the past. The achievement of enlightenment and personal tranquility; an understanding of the human's place in the natural world; acceptance of, and a feeling of harmony with, the cycles of nature, are some of his themes. For example, in "Long Hair," he explores man's relationship with nature. The opening line, "Hunting season," refers not only to the legal deer-hunting season but also to a naturally right time in the cycle of things. The pantheism of the poem, borrowed from Native American culture, comes across not so much in specific images as in an existential attitude.

Long Hair

Hunting season:

Once every year, the Deer catch human beings. They
do various things which irresistibly draw men near them;
each one selects a certain man. The Deer shoots the man,
who is then compelled to skin it and carry its meat home
and eat it. Then the Deer is inside the man. He waits
and hides in there, but the man doesn't know it. When

enough Deer have occupied enough men, they will strike
all at once. The men who don't have Deer in them will
also be taken by surprise, and everything will change
some. This is called "takeover from inside."
Deer trails:
Deer trails run on the side hills
       cross country access roads
       dirt ruts to bone-white
       board house ranches,
       tumbled down.

Waist high through manzanita,
Through sticky, prickly, crackling
       gold dry summer grass.

Deer trails lead to water,
Lead sidewise all ways
Narrowing down to one best path—
And split—
And fade away to nowhere.

Deer trails slide under freeways
       slip into cities
       swing back and forth in crops and orchards
       run up the sides of schools!

Deer spoor and crisscross dusty tracks
Are in the house: and coming out the walls:

And deer bound through my hair.

GARY SNYDER

---

1. What does Snyder mean when he says, "The Deer shoots the man"?
2. What are some ways in which Snyder has integrated the myths and images of an older, hunting culture with images of modern life?
3. How would you read the last line? Does the word "bound" have more than one possible meaning? How does it refer back to the title, "Long Hair"?

Wendell Berry is both a writer and a farmer, someone to whom a sense of place is particularly meaningful. His work often refers to specific rural places and characters, as in the following.

Creation Myth

This is a story handed down.
It is about the old days when Bill
and Florence and a lot of their kin
lived in the little tin-roofed house
beside the woods, below the hill.
Mornings, they went up the hill
to work, Florence to the house,
the men and boys to the field.
Evenings, they all came home again.
There would be talk then and laughter
and taking of ease around the porch
while the summer night closed.
But one night, McKinley, Bill's young brother,
stayed away late, and it was dark
when he started down the hill.
Not a star shone, not a window.
What he was going down into was
the dark, only his footsteps sounding
to prove he trod the ground. And Bill
who had got up to cool himself,
thinking and smoking, leaning on
the jamb of the open front door,
heard McKinley coming down,
and heard his steps beat faster
as he came, for McKinley felt the pasture's
darkness joined to all the rest
of darkness everywhere. It touched
the depths of woods and sky and grave.
In that huge dark, things that usually
stayed put might get around, as fish
in pond or slue get loose in flood.
Oh, things could be coming close

that never had come close before.
He missed the house and went on down
and crossed the draw and pounded on
where the pasture widened on the other side,
lost then for sure. Propped in the door,
Bill heard him circling, a dark star
in the dark, breathing hard, his feet
blind on the little reality
that was left. Amused, Bill smoked
his smoke, and listened. He knew where
McKinley was, though McKinley didn't.
Bill smiled in the darkness to himself,
and let McKinley run until his steps
approached something really to fear:
the quarry pool. Bill quit his pipe
then, opened the screen, and stepped out,
barefoot, on the warm boards. "McKinley!"
he said, and laid the field out clear
under McKinley's feet, and placed
the map of it in his head.

WENDELL BERRY

1. How does Berry change the idea of a "myth" from the usual meaning of the word?
2. In what sense is this poem about creation? What is created in the poem?
3. Recall other creation stories or myths you might know. How is Wendell Berry's poem like them? How is it different from the other creation myths?

Another modern poet who has made extensive and direct use of mythic or folkloric material is Anne Sexton. In her collection *Transformations* she retells several of Grimm's fairy tales. Sexton sometimes borrows the stories so directly from the originals that we might almost think they were translations. But her modern treatment and voice uniquely express Sexton's own kind of nervy humor. Looking up this collection would well reward your effort.

In all of these examples, it is important to discard one meaning we may associate with the word "myth," that a myth is something untrue. A myth might not be literally true but, being metaphorical or symbolic in its method, it may represent some deep psychological, historical, cultural, or personal reality.

Besides using older themes, myths, or literature to order and give resonance and continuity to the poet's view of the present, mythopoeia may involve other poetic tactics. Charles Olson and William Carlos Williams, among others, have used particular places to give mythic stature to their works. Olson uses the geography and history of Gloucester, Massachusetts in his *Maximus* poems, while Williams's *Paterson* similarly uses history, geography, and events related to that New Jersey city. In using place this way the poet is not really writing about a place; he or she is using it to represent an emotional or psychic landscape. Imagine how this might be done in your own poetry. What real landscape seems to be an appropriate representation of your own viewpoint? Is it the East Coast, where water and land meet and one looks back to Europe? (Hawthorne uses it this way in *The Scarlet Letter*.) Is it the West Coast, which might be seen as either a jumping-off place or the last western foothold before journeying into a Far Eastern state of mind? Do the Middle Western plains represent a level steadiness? Or does the street where you grew up seem important? In Olson and Williams the myth of place is both a metaphor and an organizing device.

The myth of place is also important to poets such as Robert Lowell, whose ancestors settled in New England. Gary Snyder's work is often infused with the landscape of the western outdoors, logging camps, forest lookouts. Others from Walt Whitman to the Beats have drawn on the large landscape of America—the myth of the big, open country, its roads and cities, its two coasts. One can also find a number of regional anthologies: poets of the Northwest; Nebraska poets; poets of the "Third Coast," that is Michigan; the New York poets, and so on. In many of these, however, the organization of poets by place seems almost accidental, simply a way of defining who happens to be in any general area at a specific, but not necessarily long, time. Poets move around a lot these days. But such collections do publicize the presence of local poets to their most accessible audience, their neighbors, a worthwhile aim; and in a few cases the individuals presented in such anthologies do use place as mythopoeia.

A different, personal myth making is involved when the poet develops a mythology of a created character. For an example, see Paul Zimmer's poem about his own continuing character, Alphonse, in Chapter 10. Another example to look for would be John Berryman's Henry, who appears in *The Dream Songs*. This Everyman sort of character, antihero, persona, alter ego of the poet, or combination of all of these, has traditional antecedents in characters such as Br'er Rabbit, Coyote, and Prometheus, who appear in a series of anecdotal episodes. By using a character such as Alphonse or Henry in a series of poems, the poet gives a sense of a full, continuing life. By creating such an alter ego, the poet transcends merely personal complaints and foibles and at the same time creates a **personal mythology,** a nice paradox.

Other poets have developed personal mythologies by more direct means. Instead of, or in some cases concurrently with, using myths of the past, literary allusions, geographical and historical metaphors, or invented characters, some writers have chosen to look to the materials of their own lives in order to find a coherent framework. Such poets are commonly called **confessional,** although the term is misleading because so-called confessional poets are not giving all the intimate details of their lives, helter-skelter. Like any other good poet, the good confessional poet shapes, selects, and interprets what he or she "confesses." What marks the confessional poet is the frankly personal tone of his or her metaphors, images, symbols, events, and characters. Taboo subjects, such as personal problems, mental illness, alcoholism, sexuality, and so on, may be broached. The "I" of the poems seems actually to be the poet, rather than any persona. In fact, we should say that the confessional poet uses himself or herself as a central metaphor, a device in Whitman's "Song of Myself," as noted by the South American writer Borges, for example.★ Borges means that the poetry seems to be a personal statement in the voice of Whitman himself and that Whitman used himself to stand for the democratic spirit of America and all the ideas expressed in his poetry. Thus, the speaker is a larger-than-life Whitman, consciously shaped and thrown onto the screen that is the poem.

One mark of the confessional poet, or the poet who uses himself or herself as metaphor, is surely the willingness to admit personal failings. Contemporary poets who have used themselves as the central figures in their own poetry include Sylvia Plath, Anne Sexton, Robert Lowell, Allen Ginsberg, W. D. Snodgrass, Charles Bukowksi, and Diane Wakoski. Before looking at examples, let us return briefly to Jung.

★The author heard Borges speak on the subject at Michigan State University in 1976.

In his autobiography, *Memories, Dreams, Reflections,* translated by R. and C. Winston, Jung says, "I have now undertaken, in my eighty-third year, to tell my personal myth. I can only make direct statements, only 'tell stories' whether or not the stories are 'true' is not the problem. The only question is whether what I tell is *my* fable, *my* truth . . . ." In Jung's context, myth has several connotations: a story of how something or someone (for example, Jung himself) came to be; a set of objects, persons, and actions that symbolically represent some *abstract* truth; a unifying fable or pattern. The personal myth, then, is the story—the set of memories, experiences, and images—that gives a coherence to an individual's psychic life. Moreover, the exploration of our private and personal myth can lead to comprehension of the whole human experience. Thus Jung, the psychologist of the archetypal, the universal, is also the psychologist of the personal.

Jung comes close to describing the poetic processes of a confessional poet. Diane Wakoski, for example, has applied the term *"personal mythology"* to the way she develops her own poetry around personal iconography of particular characters and key events: the King of Spain becomes her elusive golden lover; belly dancers, motorcyclists, and suntanned surfers are made into exotic beings; foods are made as delectable as those in any fairy tale; jewels, beasts, and the Southern California landscape become fantastic and beautiful. In a *New York Quarterly* interview, Wakoski remarked:

> I wrote poetry because I had a very narrow and circumscribed deprived life, and it was a fantasy world. And the Diane who's in my poems is not a real person. She's a person I would like to be, that I can imagine myself being, even though I put all my faults in my poems, it doesn't mean I'm not a fantasy or imagined person. I didn't create a fantasy that was unreal . . . . But the Diane in my poems really is fantasy.

If all this seems contradictory or confusing, recall Jung's distinction between stories which are true and stories which are *"my* fable, *my* truth." Remember, the truth of myths, fairy tales, folktales, is not literal truth, as in, "Yes, I really did all this, just the way I describe it in the poem." It is a subjective truth. It is the truth of Wallace Stevens's imagination which "has the strength of reality or none at all." It is the emotional truth of archetypes and the felt reality of deep images. It is John Keat's truth in "Ode on a Grecian Urn":

"Beauty is truth, truth beauty,"—that is all
Ye know on earth, and all ye need to know.

When you are writing your own poems, remember that you may give your perceptions, obsessions, and personal life a larger-than-life, mythic dimension. You will probably not have to go far from the sort of things you think about or do every day, and it is not a matter of deception. It is, rather, a matter of finding the thread or pattern of your own myth. Where are you from? How did you get here? Who were your ancestors, or who were your predecessors? What events have changed your life? What objects seem emblematic of your life? When you think of your childhood, does it have a beginning, a middle, and an end? Is there a villain in your life? Is there a heroic figure? What is the stuff of your dreams? What is the object of your quest? What are your obsessions? Any one of these personal questions may well bring up something that touches on the universal, something that others could identify with, share, and learn from.

Following are some examples of poems that have that deep resonance arising from the melding of universals with the particular and individual.

Wakoski's "The Father of My Country" is an example of several things discussed in this chapter. First, the poet borrows a figure with mythic proportions from American history. In this poem and others, she uses George Washington to represent a theme that is both archetypal and personal—that is, the search for the lost father. George Washington and the speaker's father merge in Wakoski's personal mythology. Traditionally such a search did not always involve a father but could be a quest for a patrimony or inheritance—the rightful throne, family wealth stolen by a giant, and so on. We do not know whether this is Wakoski's actual father, but the self created in the poem says that she has become what she is—"a maverick,/ a writer,/ a namer," and "a lonely woman,/ without a purpose," because her father abandoned her when she was a child. Of course, in using George Washington as a symbolic figure, Wakoski does not especially stick to history, and even though she ends the poem "Father,/ Father,/ Father,/ have you really come home?" she may no longer be referring to her father. Perhaps she is addressing a husband or lover as a father substitute, and assigning the identity George Washington to that father substitute. Wakoski is bound by neither historical fact nor personal history, but she makes creative use of both.

The Father of My Country

All fathers in Western civilization must have
a military origin. The
ruler,
governor,
yes,
he is
was the
general at one time or other.
And George Washington
won the hearts
of his country—the rough military man
with awkward
sincere
drawing-room manners.

My father;
have you ever heard me speak of him? I seldom
do. But I had a father,
and he had military origins—or my origins from
him
are military,
militant. That is, I remember him only in uniform. But of
   the navy,
30 years a chief petty officer,
always away from home.

It is rough / hard for me to speak
now.
I'm not used to talking
about him.
Not used to naming his objects/
objects
that never surrounded me.

A woodpecker with fresh bloody crest
knocks

at my mouth. Father, for the first
time I say
your name. Name rolled in thick Polish parchment scrolls,
name of Roman candle drippings when I sit at my table
alone, each night,
name of naval uniforms and name of
telegrams, name of
coming home from your aircraft carrier,
name of shiny shoes.
name of Hawaiian dolls, name
of mess spoons, name of greasy machinery, and name of
stencilled names.
Is it your blood I carry in a test tube,
my arm,
to let fall, crack, and spill on the sidewalk
in front of the men
I know,
I love,
I know, and
want? So you left my house when I was under two.
being replaced by other machinery (my sister), and
I didn't believe you left me.

     This scene: the trunk yielding treasures of
     a green fountain pen, heart shaped mirror,
     amber beads, old letters with brown ink, and
     the gopher snake stretched across the palm tree
     in the front yard with woody trunk like monkey
       skins,
     and a sunset through the skinny persimmon trees.
       You
     came walking, not even a telegram or post card from
     Tahiti. Love, love, through my heart like ink in
     the thickest nubbed pen, black and flowing into
       words
     You came, to me, and I at least six. Six doilies
     of lace, six battleship cannon, six old beer-bottles,
     six thick steaks, six love letters, six clocks

running backwards, six watermelons, and six baby
teeth, a six cornered hat on six men's heads, six
lovers at once or one lover at sixes and sevens;
how I confuse
all this with my
dream
walking the tightrope bridge
with gold knots
over
the mouth of an aenemone/ tissue spiral lips
and holding on so that the ropes burned
as if my wrists had been tied

If George Washington
had not
been the Father
of my Country
it is doubtful that I would ever have
found
a father. Father in my mouth, on my lips, in my
tongue, out of all my womanly fire,
Father I have left in my steel filing cabinet as a name on my
birth
certificate, Father I have left in the teeth pulled out at
dentists' offices and thrown into their garbage cans,
Father living in my wide cheekbones and short feet,
Father in my Polish tantrums and my American speech, Father,
    not a
holy name, not a name I cherish but the name I bear, the name
that makes me one of a kind in any phone book because
you changed it, and nobody
but us
has it,
Father who makes me dream in the dead of night of the falling
    cherry
blossoms, Father who makes me know all men will leave me
if I love them,
Father who made me a maverick,
a writer,

a namer,
name/father, sun/father, moon/father, bloody mars/father

other children said, "My father is a doctor,"
or
"My father gave me this camera,"
or
"My father took me to
the movies,"
or
"My father and I went swimming,"
but
my father is coming in a letter
once a month
for a while,
and my father
sometimes came in a telegram
but
mostly
my father came to me
in sleep, my father because I dreamed in one night that I dug
through the ash heap in back of the pepper tree and found a
    diamond
shaped like a dog, and my father called the dog and it came leaping
over to him and he walking away out of the yard down the
    road with
the dog jumping and yipping at his heels,

my father was not in the telephone book
in my city;
my father was not sleeping with my mother
at home;
my father did not care if I studied the
piano;
my father did not care what
I did;
and I thought my father was handsome and I loved him and I
    wondered
why

he left me alone so much,
so many years
in fact, but
my father made me what I am,
a lonely woman,
without a purpose, just as I was
a lonely child
without any father. I walked with words, words, and names,
names. Father was not
one of my words.
Father was not
one of my names. But now I say, "George, you have become my
    father,
in his 20th century naval uniform. George Washington, I need
    your
love; George, I want to call you Father, Father, my Father,"
Father of my country,
that is,
me. And I say the name to chant it. To sing it. To lace it around
me like weaving cloth. Like a happy child on that shining
    afternoon
in the palmtree sunset with her mother's trunk yielding treasures,
I cry and
cry,
Father,
Father,
Father,
have you really come home?

DIANE WAKOSKI

---

1. Why does Wakoski use George Washington as a substitute for her own fa-
    ther? Look for parallels between the two figures.
2. Who is the "hero" of this poem?
3. In what way could this poem be described as an attempt by the poet to un-
    derstand feelings associated with her own childhood?
4. Could this be described as a *confessional poem?* Explain.

·Of course using or creating a mythology is not the only way to give poetry resonance. Following are some groups of poems, each of which shows how a poet has recreated an old and much-used subject by giving it a fresh interpretation. In turn, the resonance of universal subjects such as renewal in nature, death, and the human response to other living things gives a sense of largeness and timelessness to the individual viewpoint. Although most of the poems in this book are from the twentieth century, the next three are earlier. William Wordsworth's sonnet, "Composed Upon Westminster Bridge," is about primal beauty: the city at daybreak, experienced in a personal encounter. If you have ever stayed up all night or risen early and found yourself enchanted by the peace and beauty of a city at an early hour—no noise, no smog, but "smokeless air"—then you will recognize the commonality of Wordsworth's experience.

Composed Upon Westminster Bridge

September 3, 1802

Earth has not anything to show more fair:
Dull would he be of soul who could pass by
A sight so touching in its majesty:
This City now doth, like a garment, wear
The beauty of the morning; silent, bare,
Ships, towers, domes, theaters, and temples lie
Open upon the fields, and to the sky;
All bright and glittering in the smokeless air.
Never did sun more beautifully steep
In his first splendor, valley, rock, or hill;
Ne'er saw I, never felt, a calm so deep!
The river glideth at his own sweet will:
Dear God! the very houses seem asleep;
And all that mighty heart is lying still!

WILLIAM WORDSWORTH

1. What are some of the words and images Wordsworth uses to convince you of the beauty of early morning?

2. Personification, a figure of speech in which nonhuman things are given human attributes, works not only to dramatize a subject in an interesting way but also helps the reader identify with the subject. Identify examples of personification in "Composed Upon Westminster Bridge." How does personification contribute to the feeling of the poem?

3. Besides using concrete image words, Wordsworth uses such words as "not anything," "Never," "Ne'er," "All," "very," and "so" to give a particular feeling to the poem. What is that feeling?

4. How does it intensify the poem for Wordsworth to address God in the next to last line?

5. Is it important to have the exact date at the beginning of the poem? Explain.

A. E. Housman's "Loveliest of Trees" is also a poem about a moment out of time, the appreciation of beauty in the present, and by association, about the passing of time. After reading Housman's poem, it might be hard ever to ignore cherry trees in blossom. Compare this to another spring poem, Williams's "Spring and All" in Chapter 4.

Loveliest of Trees

Loveliest of trees, the cherry now
Is hung with bloom along the bough,
And stands about the woodland ride
Wearing white for Eastertide

Now, of my threescore years and ten,
Twenty will not come again,
And take from seventy springs a score.
It only leaves me fifty more.

And since to look at things in bloom
Fifty springs are little room,
About the woodlands I will go
To see the Cherry hung with snow.

A. E. HOUSMAN

1. Why does Housman use the cherry tree to represent the ephemeral beauty of spring? How does focusing on the cherry tree instead of telling about the whole landscape strengthen the poem?
2. If you were writing a poem about each of the four seasons, what is one image you would choose to represent each?
3. What does it add to Housman's poem that he talks about his age and the average life span? How would the poem be different without that detail?

In "Spring and Fall," Gerard Manley Hopkins introduces the subject of death—also implied by the Housman poem, though less soberly—in conjunction with the seasons, an old and natural association.

Spring and Fall

To A Young Child

Márgarét, are you grieving
Over Goldengrove unleaving?
Leáves, líke the things of man, you
With your fresh thoughts care for, can you?
Áh! ás the heart grows older
It will come to such sights colder
By and by, nor spare a sigh
Though worlds of wanwood leafmeal lie;
And yet you will weep and know why.
Now no matter, child, the name:
Sórrow's spríngs áre the same.
Nor mouth had, no nor mind, expressed
What heart heard of, ghost guessed:
It is the blight man was born for,
It is Margaret you mourn for.

GERARD MANLEY HOPKINS

1. What does Hopkins mean in the last line?
2. What event is described in this poem? How is this event a universal as well as an individual experience?

3. This is a poem of address, as defined in Chapter 5. How does addressing the child directly strengthen the poem?

Theodore Roethke's "Root Cellar" touches instinctive feelings, such as revulsion at the "congress of stinks," to make a powerful statement about the life force.

Root Cellar

Nothing would sleep in that cellar, dank as a ditch,
Bulbs broke out of boxes hunting for chinks in the dark,
Shoots dangled and drooped,
Lolling obscenely from mildewed crates,
Hung down long yellow evil necks, like tropical snakes.
And what a congress of stinks!—
Roots ripe as old bait,
Pulpy stems, rank, silo-rich,
Leaf-mold, manure, lime, piled against slippery planks.
Nothing would give up life:
Even the dirt kept breathing a small breath.

THEODORE ROETHKE

---

1. Roethke summarizes the subject of his poem in the last two lines. How would you state this archetypal subject in your own words?
2. Does Roethke use strong or delicate language in this poem? Does he use common or fancy words? Are the image words vivid and concrete or general?
3. Startling, original images help to make an old subject new. Identify particularly unusual images in the poem.
4. Is Roethke using personification in this poem? Explain. In what way would personification be a particularly appropriate figure of speech for this subject?

The next three poems deal more directly with death. Although John Crowe Ransom's "Piazza Piece" deals with a grim subject, because of the rhyme and the melodramatic postures of the characters—"Back from my trellis, Sir, before I scream"—this sonnet has a paradoxically light tone.

Piazza Piece

—I am a gentleman in a dustcoat trying
To make you hear. Your ears are soft and small
And listen to an old man not at all,
They want the young men's whispering and sighing.
But see the roses on your trellis dying
And hear the spectral singing of the moon;
For I must have my lovely lady soon,
I am a gentleman in a dustcoat trying.
—I am a lady young in beauty waiting
Until my truelove comes, and then we kiss.
But what grey man among the vines is this
Whose words are dry and faint as in a dream?
Back from my trellis, Sir, before I scream!
I am a lady young in beauty waiting.

JOHN CROWE RANSOM

1. What is the concrete subject of this poem—that is, what happens? What is its abstract subject or idea?
2. How does John Crowe Ransom use playful, musical sounds and rhymes to give the poem an ironic tone? Does the sound of the poem go with the content or contrast with it?

In "Do Not Go Gentle into That Good Night," Dylan Thomas also uses a form often associated with lighter, more playful verse, the villanelle. But here the music becomes sonorous and dignified.

Do Not Go Gentle into That Good Night

Do not go gentle into that good night,
Old age should burn and rave at close of day;
Rage, rage against the dying of the light.

Though wise men at their end know dark is right,
Because their words had forked no lightning they
Do not go gentle into that good night.

Good men, the last wave by, crying how bright
Their frail deeds might have danced in a green bay,
Rage, rage against the dying of the light.

Wild men who caught and sang the sun in flight,
And learn, too late, they grieved it on its way,
Do not go gentle into that good night.

Grave men, near death, who see with blinding sight
Blind eyes could blaze like meteors and be gay,
Rage, rage against the dying of the light.

And you, my father, there on the sad height,
Curse, bless, me now with your fierce tears, I pray.
Do not go gentle into that good night.
Rage, rage against the dying of the light.

DYLAN THOMAS

1. Human beings react to death in various ways. What response does the
    speaker in the poem want his father to choose?
2. Notice that the poem has only two rhyming sounds, established by "night"
    and "day." Do you think the rhyme works well with the subject? Explain.
3. What are some other possible responses to death that might be used in po-
    ems? Look for examples in other poems you have read, such as "Piazza
    Piece" or the poem below by e. e. cummings.

e. e. cummings's "you are not going to, dear" is about resisting death and beating it, at least temporarily, "because you fooled the doctors." This is not only a poem about surviving but also a love poem, and the joining of these two big themes emphasizes the poignancy of the last image, where the happy and grateful lovers are pictured against the prospect of death: "we were / two alert lice in the blond hair of nothing."

you are not going to, dear. You are not going to and
i but that doesn't in the least matter. The big
fear Who held us deeply in His fist is

no longer, can you imagine it
i can't which doesn't matter
and what does is possibly this dear, that we may resume
impact with the inutile collide

once more with the imaginable, love, and eat sunlight(do
you believe it?   i begin to and that doesn't matter)which

i suggest teach us a new terror always
which shall brighten
carefully these things we consider life.
Dear i put my eyes into you but that doesn't matter
further than of old

because you fooled the doctors, i touch you with hopes and
words and with so and so: we are together, we will
kiss or smile or move. It's different too isn't it

different dear from moving as we, you
and i, used to move when i thought you were going to(but
that doesn't matter)
when you thought you were going to America.
                                        Then

moving was a matter of not keeping still; we were
two alert lice in the blond hair of nothing

                                        E. E. CUMMINGS

1. What is the universal subject in this poem?
2. Does the treatment of the subject feel personal?
3. How does cummings make an old subject new or original? Does his poem sound like anyone else's poem about death or is it somehow unique? Explain.

The last line of Emily Dickinson's "A Narrow Fellow in the Grass" is a lesson in the use of imagery. "Zero at the Bone" is exactly right and unforgettable—it appeals to the senses, and the word "bone" has a deep resonance. One of the charms of this poem is Dickinson's introduction of the serpent in the garden in such a natural and homely way. The description of starting to pick up the "narrow fellow," thinking it is a riding whip someone has dropped, is also striking. Notice that Dickinson uses the persona of a boy in this poem.

A Narrow Fellow in the Grass

A narrow fellow in the Grass
Occasionally rides—
You may have met Him—did you not
His notice sudden is—

The Grass divides as with a Comb—
A spotted shaft is seen—
And then it closes at your feet
And opens further on—

He likes a Boggy Acre
A Floor too cool for Corn—
Yet when a Boy, and Barefoot
I more than once at Noon
Have passed, I thought, a Whip lash
Unbraiding in the Sun
When stooping to secure it
It wrinkled, and was gone—

Several of Nature's People
I know, and they know me—
I feel for them a transport
Of cordiality—

But never met this Fellow
Attended, or alone
Without a tighter breathing
And Zero at the Bone—

EMILY DICKINSON

---

1. Who is the "Narrow Fellow in the Grass?" Is anything gained by not explicitly stating that information?
2. People are often startled by snakes. Emily Dickinson takes an ordinary experience and makes it extraordinary by using fresh, interesting images. What are some of the images she uses to get across her feelings about the snake?
3. What archetypal association do you make with the image of a snake? Is Dickinson's depiction of the snake like that archetypal association or contradictory to it?

Roethke, too, uses a snake; apparently snakes inspire a deep intuitive response. (See also Lawrence's "Snake" in Chapter 4.) Here, the speaker admires the beauty of the snake and its movements, and wishes to "be that thing." The last line turns the poem deftly, quietly, in a startling direction.

Snake

I saw a young snake glide
Out of the mottled shade
And hang, limp on a stone:
A thin mouth, and a tongue
Stayed, in the still air.

It turned; it drew away;
Its shadow bent in half;
It quickened, and was gone.

I felt my slow blood warm.
I longed to be that thing,
The pure, sensuous form.

And I may be, some time.

THEODORE ROETHKE

---

1. Compare the description of the snake in Roethke's poem to that in Dickinson's poem. Compare the speaker's feelings in the two poems.
2. How does Roethke transform a momentary and incidental experience into something larger than the moment? For example, what does he imply in the last line? What does he mean when he says the snake "quickened"?

Because of Roethke's last line, his poem engages another old, recurrent subject: change, the cycles of things, metamorphosis. Perhaps Roethke was thinking of evolution, or perhaps of natural death, decay, and new life. In any case, the poem is an example of the archetype of metamorphosis.

Galway Kinnell's "The Gray Heron" also considers change, but with a different tone. The situation has an "Alice in Wonderland" feel—the baby changes into a pig, and so on. The detail of the lizard's head as "a / fieldstone with an eye" is evocative and also suggests further linkages in kinds, that the creature might turn into stone or have evolved from stone, "the mineral kingdom."

The Gray Heron

It held its head still
while its body and green
legs wobbled in wide arcs

from side to side. When
it stalked out of sight,
I went after it, but all
I could find where I was
expecting to see the bird
was a three-foot-long lizard
in ill-fitting skin
and with linear mouth
expressive of the even temper
of the mineral kingdom.
It stopped and tilted its head,
which was much like
a fieldstone with an eye
in it, which was watching me
to see if I would go
or change into something else.

GALWAY KINNELL

---

1. The word **motif** means both an element in a pattern and sometimes that pattern itself. It is also sometimes used to mean a *theme* or general subject. What motif appears in the last line of "The Gray Heron" which also occurs in the Roethke poem?
2. How does the poet's depiction of the heron change in the poem? Does he mean that the heron has actually changed into a lizard or that it looks like a lizard?
3. Which words in this poem help you see the scene clearly?

Suggestions for Writing

1. Write a poem beginning with one of the lines below, chosen to suggest archetypal themes or images. Think of some real experience that would fit the line and write your poem to bring out its archetypal significance, or invent something fantastic and dreamlike. Be open to a variety of possibilities.
   a) I enter a room
   b) There is a stairway leading

c) I am flying
d) The journey lies ahead
e) I am lost
f) There is a face at the window
g) I have lost something
h) There is a strange land ahead
i) Something is about to happen
j) I am afraid
k) Falling, falling
l) I have been here before
m) The door is closed
n) The wheel turns
o) I hear the sound of water running
p) Once, long ago

When you are done, you may want to excise the first line if you can do so without ruining the poem, since it is really just a device to get started. Do not limit yourself to this list, either. Invent archetypal first lines for yourself, or invent a line and trade with someone else. Even when a whole group works from the same line, obviously many different poems will result.

2. Retell your favorite myth, folktale, or fairy tale. Find one that can be told in terms of your own life. Are you Icarus, who wanted to fly but went too high? Do you think of yourself as Cinderella or Sleeping Beauty or Prince Charming? What beanstalk have you had to climb lately? Do not be afraid of an ironic twist. Perhaps your sympathy lies with wicked stepmothers, stepsisters, and witches, who may have just been misunderstood.

Some of the things to consider in writing such a poem are:
a) Tone and diction (a modern flavor is probably desirable)
b) Direct use of narrative (sticking to the story) or allusion (telling your own story but referring to folkloric or mythic material).
c) Dimension or interpretation (how can the old story be made new, original, yours)

You need not go to classical or European sources. Remember to consider Native American or early American myths, traditions, and history. Perhaps your own ethnic background offers material.

3. Every people has one or more creation stories, and though there are similarities each story reflects its particular culture. Write a creation

story, fable, myth, or parable of the origin of things, which reflects your own culture. You might begin: "It was Monday night in nowhere / and nothing was around." Continue, building a world.

4. Write a poem on how something came to be. This is like suggestion 3, but make it narrower, more specific.

5. What journeys have you made? Write a poem in which you focus on a particular journey that changed your life. For example, did your family move when you were young? When were you allowed to journey across the street? Did you ever start on a journey and make a detour (literally or figuratively)? What was your most important journey? (It could be halfway around the world or simply across a room.) Try to give the journey a symbolic or mythic meaning, as well as a literal one. Or feel free to use another's journey instead of your own. You might combine this with one of the other suggestions for writing, retelling the story of Columbus or Sacajawea and giving it some sort of contemporary interpretation or relating the historical material to your own view of life. History is full of journeys.

6. Explore the figures of your personal mythology. Here are some exercises for your imagination to decide what those figures are.

   a) Design a deck of cards, but instead of kings, queens, jacks, and so on, put key characters and figures from your life on the cards. What image would be your ace? Who is your joker? What sort of games could you play with your cards?

   b) You are in a constellation. Who else is in your constellation? What is the shape of your constellation?

   c) You are pasting pictures into an album of your life. What pictures would go into the album, and in what order? Look for crucial events, images, and persons; look for yourself at various specific stages and places.

   d) Make a map of your psychic landscape. What are the landmarks? What are the landforms? Are there roads, mountains, bodies of water? Name them according to particular problems, experiences, people, and so forth. Consider four figures to be identified with the four directions of the compass. Who or what would they be, and why?

   e) Your life is a script for an adventure story. Who are the villains and the heroes? Develop characterizations that dramatize them. What is your persona in this adventure?

Use one of these systems to develop a poem or series of poems using your personal mythology.

7. Write a poem about one of the great recurrent themes: love, death, metamorphosis, the revitalizing power of nature, the seasons, art, or variations on these. Relate the theme specifically to your own life.

8. Do you have any recurrent dreams? Write a poem in which you explore the meaning of such a dream. Chances are you will be dealing with an archetype whether or not you recognize it.

9. Choose one of the poems from this chapter, or some other poem about which you have a strong feeling. Determine what the *theme*—the abstract subject—of the poem is, distinguishing theme from *imagery* or content—the concrete subject. For example, a poem may be about finding a run-over dog (its concrete subject) and about the immutability of death (its abstract subject). Write your poem on the same abstract subject as your model, but make your concrete subject so different that no one would say the two poems were alike.

10. Write a poem using a real place in your life in an important way.

11. Birds, snakes, bears, dinosaurs—what kind of animal or animals could you endow with mythic power or use to say something about life and human beings? Write about animals.

12. Write about a "strange encounter" in your life.

13. Write a poem on the subject of changes, that is, transformations.

13

Games and Experiments

The sense of play is important in poetry, as it is in any art. Like Picasso, who created a bull's head out of a bicycle seat and handlebars, the poet experiments, plays jokes, tinkers with structure, creates new and amusing contexts and relationships, dabbles with language as if it were clay or fingerpaint, and challenges his or her own wits as if the poem were something between chess and a crossword game.

Many of the suggestions for writing poetry in this book present problems calculated to challenge creativity. In that sense, they are problem-solving games. But the examples and exercises of this chapter are much more directly like experiments and games. For example, a poem may be an explicit riddle, or at the least we may have to guess its meaning from clues the poet gives us. Such a poem is "The Reed," translated from the Anglo-Saxon by Burton Raffel:

Riddle #60: The Reed

(Probably a love message in the form of a riddle.)
I grew where life had come to me, along
The sandy shore, where the sea foamed in
Below a cliff. Men came
To my empty land only by accident.
But every dawn a brown wave swept
Around me with watery arms. How
Could I ever imagine a time when, mouthless,
I'd sing across the benches where mead

Was poured, and carry secret speech?
What a strange and wonderful thing to someone
Who puzzles, but neither sees nor knows,
That the point of a knife and a strong right hand
Should press and carve me, a keen blade
And the mind of a man joined together
To make me a message-bearer to your ears
Alone, boldly bringing you what no one
Else could carry and no one hears!

ANONYMOUS ANGLO-SAXON
Translated by Burton Raffel

"The Reed" uses the device of personification by allowing the reed itself to speak of its existence. This idea of depicting an inanimate object as being able to speak and giving clues to its own identity is one *convention* of the **riddle form.** Another characteristic of the riddle is the use of a puzzling statement, something which seems impossible, such as "mouthless, / I'd sing," which becomes clear after one discovers the answer to the riddle.

A modern work which seems like a riddle and whose title tells the subject is Anne Stevenson's "The Television":

The Television

Hug me, mother of noise,
Find me a hiding place.
I am afraid of my voice.
I do not like my face.

ANNE STEVENSON

Another modern example that is not explicitly called a riddle, but seems like one, is the following passage from the first part of Theodore Roethke's "The Lost Son":

The shape of a rat?
    It's bigger than that.
    It's less than a leg
    And more than a nose,
    Just under the water
    It usually goes.

    Is it soft like a mouse?
    Can it wrinkle its nose?
    Could it come in the house
    On the tips of its toes?

    Take the skin of a cat
    And the back of an eel,
    Then roll them in grease,—
    That's the way it would feel.

    It's sleek as an otter
    With wide webby toes
    Just under the water
    It usually goes.

Roethke's lines are riddlelike, but he is aiming for emotional effect, not the answer to a riddle. What sort of thing do these extraordinary images conjure up, and how do you feel about what is suggested? There is no simple answer to this one.

1. Of these three examples—"The Reed," "The Television," "The Lost Son"—which one seems most like riddles you know? Explain.
2. Who is speaking in each poem? Is it always possible to know? To make a good guess? Is the speaker important?
3. In each of the three poems, what might be the author's point in not stating the subject in the poem? What does the riddle form do for the poem?
4. Is any one poem clearer or more puzzling than the others? Why?
5. What are some ways in which riddles are like poems?

But Is It Poetry? is a small-press anthology of one-line poems, edited by Duane Ackerson. The one-line poem often seems like a riddle, with the title as the answer. Part of the pleasure in these one-liners is to make that quick leap from puzzlement to understanding at how the writers have made their statements in a surprising and revealing way. In each of these poems, some hitherto unnoticed connection is made.

Rear View Mirror

I look back, see myself looking back.

PETER COOLEY

Stone and the Obliging Pond

Bull's Eye: the water cries out.

FELIX POLLAK AND DUANE ACKERSON

Family Squabble

Rocking the boat in the bathtub

GREG KUZMA

Icicles on Telephone Wires

Messages have grown beards waiting.

FELIX POLLAK AND DUANE ACKERSON

---

1. What is the importance of the titles in these one-line poems?
2. Is it possible to state the meaning of each poem in different words and still retain the feeling or effect of the poem? Try it.

Notice that "Stone and the Obliging Pond" and "Icicles on Telephone Wires" have two authors. We do not know who is responsible for what in Pollak and Ackerson's collaborations, but we can imagine playing a game with a poet friend in which one person gives a title while the other must supply a one-line poem. Imagine half-a-dozen people making a one-line poem for "Car Tracks in the Snow," "The Smoking Oven," "Alphabet Soup," or "Candy Hearts." Each would come up with a different one-line poem for the same title. Perhaps one or more of these would be worth keeping, perhaps not, but the real point would be the enjoyment of playing with words. If it got a little silly, fine.

There are many other possibilities for collaborative poems and word games. Here are two poems that bear the following introduction: "These collaborative poems were composed through the mail, between Minnesota and Michigan, with each author adding two lines. The period of composition was usually about three months."

Part of the Waking

In the morning, even before
the dog is awake
I have put on all
my dreaming clothes and walked outside
across the lawn with my shoes
in my hand.

But this will not be enough.
The touch of the grass will taste like green teeth,
and the hammock, stretched between the unpruned apple trees,
can barely hold the day's weight. I must keep saying to myself
lean back, back far enough until you see
the apples fade from red to pale blue
and feel the ground underneath inhaling,
pulling through the squares of rope
one by one like pieces of sleep.

JACK DRISCOLL AND WILLIAM MEISSNER

First Kiss

When he first discovered his dentures
in the garden, he put them
in a glass of cut flowers, watched them
sprout water lilies between the teeth.
Each flower frightened his wife like
a snake asleep in her clay pot.
When he smiled, his gums
were pale roses pressed for years
against the fishbowl of her dreams.
It was always that way between them,
the soft bites underwater, the kisses
that leave a taste for decades in their mouths.

JACK DRISCOLL AND WILLIAM MEISSNER

1.   Do the poems seem as if they were written by two different people? Why or why not?
2.   What would be gained from writing a poem in this cooperative way? What, if anything, would be lost?
3.   In what sense are these *surrealistic* poems?

Of course it would be impossible to foresee where something like this would end up. Each participant is dependent on lines the other feeds him, and at the same time each can turn the poem with his own line. Also, these were done over the length of time it took to mail things back and forth, instead of on the spot, which would influence the result.

A *manipulated poem* is one in which certain requirements are set or certain steps are followed. Without fully planning or anticipating the results, the writer will produce something that is poemlike if not actually a poem. Manipulated-poetry exercises are often useful at the beginning of workshops or writing groups, to get people together and to suggest assumptions we make about poetry, which can then be questioned, clarified, accepted or rejected.

For example, here is a manipulated poem for one to six participants. If you try the whole thing yourself, concentrate on each line, one at a time, without anticipating the next. If the poem is passed around for different people to contribute lines, the paper should be folded back so that each person writes without knowing what the previous line has been.

A Manipulated Six-Line Poem

Line 1. Write a line, a sentence, with a color in it (or two colors).
Line 2. Make a one-line statement about a town.
Line 3. Say something about a time of year, a season, or the weather.
Line 4. Finish a sentence that begins "I wish."
Line 5. Say something about a friend or a famous person.
Line 6. Finish a sentence beginning with the words, "Next year at this time."

Many variations on these lines are possible. For example: "Describe what you would see from a hot-air balloon or a submarine" or "State the first thing you saw when you woke up this morning." The point is to evoke concrete imagery that might seem mysterious or interesting, without explaining it.

Another approach would be to use a set of slightly off-the-wall questions calculated to produce unexpected answers with a certain emotional character because of their out-of-context quality. The only requirement for this exercise is that the answers be complete statements. Following is a suggested set of questions. Give a one-sentence answer to each one in this order:

Why Did You Do It?

1. Why did you do it?
2. What was the texture of the air?
3. What was the sound (or color or smell) of the weather?
4. Was there a stranger?
5. Why did you do it? (Different answer than 1.)

6. Were promises made?
7. Would you do it again?
8. Why did you do it? (Different answer than 1 and 5.)
9. Why did you do it? (Different answer than 1, 5, and 8.)

A room full of twenty different writers will come up with twenty different configurations or stories: I did it because I wanted to. / The air was like silk. / The storm smelled like honey and peaches . . . and so on. Repetition of some of the questions helps give the exercise a sense of continuity. Use these questions or make up your own.

This exercise recalls the subject of configuration, or gestalt, discussed in Chapter 7. Even if no connection between the various lines has been planned, we will start to see connection because the mind tends to find patterns, whether or not patterns are intended. An instructive thing about this game is that it shows one way poems can be structured: each line is conceived and exists as a separate grammatical unit, but, nevertheless, all the lines together make a whole. The self-contained lines even establish a free-form periodic rhythm.

Another manipulated form for loosening up, which plays with language and free association, is what might be called a *thought line*. The simplest thought line begins with an abstraction, such as *life, love, death,* or *hate*. Then, simply free associate from that word in a continuous curving line, up and down, upside down, around, letting the words snake from one end of the paper to the other and back again.

Such exercises can also focus on questions such as whether or not art can be accidental or **aleatory**. Stephen Daedulus, in James Joyce's *Portrait of the Artist as a Young Man,* asks, if a man hacking at a block of wood accidentally produces the image of a cow, is that art? Likewise, is collaboration valid? How is continuity to be maintained in a poem, and to what extent do line breaks determine whether or not we see something as a poem? Beyond such philosophy, of course, the results of exercises can be fascinating and amusing.

Instead of using several subjects in a manipulated poem, such as the weather, far-off places, wishes, or the passing of time, we might choose just one. Color, especially, is a powerful ingredient in poetry and can be both an organizing principle and a means to carry the weight of feeling in a poem. As an exercise, free associate on a large piece of paper using

a colored marker, and let your imagination play off the color of the pen.
For example, imagine this association written in the colors of ink it names:

> This is a blue week or
> a blue season, iced deep and down blue.
> In it, I will do only blue things:
> buy blue shoes, put blue make-up on my eyes,
> read a blue book.
> I will study my veins a lot
> this week, knit blue wool
> into something to transform the wearer.
> Look at the sky.
>
> Now this is my orange pen.
> My orange pen writes
> all the opposite things
> my blue pen has never seen,
> its complement. A pumpkin.
> An orange. A carrot. Deep
> rooted orange. I believe
> it is my most edible pen,
> so it always returns to my mouth.
>
> Yellow, fearful yellow pen that moves
> like the hand that having writ, et cetera,
> it writes of age and the aged sun,
> scribbles a week of dying leaves,
> tawny grass and the ends of seasons.
> Jaundiced pen,
>
> it drives me to snatch up the green pen,
> but the green soon gives flower to the purple,
> and the flower gives fruit to the red,
> the magenta, the carmine, and soon
> this bloody color has drained me.
>
> Pale, barely two dimensional,
> I have only enough strength
> to reach for the black pen, my salvation.
> With it, I sign my name.

Even abandoning your colored pen for black-and-white type, you will want to think about the mental and visual effect of color. A poet who has made consistent and remarkable use of color in his poetry is Wallace Stevens. Notice how color is linked to transformations of the imagination in the following:

A Rabbit as King of the Ghosts

The difficulty to think at the end of day,
When the shapeless shadow covers the sun
And nothing is left except light on your fur—

There was the cat slopping its milk all day,
Fat cat, red tongue, green mind, white milk
And August the most peaceful month.

To be, in the grass, in the peacefullest time,
Without that monument of cat,
The cat forgotten in the moon;

And to feel the light is a rabbit-light,
In which everything is meant for you
And nothing need be explained;

Then there is nothing to think of. It comes of itself;
And east rushes west and west rushes down,
No matter. The grass is full

And full of yourself. The trees around are for you,
The whole of the wideness of night is for you,
A self that touches all edges,

You become a self that fills the four corners of night.
The red cat hides away in the fur-light
And there you are humped high, humped up,

You are humped higher and higher, black as stone—
You sit with your head like a carving in space
And the little green cat is a bug in the grass.

WALLACE STEVENS

1. Who is speaking? Who is the "you" mentioned in the poem? Is this a poem
   of address or a poem in persona?
2. What colors does Stevens use in the poem? Does he use any of them more
   than once? Is there any pattern in his use of colors?

At the end of the poem the rabbit is dominant, a Walter Mitty of rabbits, a veritable giant of a rabbit, "your head like a carving in space,"
while the cat has been reduced to a "little green cat" and "a bug in the
grass." Stevens's poem is more than a game, but much of the wonderful
feeling of the poem is playful and wistful at the same time.

Visual play with words is possible in many ways. *Used words,* for
example, refers to making a visual *collage* of words cut from magazines,
newspapers, cereal boxes, or any other printed source. Words can be cut
out and pasted together to make a preconceived statement, or the process
can be more accidental and less linear. Cut out a whole bagful of words
and then divide the used words among members of a workshop. Work
on a pile of words by yourself or with someone else. Paste down the collage, or simply put it back in the bag when you are done. Someone else
can use the same words to say something quite different. We have already
discussed a related process in Chapter 8, with regard to found poetry. In
this case, however, it is a matter of using the typography of words from
different sources rather than their allusory qualities, although the ghost of
allusion lurks in a visual-collage poem.

An exercise like this reminds us that the words we use in writing have
already been used by others, over and over, and it remains for each of us
to use them in a new way, to somehow refresh the old words. All of our
words are, in effect, used words. Have you ever looked at a brilliant poem
or novel and said to yourself: "I know all the words that writer used. Why
couldn't I have put them together like that?" One famous definition for
poetry is Coleridge's, "The best words in the best order," but it appears

that all our used words have many possible orders. Another benefit of the used words, or collage, exercise is that it imparts a concrete feeling for the size and space of the language, the way in which the words are separate pieces that can be moved around and put together.

From collage poems it is a short step to concrete poetry, which has already been mentioned in Chapter 1 in connection with Mary Ellen Solt's "Lilac." To experiment with concrete poetry, start with something as simple as using the letters of a word to make a picture of the thing to which the word refers, as in this depiction of a violet.

What could you do with the words for "train," "sunset," or "hunger"? Concrete poetry represents a combination of the visual and verbal. The term **concrete** implies that the poem is itself only, and that there is no abstract meaning to be drawn from it. Various practitioners, dissatisfied with the term, have invented other designations: *image poetry, word pictures, picture poems,* and so on, but the term concrete poetry seems to stick, and it is useful because it means more or less the same thing to most people.

A 1967 issue of *The Chicago Review* was devoted to concrete poetry; it included everything from audiovisual puns to a series of images of letters blown up in size until the curve of a single "a" filled the page. Advertising art and visual jokes, such as the word "cold" written with jiggly, shivering lines or with icicles drawn hanging off the letters, use this kind of verbal and visual play, and it is easy to think of other simple applications of this idea. But good concrete poetry is not so easy. The French poet Guillaume Apollinaire wrote lyric poetry as well as concrete poetry, and his concrete works have a lyrical quality to them. One of the older examples of picture poetry is George Herbert's "Easter Wings," written in the early seventeenth century, in which Herbert meditates about losing and regaining spiritual grace.

Easter Wings

Lord, who createdst man in wealth and store,
Though foolishly he lost the same,
Decaying more and more
Till he became
Most poor:
With thee
O let me rise
As larks, harmoniously,
And sing this day thy victories:
Then shall the fall further the flight in me.

My tender age in sorrow did begin;
And still with sicknesses and shame
Thou didst so punish sin,
That I became
Most thin.
With thee
Let me combine,
And feel this day thy victory;
For, if I imp my wing on thine,
Affliction shall advance the flight in me.

GEORGE HERBERT

---

1. Does the length of the lines relate to the content of the lines in any way? Notice particularly such lines as "Most poor:" and "Most thin." Is the length of any other lines significant?
2. Look at "Easter Wings" overall and from different directions. Do you see a picture in the shape of the poem?
3. Does the appearance of the poem add anything to the poem? For instance, does it strengthen the meaning of the poem or make it more interesting or pleasing?

Modern concrete poets use language in a variety of ways. Sometimes the appeal is mainly to the eye, while the repetition of a word may emphasize its sound. Richard Kostelanetz's concrete poems "Disintegration" and "Concentric," which visualize their meanings, are examples of the former. Aram Saroyan's "Crickets" simply repeats the word crickets in a line down the page so many times that we are reminded of the sound of crickets. Consider the following examples and how each is a concrete representation of its subject as well as how the method and degree of concreteness vary. Perhaps you will want to look back to Chapter 1 to include Mary Ellen Solt's "Lilac" in this comparison.

Night Practice

I
will
remember
with my breath
to make a mountain,
with my sucked-in breath
a valley, with my pushed-out
breath a mountain. I will make
a valley wider than the whisper, I
will make a higher mountain than the cry;
will with my will breathe a mountain, I will
with my will breathe a valley. I will push out
a mountain, suck in a valley, deeper than the shout
YOU MUST DIE, harder, heavier, sharper, a mountain than
the truth YOU MUST DIE. I will remember, My breath will
make a mountain. My will will remember to will. I, sucking, pushing, I will breathe a valley, I will breathe a mountain.

MAY SWENSON

---

1. How does "Night Practice" imitate its subject?
2. Swenson has created a picture poem, but she also plays with other senses besides sight. How does Swenson use repetition of sounds? How does the sound of the poem imitate the subject? If you read the poem aloud, does it make you conscious of your breath?

The way Bob Heman's poem looks on the page is important but in a different way than Swenson's, Solt's or Herbert's. Swenson brought in the element of breath and voice. Heman adds another active element. The poem itself becomes a kind of game that does not *need* to be played. One can imagine playing it—and that suffices.

Guilt

the cat
you released
in the woods
is making its way
slowly back to you

the cat
you released
in the woods
is making its way
slowly back to you

make the cube
roll it and read the upturned side
roll it again and read the upturned side
continue doing this
stop when you feel like it

the cat
you released
in the woods
is making its way
slowly back to you

the cat
you released
in the woods
is making its way
slowly back to you

the cat
you released
in the woods
is making its way
slowly back to you

the cat
you released
in the woods
is making its way
slowly back to you

BOB HEMAN

1. What would be the effect of making the poem into a cube, rolling the cube, and reading from it?
2. How does Heman's title help reinforce the feeling of the game?

Sound is important in all poetry, unless we except such examples as "Lilac." Even in this case, as we read the poem, the echo of the title or of the letters as sound in the mind must be an aspect of meaning. In some works, the sound plays a part that is not unlike the visual effect of concrete poems. The device of using a word, or a group of words, to imitate the sound named is called **onomatopoeia.** Following are two poems that go beyond the simple onomatopoeia of "swish, swish" or "bang, bang" to make sound into an immediate event, integral to the meaning of the poem.

Earthy Anecdote

Every time the bucks went clattering
Over Oklahoma
A firecat bristled in the way.

Wherever they went,
They went clattering,
Until they swerved
In a swift, circular line
To the right,
Because of the firecat.

Or until they swerved
In a swift, circular line
To the left,
Because of the firecat.

The bucks clattered.
The firecat went leaping,
To the right, to the left,
And
Bristled in the way.

Later, the firecat closed his bright eyes
And slept.

WALLACE STEVENS

1. In what way does Stevens use sound to recreate the subject of the poem?
2. Stevens was interested in the relationship between imagination and reality. Which of these does his title suggest? Which does the poem itself suggest? Is it fair to say that Stevens is playing a game with the reader's imagination?

Analysis of Baseball

It's about
the ball,
the bat,
and the mitt.
Ball hits
bat, or it
hits mitt.
Bat doesn't
hit ball, bat
meets it.
Ball bounces
off bat, flies
air, or thuds
ground (dud)
or it
fits mitt.

Bat waits
for ball
to mate.
Ball hates
to take bat's
bait. Ball
flirts, bat's
late, don't
keep the date.
Ball goes in
(thwack) to mitt,
and goes out
(thwack) back
to mitt.

Ball fits
mitt, but
not all
the time.
Sometimes
ball gets hit
(pow) when bat
meets it,
and sails
to a place
where mitt
has to quit
in disgrace.
That's about
the bases
loaded,
about 40,000
fans exploded.

It's about
the ball,
the bat,
the mitt,
the bases
and the fans.
It's done
on a diamond,
and for fun.
It's about
home, and it's
about run.

MAY SWENSON

1. What do you notice about the appearance of May Swenson's poem?
2. When you read "Analysis of Baseball" aloud, what do you notice about the sound of it?
3. Would you call this more of a picture poem or a sound poem?

Another way to play with words visually and concretely is to use the words to fill in the shape of something. That is, do not build a shape out of words, as in Herbert's "Easter Wings" or Swenson's "Night Practice," but simply draw a shape and fill it with words. Outline your own hand, for example, and pattern it with words describing things you touch, or lie down on a big sheet of butcher paper, have someone make an outline of your whole body, and fill it with things about yourself. You could do this over a period of time, creating a sort of visual diary. You could draw in your features with words, such as "My eyes have seen . . . " to make your eyes, or "Tooth, tooth, tooth, crown, tooth" written inside of an outlined mouth. Any of these exercises can be as simple or sophisticated as you care to make them.

All of these visual suggestions have to do with the concrete style of the poem itself, but there are other ways of joining poetry with the visual arts. State arts councils or city arts groups have sponsored programs, such as Poetry in Public Places, which involve poems short enough to be read by passersby or which lend themselves to a poster presentation. These poems are displayed on buses, billboards, and so on. Small presses have published poster poems that are sometimes concrete poems, although many of them are simply high-quality posters on which a poem is presented in fine type, sometimes accompanied by an illustration. Some presses have come out with poetry postcards ranging from artful presentations of short poems to outrageous puns and visual jokes. If you are in a writing workshop with a convenient way to display such things, you might think in terms of a graffiti board—signed or anonymous poems and word play, scribbled, posted, or drawn on a large piece of butcher paper tacked up in some public place—an open invitation to others to contribute.

Besides experimenting with poems and wordplay in riddles, concrete and visual forms, sound poems and other approaches, think about poetry as it might blend with other mediums—comic strips or film, for example. Experimental poetry collages exist consisting of words "spoken" in cartoon balloons by people or objects cut out of magazines or photos. Some of these experiments bring to mind the French surrealists and the dadaists. In his *Scientific American* column, "Mathematical Games" (February 1977), Martin Gardner discusses a contemporary French group, the Oulipo, devoted to what he calls "recreational linguistics." The recreations that best relate to poetry include the following:

Flip Book. Lines of poems are written on pages which have been sliced horizontally so that they form a book in which pages may be flipped to show different combinations of lines. Gardner describes the Oulipo's *A Hundred Thousand Billion Poems,* in which the pages are sliced into fourteen strips, "all structurally perfect and making sense."

Lipogram. This is a work that omits one or more letters of the alphabet, for example, a long poem that omits the letter "e."

Palindrome. Whether it is one line or longer, this reads the same backward and forward ("Madam, I'm Adam"). Clearly this is of limited application in poetry, but it is offered here as a challenge to those who enjoy wordplay.

Permutations. Gardner describes various kinds of permutations, ranging from the splicing of front and back halves of different proverbs to the substitution of randomly selected words into a known work. A permutation might be set up so that it would appear as two poems running down two columns on opposite halves of the same page, but it could be read across the page as one poem; or lines could alternate in some other way. Permutations could also be achieved by computer or by a mathematical plan. One example mentioned by Gardner is the Möbius strip with a different poem written on each side of a strip of paper, the two poems becoming one when the strip is connected.

Isogrammatic Poems. A poem is written containing only the letters that appear in a specified word.

Snowball Sentences. Each word is one letter longer than the preceding word. This could be adapted to each word in a line or in a stanza.

Hidden-Structure Poems. Some secret structure, meaningful or not, is invented, and a poem is developed within its restrictions. This can be an acrostic in which the first letter of each line spells the name of a person or a statement of some sort; or the first word of each line might begin with the last letter of the preceding line. Diane Wakoski's "Justice Is Reason Enough" is structured on its first line, "He who was once my brother"; the first letter of each line spells out this phrase. (The *t* line was deleted in revision, but one need not keep a structure wholly intact.)

Gardner's article tells much more about the Oulipo and various examples of eccentric wordplay. Refer to it if you would like to pursue the subject in greater depth. Meanwhile, experiment with these exercises; if you get a good poem out of one, fine, but if you simply enjoy the wordplay, that is good, too.

Here is a word game that I have used with worthwhile results in a number of writing workshops. Choose some polysyllabic word (such as *polysyllabic*). Give yourself as much time as you want and see how many words you can make out if it, repeating letters more times than they appear in the original word, if you wish. When you have a good-sized list, see if you can form some nonsensical or serious poem or statement. Use only one word to a line in your poem and use the original word as a title. For example:

Sincerely

Since
I
lie
nicely
I
sin
nicely.

Situation

I
sit
at
a
station.

Napoleon

O
pale
Napoleon
lone
one,
lean
on
no one.

Malevolence

No
love?
Leave.
Move
on.
Calm
cove,
a
lone
vale.

Grapefruit

Fear
fat?
Fit
gear.
Eat
a
grapefruit.

This exercise, like others in this chapter, is an enjoyable warm-up for a writing group, like doing push-ups or jumping jacks, except that one does not get out of breath.

Suggestions for Writing

Since the suggestions for writing have been explained in the chapter itself, here is simply a review of the possibilities covered. Refer to the chapter for explanations:

1. Riddles

2. One-line poems

3. Collaborations

4. Manipulated poems

5. Color associations

6. Thought lines

7. Concrete and visual poetry

8. Poetry written inside shapes

9. Sound poetry

10. Posters, postcards, and other display forms

11. Mixed-media poetry

12. Recreational linguistics: scrambled poems, snowballs, alphabetic sentences, flip books, lipograms, palindromes, exercises in randomness, Möbius construction, hidden structure poems, permutations

13. Poems out of letters from a polysyllabic word

14

Then and Now

To read the poetry of our contemporaries and predecessors is to live in an atmosphere of charged language and charged ideas. To try to write without reading the works of others and without knowing anything of those before us is like trying to grow flowers in cement. No mulch. Of course it can be overwhelming; there are so many books, so many names. But the writer has the luxury of being able to pick around. Browse your library. Look into anthologies. Go through the collected and selected works of single authors. Look for first books by young authors in small editions. Look for prize-winning collections. Read the poems that are tucked here and there in magazines. Don't forget to look for international authors—read Pablo Neruda, César Vallejo, Anna Akhmatova, Tomas Tranströmer, Guillaume Apollinaire. If there are poetry readings in your area, go to them and listen until you understand what charges you up and what doesn't. If people tell you the names of poets whose works they like, find books by these poets and read them. Stand in bookstores reading what you find on the shelves until you find the books you want to read over and over. Buy those and take them home.

Following are some suggestions for areas you might like to pursue. With the other poems and authors you'll find in this book and elsewhere, they can provide a starting place for you to familiarize yourself with modern and contemporary poetry.

Ask various poets what one should read in order to become a poet, and answers will range from *Beowulf* to *The New York Times*. Ask what the most important events in the history of poetry are, and answers may range from the birth of Shakespeare to the invention of the typewriter.

One poet says, "I didn't understand poetry until I discovered 'Gilgamesh,'" an ancient Babylonian poem based on even more ancient

319

Sumerian mythology. Another declares that Edmund Spenser's "The Faerie Queene" is the masterwork or that the King James Bible is the cornerstone of modern free verse. Still another advises: "Don't read poetry. Read science. I read science. I write poetry."

The only response to all of this is that we have a richness to enjoy and learn from—more, in fact, that any single lifetime would allow. Poetry is such an eclectic art that it is impossible to circumscribe or neatly package all that might contribute to its making. The main thing is to get into it. Read everything you can. Be open to possibilities. Try anything that interests you. Write and write and write some more.

The more you learn about poetry, the more you will see echoes of one poet in another. Tracing influence is not our main concern here, except to note that all poets profit from the influence and experience of their predecessors and of their contemporaries.

At the same time, it's important to remember that poetry is continually changing, continually being reinvented. In *A History of Modern Poetry: From the 1890's to the High Modernist Mode,* David Perkins observes about American poets of the early twentieth century: "On the whole, American poetry was written by men and women who taught themselves, without being exposed to either the discipline or the intimidation of an aware criticism at the start of their careers."

Later in the book he writes about Ezra Pound:

> Pound explained that poetry is not an amateur hobby. It should be practiced professionally, as a craft; one studies it, he said, in several languages; one labors at technique; one weighs and ponders in conscious self-criticism. And yet the amateur atmosphere of American poetry at the turn of the century cannot have been wholly disadvantageous, if only because Robinson, Frost, Pound, Williams, Sandburg, Masters, Eliot, and Stevens grew up in it—better poets than many reared in the more professionally sophisticated and critically watchful milieu of the last forty years.

Translated into advice for the student poet, this means, learn your craft and tradition but do not be intimidated by critics or literary history. Follow models when they work; forget them when they do not.

It is sometimes said that modern American poetry began in 1855 with the publication of Walt Whitman's *Leaves of Grass,* in its first edition a collection of twelve poems with an introduction by the poet.

Whitman self-published this edition of his poems. Setting a brash example for his successors, he wrote enthusiastic reviews of his own work under a pseudonym. Transcendentalist writer Ralph Waldo Emerson, to whom Whitman sent a copy, praised the poems, but otherwise they were not well received by his contemporaries. The reason for this lack of acceptance may be found obversely in Pound's "Salutation the Second," written many years later:

> You were praised, my books,
>   because I had just come from the country;
> I was twenty years behind the times
>   so you found an audience ready.

Pound, himself a highly influential modern American poet and critic, recognized that readers are often more accepting of familiar things than of the new and that a writer may meet with greater approval with his less original works. Perhaps Whitman found an audience even less ready than most. It is interesting to note that *Leaves of Grass* was published in the same year as another attempt to create the American epic poem, Longfellow's "Hiawatha," although the latter is no longer read seriously. Whitman's reputation has waxed and waned and waxed again since 1855, but whether they resist or embrace him, modern poets have had to deal with the example of Whitman, as Pound acknowledged:

A Pact

I make a pact with you, Walt Whitman—
I have detested you long enough.
I come to you as a grown child
Who has had a pig-headed father;
I am old enough now to make friends.
It was you that broke the new wood,
Now is the time for carving.
We have one sap and one root—
Let there be commerce between us.

EZRA POUND

The point is that American poetry before Whitman was not so uniquely American. Whitman used long, loosely constructed unrhymed lines, of varying lengths and rhythms. He used common language and wrote about common, earthy subjects. Out of Whitman came the break with the more formal English tradition, and this break has continued into the present to foster the strongest, most original strain in modern American poetry.

Because so much twentieth-century poetry is written in free verse, that aspect of Whitman alone is enough to place him at the source of a dominant stream in poetry. The use of free verse by Whitman is not merely a technical matter but also a philosophical one. Repeatedly Whitman expressed a desire to be close to nature and free of influences that prevent that relationship, as in these lines from "Song of Myself":

> I harbor for good or bad, I permit to speak at every hazard,
> Nature without check with original energy.

Seeking to create a fresh, new poetry appropriate to his time and place, Whitman rejected the strictures of tradition, including traditional forms. He improvised rhythms and structures to suit the subject and emotions of the poem.

Of course Whitman was not writing in a cultural or historical vacuum. His individualism grew naturally in the atmosphere of the American transcendentalist movement. Henry David Thoreau's *Walden* was published in 1854, the year preceding the publication of *Leaves of Grass.* Emerson, in his essay "Self Reliance," wrote: "Great works of art have no more affecting lesson for us than this. They teach us to abide by our spontaneous impression." This is what Whitman attempted and advocated.

The assertion of the goodness of nature and, by association, the worth of the individual links another characteristic in Whitman to later American poetry. That is, he used himself as an important unifying element in the work. The poet speaks in the first person, using his own name, and declares his relationship to the universe; of course, the character he is in his poetry and the poet in person are not identical. Critic Malcolm Cowley pointed out, in the 1959 republication of the original 1855 *Leaves of Grass,* that Whitman distinguished between himself as author, Walter Whitman, and himself as *persona* or speaker, "Walt Whitman, an American, one of the roughs, a kosmos," who speaks for universal human experience. The individual identity is there, but shaped to become a representative of something larger than one person:

Through me many long dumb voices,
Voices of the interminable generations of prisoners and slaves,
Voices of the diseased and despairing and of thieves and dwarfs,
Voices of cycles of preparation and accretion,
And of the threads that connect the stars, and of wombs and of the
    father-stuff,
And of the rights of them the others are down upon,
Of the deformed, trivial, flat, foolish, despised,
Fog in the air, beetles rolling balls of dung.

His was not to be a poetry dealing only with the ideal and exalted, but also a democratic poetry, asserting the worth of the lowly, the oppressed, and the humble.

The use of free verse, long lines, and open structure; the use of *I* both in a personal and universal mode; the use of the American landscape to create a myth of place; a prevalent democratic idealism; the use of the list as a structure and the use of eclectic subject matter; the expression of mystical union with all of life; the combining of feeling and music with a philosophical argument; these are some of the things that are meant when one speaks of the Whitmanian tradition.

Echoes of Whitman abound in modern poetry. Early in the twentieth century Edgar Lee Masters wrote about the lives of ordinary Americans and paid tribute to Whitman, as in this excerpt from "Petit the Poet":

Life all around me here in the village:
Tragedy, comedy, valor and truth,
Courage, constancy, heroism, failure—
All in the loom, and oh what patterns!
Woodlands, meadows, streams and rivers—
Blind to all of it all my life long.
Triolets, villanelles, rondels, rondeaus,
Seed in a dry pod, tick, tick, tick,
Tick, tick, tick, what little iambics.
While Homer and Whitman roared in the pines?

Laboring over imitations of past forms, Petit is blind to "life all around me here in the village," but Whitman, who immersed himself in "life . . . in the village," is identified with Homer, the greatest of the epic poets.

Robinson Jeffers makes no specific reference to Whitman in the following poem, but his long unrhymed lines and the expressed desire to be in harmony with nature, even nature expressed in the body of a vulture, are reminiscent of Whitman.

Vulture

I had walked since dawn and lay down to rest on a bare hillside
Above the ocean. I saw through half-shut eyelids a vulture
   wheeling high up in heaven,
And presently it passed again, but lower and nearer, its orbit
   narrowing, I understood then
That I was under inspection. I lay death-still and heard the flight-
   feathers
Whistle above me and make their circle and come nearer.
I could see the naked red head between the great wings
Bear downward staring. I said, "My dear bird, we are wasting time
   here.
These old bones will still work; they are not for you." But how
   beautiful he looked, gliding down
On those great sails; how beautiful he looked, veering away in the
   sea-light over the precipice. I tell you solemnly
That I was sorry to have disappointed him. To be eaten by that
   beak and become part of him, to share those wings and those
   eyes—
What a sublime end of one's body, what an enskyment; what a life
   after death.

ROBINSON JEFFERS

     Of course poets do not simply imitate one another—even the word "influence" may not be an accurate description for what occurs. Each of these poets learned from Whitman and yet each is an original. Perhaps what we take from predecessors is a sense of permission—of possibilities opening, of processes to be extended. Another word for this opening up of possibilities may be "inspiration." Sometimes inspiration or influence is direct and acknowledged, as in this poem by Allen Ginsberg, where the poet identifies with Whitman as friend, mentor, and model. Notice how Ginsberg gives his poem a Whitmanesque rolling, expansive sound by using lists and long lines.

A Supermarket in California

What thoughts I have of you tonight, Walt Whitman,
for I walked down the sidestreets under the trees with a
headache self-conscious looking at the full moon.

In my hungry fatigue, and shopping for images, I went
into the neon fruit supermarket, dreaming of your enum-
erations!

What peaches and what penumbras! Whole families
shopping at night! Aisles full of husbands! Wives in the
avocados, babies in the tomatoes!—and you, Garcia Lorca,
what were you doing down by the watermelons?

I saw you, Walt Whitman, childless, lonely old grubber,
poking among the meats in the refrigerator and eyeing the
grocery boys.

I heard you asking questions of each: Who killed the
pork chops? What price bananas? Are you my Angel?

I wandered in and out of the brilliant stacks of cans
following you, and followed in my imagination by the
store detective.

We strode down the open corridors together in our
solitary fancy tasting artichokes, possessing every frozen
delicacy, and never passing the cashier.

Where are we going, Walt Whitman? The doors close
in an hour. Which way does your beard point tonight?

(I touch your book and dream of our odyssey in the
supermarket and feel absurd.)

Will we walk all night through solitary streets? The
trees add shade to shade, lights out in the houses, we'll
both be lonely.

Will we stroll dreaming of the lost America of love
past blue automobiles in driveways, home to our silent
cottage?

Ah, dear father, graybeard, lonely old courage-teacher,
what America did you have when Charon quit poling his

ferry and you got out on a smoking bank and stood watching the boat disappear on the black waters of Lethe?

Berkeley 1955

ALLEN GINSBERG

At other times a flowering of ideas may be more indirectly part of a cultural and political climate, so that we are reminded of Whitman in such diverse, contemporary voices as the song lyrics of Bob Dylan and the poetry of Adrienne Rich. The following lines from Whitman's "Song of Myself" might have appeared in an early Dylan song without seeming out of place:

> I have heard what the talkers were talking, the talk of the beginning
>   and the end,
> But I do not talk of the beginning or the end.

These same lines might well have inspired Adrienne Rich's "Planetarium." Here is an excerpt from her poem:

> I have been standing all my life in the
> direct path of a battery of signals
> the most accurately transmitted most
> untranslatable language in the universe
> I am a galactic cloud so deep   so invo-
> luted that a light wave could take 15
> years to travel through me   And has
> taken   I am an instrument in the shape
> of a woman trying to translate pulsations
> into images   for the relief of the body
> and the reconstruction of the mind.

Whitman, of course, is not the whole story. Other American precursors of contemporary poets include Emily Dickinson and Edgar Allan Poe.

If Whitman's poems are great, sprawling vistas, macrocosms, Emily Dickinson's are small, perfect gardens, microcosms. It is valuable to notice the different range of experience in these poets' lives, for often we think of the poet in the *romantic* model as one who must travel, go among all kinds of people, live both the high and the low life in order to write well. Unlike Whitman, Emily Dickinson made no attempt to lead a public poet's life. She lived in Amherst, Massachusetts, and became over the years more and more an eccentric recluse. Yet her imaginative genius allowed her to encompass the greatest extremes of consciousness in her poetry.

The poems of Dickinson are short, marked by restraint and wit, by startling metaphors and images drawn from imagination and from nature as she observed it in her own garden. Here is an example.

A Bird Came Down the Walk

A Bird came down the Walk—
He did not know I saw—
He bit an Angleworm in halves
And ate the fellow, raw,

And then he drank a Dew
From a convenient Grass—
And then hopped sidewise to the Wall
To let a Beetle pass—

He glanced with rapid eyes
That hurried all around—
They looked like frightened Beads, I thought—
He stirred his Velvet Head

Like one in danger, Cautious,
I offered him a Crumb
And he unrolled his feathers
And rowed him softer home—

Than Oars divide the Ocean,
Too silver for a seam—
Or Butterflies, off Banks of Noon
Leap, plashless as they swim.

EMILY DICKINSON

Since nearly all of Dickinson's poems were published only after her death, they did not find an audience until many years after they were written, and even now it is more difficult to point out the followers of Dickinson than those of Whitman. Perhaps we could compare Dickinson's poetry to that of the *imagists,* modern writers who emphasize succinct, concrete language and striking images. Other poets come to mind including Robert Frost, who often wrote of nature with an ironic twist; e.e. cummings, who sharpened the traditional lyric into a work of modern sculpture; Marianne Moore, another writer who gave a modest demeanor to the enigmatic imagination of a sphinx; May Swenson, who looked at the world with a close and startling scrutiny; or William Stafford, another poet whose quietness masks an unconventional metaphysicality. Although her work is greatly admired by later poets, and though she undoubtedly has been of great influence, Dickinson was such an original genius the lines of her influence are not necessarily clear.

The influence of Edgar Allan Poe may seem less clear than that of either Dickinson or Whitman when we compare his poems with works by twentieth-century poets. He is now most respected for his short stories, while his poetry, because of its artificiality and heavy *gothic* effects, seems at odds with the more natural language and relaxed rhythms of more recent poetry. However, his poetry, and especially his poetic theory, were admired by the *French symbolists* of the late nineteenth century, and Poe's influence returned to American poetry by that indirect route. **Symbolism** was a *romantic* movement in which the poet sought to communicate emotion in various ways, such as by emphasizing the musical qualities in language and by using strange or mysterious imagery to represent abstract, subjective experience. Consider the emphasis on mood or atmosphere, the dense sound structures, and the exotic imagery in the following lines from Poe's "Ulalume—A Ballad";

And now, as the night was senescent,
   And star-dials pointed to morn—
   As the star-dials hinted to morn—
At the end of our path a liquescent
   And nebulous lustre was born,
Out of which a miraculous crescent
   Arose with a duplicate horn—
Astarte's bediamonded crescent,
   Distinct with its duplicate horn.

The *Princeton Encyclopedia of Poetry and Poetics* (1974) says this about Poe's influence on the French symbolists:

> More important than his poems, Poe's theories proclaimed the idea of an absolute Beauty and the importance of the poem "written solely for the poem's sake"; urged in poetry "a certain taint of sadness," the need for images with indefinite sensations, and the "absolute essentiality" and vast importance of music; and represented the poet as a thoroughly conscious artist. [p. 837]

The French symbolists influenced not only subsequent art movements, **dadaism** and **surrealism,** but also various English-speaking poets, including the Irish poet William Butler Yeats, who experimented with **automatic writing** in his search for **symbols.** T. S. Eliot read and was influenced by Yeats, and Eliot's theory of the **objective correlative** (Chapter 12) involves the search for symbols or images to express the emotional life, combined with the idea that the poet is a "thoroughly conscious artist."

These, then, are the most visible precursors of modern and contemporary poetry: Whitman, Dickinson, and Poe. From Whitman and from Poe (via the French symbolists) particularly are seen two separate, sometimes contradictory, sometimes intersecting lines of influence. Whitman represents the long poem, the long free-verse line, and a more open, personal, and American strain; Poe represents the rhymed, metrical, shorter poem in a more deliberately artificial mode. That this is an oversimplification is clear when we look at the explosion of modernists around the beginning of the twentieth century and the variety encompassed within the idea of modernism.

Perhaps the most influential of the modern poets was Ezra Pound, whose "Cantos" can be considered alongside T. S. Eliot's long work, "The Waste Land." As leader of the imagist movement, Pound advocated succinctness, concreteness, and *open* or **organic form** in poetry (as opposed to traditional form imposed upon the material). Pound insisted that rhythms and line breaks should arise from the material and the emotion inherent in the material. The speech of poetry should feel natural, not artificial. Eliot's "The Waste Land," which expressed a need to control and unify a fragmented world, and which was accompanied by scholarly apparatus, seemed to move away from these values. For this reason, William

Carlos Williams—who had been working in his own poetry toward freer form and a more natural, less adorned style and imagery—once said that the publication of "The Waste Land" had put modern poetry back twenty years. Eliot's influence is associated with later "formalists" or "academics" who were prominent through the following decades. The influence of Pound and Williams is associated with the resurgence of a more open, indigenous poetry during the Fifties. And yet we must remember that Pound advised Eliot and edited "The Waste Land" and that the poem was influenced by the imagist movement. There are many more points at which divergent tendencies intersect.

The early twentieth century was an intense period of activity. *Poetry* magazine, founded in 1912, published Robert Frost, Amy Lowell, Ezra Pound, T. S. Eliot, Gertrude Stein, Carl Sandburg, and many other moderns, all before 1920. The fractured syntax and technical experimentation of e. e. cummings, who first published a book of poetry in 1923, still embody for many readers the very sense of the word **modern.** Yet, his lyrical subjects and attitudes seem almost traditional beside the work of Gertrude Stein, whose work appears in Chapter 1 and who experimented with language as modern artists experimented with visual imagery, fracturing it into strange, new arrangements.

Robert Frost, John Crowe Ransom, Wallace Stevens, Hilda Doolittle (HD), Robinson Jeffers, Ezra Pound, Marianne Moore, Allen Tate, Langston Hughes, and William Carlos Williams all published throughout the Twenties. Clearly it should come as no surprise that modern poetry has been around for quite some time now, although some of the battles of the moderns continue to be waged in various forms.

One example of this was the publication of two important anthologies, at about the same time, near the end of the Fifties: *The New Poets of England and America* (edited by Donald Hall, Robert Pack, and Louis Simpson, 1957) and *The New American Poetry* (edited by Donald Allen, 1960). Each anthology attempted to define a generation of poets—the same generation —and yet not a single poet appeared in both anthologies in their first editions. Simply by linking England and America, the first took a more traditional approach, and the poets included in this collection tended to use more traditional, *closed* forms. On the other hand, the Allen anthology represented the antiestablishment poetry of *open forms* and included the *Beats,* the *objectivists,* the *Black Mountain* poets, various poets who publicly read their work at that time around San Francisco and who shared an interest in Far Eastern and esoteric philosophy, and others.

Some of the poets of *The New Poets of England and America* never-theless developed a more open poetry, and some—particularly W. D. Snodgrass, whose "Heart's Needle" is excerpted in Chapter 3—led the movement to *confessional poetry*. Snodgrass dealt openly with personal problems of divorce and child custody, of self-doubt and suffering, while retaining the *structure* of **rhyme** and **meter,** perhaps broadening the def-inition of "open" poetry to mean personal openness even while working within "closed" form. Other poets such as Anne Sexton and Sylvia Plath were influenced by this personal openness in Snodgrass as well as by Lowell, although, unlike Snodgrass, many of the confessional writers tended to develop an increasingly *ironic* tone, as if to distance or somehow manage the pain of the personal.

Neither of these anthologies adequately represented minority or women poets. During the Twenties, a literary movement among African-Americans was known as the **Harlem Renaissance.** The poets Langston Hughes, Jean Toomer, and Countee Cullen were among its best-known writers; Helene Johnson was another writer of the time whose poetry dealt specifically with themes of "black pride." During the Sixties, and in con-nection with the civil-rights movement, there was a flowering of the po-etry of black consciousness, often political and asserting an international black identity. For example, LeRoi Jones, whose works appeared in *The New American Poetry* in 1960, changed his name to Imamu Amiri Baraka in 1966 to show identification with an African heritage; his poetry demon-strates a marked political content. Many other African-American poets explore themes of black pride and ethnic, folkloric, or traditional mater-ial. Overall there has been an increase in the availability of publications by African-American poets, both by large publishers and by independent presses.

Lawson Inada, Garrett Hongo, and Mei-mei Brussenberge are three writers represented here who have tapped the Asian-American connec-tion. Such new poetry as theirs is distinctly American but infused with a rich mix of older cultures. Leslie Silko incorporates ethnic imagery and the landscape of the American Southwest into poems that combine mod-ernist values with a Native American viewpoint. *Voices of the Rainbow,* edited by Kenneth Rosen, brought together Native American poets in 1975, at a time when such collections were much rarer than now, sig-nalling a growth in awareness of the diversity of voices in American po-etry. During the summer of 1992, a festival of native North American writers at the University of Oklahoma brought together from across the country such varied poets as Joe Bruchac, Elizabeth Woody, Joy Harjo, and many others. Other poets write out of ethnic awareness whether that awareness has been a matter of lifelong involvement or a more recent discovery of cultural roots.

Earlier, at mid-century, while American poetry was discovering its own diversity and developing a sense of confidence in its own national literature, it was also in danger of becoming too insular, monolingual, and self-absorbed, as Robert Bly reminded readers when he founded his magazine *The Fifties,* later to become *The Sixties* and *The Seventies.* In this influential magazine, Bly urged readers to become more cosmopolitan, to look to the poetries of other cultures. In particular, he published translations of European and South American surrealists. Poet Jerome Rothenberg edited the influential *Technicians of the Sacred* (1968), subtitled "A Range of Poetries from Africa, America, Asia, and Oceania," thus advancing the field of *ethnopoetics,* the study of the poetry of a culture.

In various connections, poetry has become politicized. Obscenity charges against Allen Ginsberg's *Howl and Other Poems,* published by City Lights in 1956, became a focus for free-speech demonstrations in San Francisco and elsewhere. During the Vietnam War in the sixties and early seventies, the poetry of protest and the **poetry reading** as political demonstration were both revived. *Happenings,* forms of pop-art related to the earlier dadaist performances, involved improvisation and public spectacle or confrontation and sometimes included poetry readings to generate emotion or support for a cause.

Women writers, tired of virtually all-male anthologies and a male-oriented literary establishment, with the support of the women's movement of the early 1970s, established *little magazines* devoted to women's writing and the feminist point of view. An important early anthology of the women's movement in poetry was *No More Masks,* which collected the works of women poets from the beginning of the twentieth century to the early seventies. Besides being published in books and magazines aimed at feminist audiences, women are now more widely published in general than only twenty years ago. For an analysis of the nature of the difficulties faced by women poets, read Alicia Ostriker's excellent book *Stealing the Language.* As Ostriker demonstrates, for many women poets it has been a painful but clarifying experience to recognize that some of the master poets they most admired and learned from nevertheless patronized and dismissed their work.

Poetry readings have become increasingly common since Dylan Thomas toured the United States and the Beats took their poetry to the coffee shops of San Francisco in the Fifties. Nowadays universities constitute the most consistent, large audience for poetry in America, but in many cities poetry readings are held in cafes, bookstores, and elsewhere.

The financial support of the National Endowment of the Arts, especially during the seventies, encouraged the growth of state programs that sent poets into the public schools as teachers, workshop directors, and visiting readers. The program provided financial support for professional poets to practice their art in connection with teaching in a way that had not previously been available. Recent debates over the role of government-funded programs for the arts are still unresolved, and so the future of such support is uncertain. But it is clear that in the past twenty years such support, while never large compared to other government programs, has had a widespread effect in the form of outreach programs, publications, and financial support for writers. Perhaps, in part, encouraged by such programs, universities across the country have developed graduate programs in creative writing. Such programs are designed to prepare the student for a career that combines writing and teaching. Outside degree programs, many colleges and universities sponsor summer creative writing workshops. More than ever, it is possible for just about anyone who wants to take a course in creative writing to do so without going very far from home.

At the end of the twentieth century, poetry has developed several new kinks, or new versions of old ones. One of these is the **New Formalism,** basically a new interest in writing in *forms*. The New Formalism has been interpreted variously as an expression of a new conservativism in American politics, which can be seen as repressive and retrograde, or as a welcome change in a too permissive society, depending on one's own inclinations. The debate over the new formalism has given rise to such various discussions in print as "The New Conservatism in American Poetry" by Diane Wakoski (*American Book Review* May/June 1986) and "Metrical Illiteracy" by Brad Leithauser (*The New Criterion* Jan. 1983) One writer who says he is not a New Formalist says nevertheless that after years of writing free verse he has begun to use more rhyme, meter, and form in his poetry again, because "I wanted pressure on the words" and "I wanted a quality I could only think to call *traction*" (Eric Torgerson, *AWP Chronicle,* May 1991). In most cases the movement also represents a reaction against the romantic poem of personal experience and a move toward a more *classical* stance.

Poets generally do what they find interesting and challenging. Like other schools and movements, the New Formalism is an expression of this fact.

Eschewing the personal statement even more definitely is *language poetry*. Language poetry is experimental in the tradition of Gertrude Stein, working with language in such a way that its inner workings and meanings become apparent or are somehow transformed or taken apart. In "1NK M4THEMAT1CS 4N INTRODUCT1ON TO L4NGU4GE POETRY," Joel Lewis cites a poem in which there are no verbs, a poem made of one-word lines, a poem made up of "interrogative sentences," and so on (*Poets and Writers* September–October 1990). Language poetry involves word play, both visual and aural, and is related to other experimental poetries.

Another direction in poetry has been identified by Edward Field, in an article in *Poets and Writers* (July/August 1992), as "Neopop," a movement entirely different from both the New Formalism and language poetry in that it is generally very free-form, anecdotal, and I-centered. Another writer, Charles Webb, in *The MacGuffin* (Vol. IX, No. 2, 1992), writes about "The Myth of Maturity." Referring to some of the same poets Field mentions and to more or less the same phenomenon as Field's "Neopop," Webb claims that the idea of maturity has been used against populist poetry. He says that simple language, vulgarity, outrageous humor, rough style, and easy accessibility are all qualities of such populist poetry, qualities eschewed by critics who judge poetry on the basis of its "maturity." Both authors feel that populist poetry, often read to responsive audiences in bars, cafes, and at festivals and other informal, public settings, is a lively and vital movement similar in origins and goals to the earlier Beat movement. Representative authors cited include Charles Bukowski, Gerald Locklin, Jana Harris, and Ron Koertge.

Other discussions and arguments on poetry range from whether anyone these days is interested in poetry at all to whether we ought somehow to limit the ever-growing numbers of poets writing and publishing in ever-growing numbers of little magazines. This proliferation of poets and publications away from the traditional center of the publishing business, New York, has given rise to definitions of poetry in terms of regional character, as in *The New Geography of Poets,* published by University of Arkansas Press in 1992. The organization of this anthology by region tells us something about the way in which American poets, more than ever, appear in every part of the country. Any discussion of whether poetry is a viable form of literature these days reminds me of Hayden Carruth's introductory remarks to his excellent anthology, *The Voice That Is Great Within Us, American Poetry of the Twentieth Century,* where he says that when he was younger he was afraid the age of greatness was past. Happily he came to realize that his own time was "equally interesting" to that of Pound, Eliot, and the other figures who loomed large at the beginning of the century. Carruth's collection, first published in 1970, demonstrates the continuing vitality of poetry and provides a hefty and satisfying sampler of twentieth-century poems up to that time. *A New Geography of Poets* and other recent collections continue the dialogue.

One thing we all must realize is that the myth of the ivory tower poet is a false one. The quietest and most reclusive poet is intensely immersed and engaged in the experience of what it means to be alive in a particular time and place. The community of the word, quarrelsome and shifting as any self-creating entity, is a broad one, with lots of room. Read. Write. Set out the blank page and continue the invention.

APPENDIX
Publishing Alternatives

The idea of publishing is enticing to most writers. Presenting one's work to an audience is a natural completion of the work itself. But the process of trying to get published should be approached with a clear sense of what is involved and a knowledge of some of the alternatives. Should you, if you are a novice with half-a-dozen more-or-less finished poems, start addressing envelopes to magazine editors? Probably not, unless you are starting that legendary process of papering a wall with rejection slips or unless you are so convinced that your poems are going to be accepted that you cannot stop yourself.

There are many reasons for the beginning writer to avoid the whole business of manuscript submissions for a while. Submitting for publication too early may interfere with your development as a poet. Even a genius who is a polished and original writer may not want to publish. Look at Emily Dickinson; only a handful of her poems appeared during her lifetime, and those without her assent. The rest of her work was published after her death. Remember her poem from Chapter 5? "How dreary—to be—Somebody!/ How public—like a Frog—."

You have to think about what you want from publication. You will not get rich from it, nor usually even make a living. Even large-circulation magazines pay relatively modest fees for poetry, and such magazines get hundreds of submissions but publish few poems. **Small-press** magazines, the main market for poetry, often pay you in copies of the magazine in which your work appears—not dozens of copies for you to sell, but perhaps two copies, one for you and one for your best friend.

Most poets find related work to support their writing, such as teaching, editing, and giving readings or workshops, or they practice some other profession entirely. Wallace Stevens was in the insurance business; William Carlos Williams was a doctor; James Dickey and Erica Jong were two well-published poets who became commercially successful writers when they published best-selling novels. A poet who wins a major prize may command large fees for readings but still not make enough to live on from poetry sales. It appears that poets are moonlighters by necessity. If, however, it should happen that one day you can actually support yourself by publishing poetry, you will be twice as pleased for not having expected it.

Sending poems out to magazines involves time and expense. A self-addressed, stamped envelope (known as **SASE**) must be included; so double the cost of postage for each submission. Fairly often poems come back looking wrinkled or handled and need to be typed fresh for each submission. Computers and word processors have greatly simplified the process of reprinting manuscripts stored on disk, but still, you have to take into account the cost each time you run a new copy. As entertainment, submitting poems for publication is cheaper than going to the movies, but even if the poems are eventually accepted, you still might have to try ten different magazines over a couple of years or more, a substantial commitment in time and attention.

Economic considerations aside, ask yourself what you want from an *audience* of readers. If a poem is accepted by a mass-circulation magazine, you will be able to walk up to your neighborhood newsstand and see your name in print; so can your friends, relatives, and the teacher who thought you would never amount to anything. That will be gratifying, but most of your audience will remain anonymous, invisible, and silent.

Small-press publications are more personal. The editor, possibly a poet too, will certainly read your poem, and maybe the editor's friends and the other people who have poems in the magazine, unless they are the type who read only their own poems. The magazine subscribers, who are probably also poets, may read your poems, some of them wondering why the editor picked your work instead of their own. In other words, your audience will be the community of other poets, which is not bad. In fact, other poets may be the best audience you could hope for. But keep in mind that there are over 5000 markets listed in *The International Directory of Little Magazines and Small Presses*. Press runs for little magazines may be no more than 200–300, sometimes more, but in any case, distribution is limited. That is why they are called little magazines, and relatively few people are going to see your poem in one. The rewards of small-press publishing are slow and cumulative and personal.

If you are still convinced that publication is something you really want to try, there are good reasons for doing it. At a certain point in a poet's career, the very act of submitting work to editors can be a positive, creative force, even if acceptances are few and far between. Just remember, rejection can have a destructive effect, undermining your confidence and leading you to think too much of the opinions of strangers. But if you feel tough enough, and if competition brings out the best in you, then submitting work may make you look at your poetry more professionally, more critically, more imaginatively.

If you decide to submit poems for publication, do a good job of presenting them. Make sure your typewriter or printer ribbon is fresh and black. Pale, gray-looking text is hard to read and looks amateurish. The general availability of the very technology that makes it easier to reprint crisp, bright copies of a poem may make editors impatient with the irregularity of type on older typewriters or the creased look of submissions that have been around. This doesn't mean that you have to have a computer in order to submit poetry, but, whatever means you use, your manuscript should be sharp, easy to read, and well organized on the page. If you have a choice of fonts, choose a sensible business like type face—decorative scripts detract from the poem and may be difficult to read.

Three poems in one envelope make a good-sized batch to send out at once, though of course you may send more. Three poems will give the editor some choice and an idea of your range without overcrowding the envelope. Use a business-sized envelope and fold the poems into thirds, as you would a business letter. Don't forget to include the SASE. A larger bunch of poems, say more than a dozen pages, should go flat in a large envelope. Your name and address should appear on every poem at the top, either in the left or right corner. Situating your poem on the page can be a matter of personal taste to the extent that you can center the title and establish the left margin so that the poem is more or less centered, or you can simply use a standard left margin and line up both poem and title to the left, or line up the poem to the left and center the title over the poem. Remember that part of the appeal of a poem is to the eye and arrange your poems on the page accordingly. Whether you align close to center or align left, remember to leave margins at the top and bottom. A poem squeezed onto a page all the way to the bottom looks awkward and

the appearance may influence the way it is read. Although typed manuscripts usually should be double-spaced, in poetry this is optional. Double-
spacing may be preferred and is probably more common because it is
easier to read, but single-spacing can be used, especially when the poet
feels it is important that the reader see the form of the poem at a glance,
in its entirety, all on one page.

Whatever form you use, never send away the only copy of a poem.
Even if you make very small changes be sure to make a file copy for yourself of the most recent version. If you work on a computer or word
processor, be sure to make backup copies of work on disks and always
keep a hard copy as well. Computers have been known to fail, and sometimes other small disasters occur to wipe out a record on disk. I personally have had two such experiences. One was having my computer stolen,
and the other was having someone who was using my computer for an
evening accidentally erase the contents of my hard disk. The first time I
hadn't been using a computer very long and I didn't have backups. For-
tunately I got my computer back, hard disk intact. I learned from that experience, so when the second mishap occurred, I had backups to restore
what I'd lost. If you care about your works, always print hard copies for
your files and make backups of your disks. If you are typing, keep a car-
bon or photocopy on file and make note of any revisions however slight.

When you send work out, depending on the magazine and what you
know about its editorial staff, you can address your envelope simply to the
"Poetry Editor" or to a particular editor by name, if you know the name.
Check the editorial information at the front of the magazine or look to a
source such as *The International Directory of Little Magazines and Small
Presses* (Dustbooks, Len Fulton, editor) or *The Poet's Market* (Writer's Digest Books) for more specific information on editors' names or submission requirements.

You don't really need a cover letter when submitting poetry. If you
send work to a poetry magazine or address your envelope to the poetry
editor, your intent will be obvious. If you want to send some sort of cover
letter make it short. Don't dwell on explanations of your poems but let
the works speak for themselves. So what do you say in a cover letter to
a poetry editor? To begin with, if you've read the magazine to which
you're submitting work (and it would be a good idea for you to have
done so), you might mention something you particularly liked in it. Be
specific if this is your approach. Or you can say something as simple and
casual as "Dear Editor, I hope you'll be interested in the enclosed poems."
This doesn't do much so far as communication goes, but it does add a

person-to-person voice to the submission. Other kinds of information that may be included in a cover letter include professional credits, particularly if you've just won a poetry prize or had a book published, or background information that may interest the editor and which reflects on your submissions: "I grew up on an island in the Puget Sound" or "These poems are based on conversations with older family members in the logging business." If you choose to include a cover letter, whatever you say, make it short and to the point. If the editor responds in a friendly way so as to invite dialogue, you can get into more of a correspondence later on.

When you send work out, remember, you need to keep a clear record of when and where you sent it. File cards or pieces of typing paper quartered to make a card-sized packet are one option for a tracking system. Put the name of the poem at the top of a card and then record submission activity with dates of submission and responses on that card. Computer records can be convenient but as with the manuscripts themselves, be sure to keep a backup in case your computer crashes. A hard copy of your submission record is a good idea too.

In some cases when rejecting work, an editor will offer advice for revision. This is a clue to his or her particular preferences; but there are many kinds of editors, and one person's taste may not be yours. Take such advice for what it is worth—if you find it useful and objective, fine, but keep in mind that it is *not* the last word. Also, unless the editor specifically invites you to return a particular manuscript after revision, do not expect to get acceptance if you make the suggested changes and send it back. Some editors feel they ought to be helpful and encouraging, but whatever comments are offered, in the end the editor is saying, "I didn't accept this because I accepted other poems I like better." Try a magazine you like more than once, and if the editor says to send more, follow through; but also try your work elsewhere. If you decide to submit for publication, go for it on a regular basis. Don't fall into the trap of giving up on a poem you believe in just because it's rejected. Try a different magazine right away. It can help you keep your work moving if you make a list of possible markets when you first start submitting. Then, if a poem comes back, you will already have decided where to send it next and you won't waste time mourning the rejection and uncertain of what to do. Finally, avoid anger at the editor who rejects your work. The rejection may feel personal, but it is not.

One sound, old piece of advice is to read. Read the anthologies, read the magazines, read the work of your contemporaries. It would be an act of foolish arrogance to try publishing without ever having read contemporary poetry. Mass-circulation magazines are easy to find. Also examine the *International Directory* mentioned above. This annual guide lists publications alphabetically and contains geographical and special-interest indexes. Title and address are followed by editors' names, a description of the publication, subscription cost, contributor's payment (if any), frequency of appearance, names of recent contributors, comments on the magazine's particular bias, information on format and print runs, and so on. Submission decisions could be based entirely on this secondary source; however, many of the magazines also offer a sample copy for a low price. It seems a better idea to buy some magazines that interest you and to subscribe to a few others that you admire, to avoid wasting both your time and an editor's by submitting to a publication you've never seen and that does not really publish your kind of work.

A word of warning: Some small-press magazines come out at highly irregular intervals. A "one year" subscription may turn out to mean four issues spaced over three years—if the editor runs low on money, or goes through a personal crisis, or takes a vacation to Morocco. The ephemeral nature of some small-press publications may be disturbing, especially to librarians, but really it is the nature of the business and an unavoidable side effect of individual, autonomous small-press editorship. This irregularity means that you sometimes need to be patient when submitting work to small-press magazines as well. The directory listings usually give some idea of how long you can expect to wait to hear from an editor. Six months is not an unusual wait, either because the editor can't get to it any sooner or because manuscripts are being accepted on a particular schedule, such as once or twice a year. Magazines associated with colleges and universities often run on an academic schedule and may not read manuscripts during the summer, for example.

Given the long wait to hear from editors, writers inevitably consider multiple submissions, that is, sending work to more than one magazine at once. Many editors, however, specifically say that they will not consider multiple submissions. They want to be sure that their time spent reading manuscripts will not be wasted and they object to the idea of poets blanketing the markets in mass mailings instead of carefully selecting a particular magazine for particular work. Other editors say that multiple submissions are fine with them. There have been numerous discussions of this subject both in print and at writer's conferences. Generally it's probably a good idea not to do multiple submissions unless an editor specifically says that this is an acceptable practice. That's the conservative approach and the one I'm most comfortable with, but not everyone agrees. If you find the long wait for replies intolerable, make your own policy on this issue as fairly as you can and inform editors that you are submitting work to more than one magazine at once.

If you do practice multiple submissions, remember that you should immediately notify the various magazines to which you've submitted a poem if that poem is accepted by someone else. What is definitely *not* acceptable is publishing something in more than one magazine without informing the editors. A submission to a magazine signals that the work has not been published and that it is being offered for first-time publication. Sometimes, however, magazines call for previously published works for anthologies or special theme issues. When submitting previously published work, be sure that you understand your copyright agreement with the original publisher of the work and seek permission and give credit as appropriate.

Poets are naturally concerned about copyright when they publish, but with poetry in small-press magazines, it's usually no problem to retain ownership of publication rights. There may be a notice in the front of the magazine with regard to all rights being returned to the author after publication. Some magazines are extremely casual about this. Others, particularly large-distribution magazines paying substantial fees, have more formal, legal contracts. When in doubt, ask. When poems are published in a book, the question of reprint rights is apt to be more formal. Unless they have returned all rights to the author, book publishers will usually expect a share of any reprint fees as well as an acknowledgment, and this is considered a fair return for the original publisher.

In general, maintain control of your own work as much as possible, but remember that publishing is a cooperative venture. Most editors want to work with you rather than take advantage. Just be sure that you understand what's involved with copyright and with any particular transaction. Poets & Writers, Inc., which publishes *Poets & Writers* magazine and other service publications for writers, puts out *A Writer's Guide to Copyright*. To order this publication, write to Poets & Writers, Inc., 72 Spring Street, New York, NY 10012, or call 212-226-3586.

Besides sending work out, some writers choose to self-publish. Self-publication usually involves a whole book manuscript rather than individual poems, though it can be satisfying to publish broadsides, that is, single-page, interestingly designed publications of poems. There are various ways and degrees of self-publication. Self-publication can involve anything from handsetting poems on an old-fashioned letter press to paying a commercial "vanity press" to produce a whole book for you. You can type, lay out, and paste up a manuscript, and hire a quick printer to make copies which you distribute to friends and relatives. You can even make an edition of one or more handmade books, hand-lettered or typed, sewn or stapled, and decorated with your own or a friend's artwork. Self-publication can range from a desperate attempt to buy publication to a creative expression of the individual. Before you decide to self-publish, consider the advantages and disadvantages. When you submit work and have it accepted by a magazine or book publisher, you have achieved a certain stamp of approval from someone else, which can help your confidence and give your work a public validity. When you self-publish you are going on your own opinion alone and thus lack that external measure of success. In self-publication you must be sure that you believe in your work enough to stand behind it—otherwise the self-published work may become an embarrassment. Some poets will say that you should not self-publish until you have exhausted all possibilities of finding an outside publisher. Then, you can either take this as a judgment on your work and give up on it, or you can choose to publish it yourself.

Self-publication can be expensive and take away energy you could use writing. If you use your neighborhood printer, you can save money by doing the typesetting, layout, and editing yourself, if you have the means. If you go to a commercial vanity publisher it will be quite expensive and you'll still have to distribute and sell the book yourself. Moreover, the recognizable vanity press imprint may actually detract from public opinion of your work if that publisher has a reputation for printing anything so long as the writer pays enough for it. Finally, self-publication may cause you to rush into print work that you'll later surpass and which you'll wish you'd not published. A 1976 issue of *Coda* magazine (November/December) cites the drawbacks and merits of vanity-press publications. Well-known poet A. R. Ammons first published under a vanity-press imprint and does not regret it. However, his career was not really launched until ten years later, when he published a prize-winning book of poetry with a non-vanity, university-press series. Most of the writers interviewed did not favor vanity-press publishing, citing expense, the stigma, and lack of author control as disadvantages. The vanity press does not necessarily bind a book until it has guaranteed sales, and the author does not usually own the book, but must buy copies like anyone else. *Coda* (now known as *Poets & Writers* magazine) recommends that anyone thinking of signing a vanity-press contract should have a lawyer check it over for possible problems and make sure that all the conditions are clearly understood.

The consensus seems to be that while vanity publishers usually deliver what they advertise, it is an expensive and not particularly satisfying way to publish, whereas small-press self-publication under your own imprint is both more honest and more rewarding if you do want to publish your own work. There are a number of publications available detailing the procedures of self-publication, and printers are usually friendly and helpful. If you run into one printer who is not, find another. Make sure that you understand all the costs of self-publication, have some sort of plan for distribution, and determine a realistic number of copies to produce, whether you think you will be able to sell fifty or a thousand.

Besides vanity publishers of books and chapbooks, there are some presses that publish an annual writing anthology, with a substantial entry fee, often aimed at the college or high-school market. These publishers seem mainly interested in the profit from such fees and from the orders from relatives and friends of the student whose work will be included. If you are tempted by one of these offers, try to get a look at an earlier volume. If the work seems poorly chosen, poorly assembled, and produced in a cheap, crowded format, probably this too is an exploitative vanity publisher.

On the other hand, because of large numbers of submissions and the expenses of operating, reputable publishing ventures, prize-winning book series, or well-known annual poetry contests may ask for a reading fee when you submit a manuscript. If you are uncertain of whether this is money well-spent, look at previous work from that press or ask the advice of a professional writer or writing teacher.

Questions about self-publication generally relate to book-length manuscripts. You should remember, it costs nothing more than postage and materials to submit work to magazines. You should probably have some success with magazine publishing before you pay fees to enter contests and certainly before you get into the process of putting together a whole book manuscript, either to submit to an editor or to publish yourself.

The lure of publishing is bound to be attractive to most poets. The desire to speak to others, after all, is one reason we write. If you would like to try publication but don't feel ready for either the small or large presses, maybe you will want to put together an assemblage in your writing workshop or among friends. An assemblage is an autonomous form of publication in which each writer in the publication produces his or her own page or pages. The writers then assemble the work, staple it, and distribute it within the group. In planning for an assemblage, it's necessary to decide ahead of time on the maximum number of pages allowed to each author, the overall dimensions of the page, and a cover for the whole collection. Otherwise each writer makes his or her own decisions about content and presentation. Assemblages have been carried out by small amateur groups as well as by large groups of professional writers mailing their pages from all over the country to one central assembling and distribution point.

Another possible project for small-scale publication is a **chapbook** of poems. A chapbook is a pamphlet-sized book, usually containing no more than a dozen or so poems. They are apt to be small editions containing poems with some sort of thematic unity or particular focus. Some small-press publishers and contests specialize in chapbooks. A self-published chapbook has some of the character of an artist's print, in that it can be a self-designed, self-produced work of art.

Whether you choose to submit work for publication or not, remember that publication should serve the interests of poetry. When you publish, you have a right to expect that your work will be presented well on the page, without errors, that it will be distributed, and that you will be paid according to agreement, whether payment is a matter of money or simply copies of the publication. Don't submit work if rejection is going to send you into a tailspin or just because you think it is something writers do. Submit work if it will help you grow as a poet and if you feel that you are ready for the risks and satisfactions involved.

SOME REFERENCES AND ADDRESSES

Poets & Writers. A writer's newsletter, published by Poets & Writers, Inc. (72 Spring Street, New York, NY 10012; telephone 212-226-3586). A nonprofit corporation, it is supported by the National Endowment for the Arts and the New York State Council on the Arts, as well as by contributions from individuals and other sources. *Poets & Writers* is published six times a year and contains practical advice to writers and informative articles on a wide range of subjects including taxes, presses, contests, and grants and awards to writers. Writing-related events such as bookfairs are announced, and a "wants" list is posted for anthologies and magazines looking for submissions. Since *Poets & Writers* is a professional publication, it may be of limited use to student writers, but focus articles on specific poets can be of interest and the "wants" column may supply ideas for poems. Poets & Writers, Inc. also publishes guides to literary bookstores, copyright, readings and workshops, writers conferences, and *A Directory of American Poets and Fiction Writers.*

Writer's Guide to Copyright. Also published by Poets & Writers, Inc. (72 Spring Street, New York, NY 10012). This inexpensive booklet explains the Copyright Law.

International Directory of Little Magazines and Small Presses. Published by Dustbooks and edited by Len Fulton (P.O. Box 100, Paradise, CA 95967). Since 1964, when it was a forty-page volume, this directory has been published annually. It now has over nine hundred pages and lists over 5000 markets for writers, with addresses and information about types of work published, submission requirements, subscription costs, writers previously published, reply time, and other information. Entries are listed alphabetically and also by region and area of interest (such as dreams, environment, feminism, gardening etc.) Not all of these are poetry markets, of course, but many are.

The Poet's Market and *The Writer's Market.* These are annual publishing guides, mainly about commercial markets, though *The Poet's Market* and the poetry section of *The Writer's Market* both include some small press and literary markets. Readily available in libraries and bookstores, they are published by Writer's Digest Books.

Printing It. Edited by Clifford Burke (Wingbow 1974). Instructions for offset—"Graphic techniques for the impecunious."

Publish-It-Yourself Handbook: Literary Tradition & How-to. Ed. Bill Henderson. (3rd revised edition, Pushcart Press 1987). A friendly, practical book on the subject of self-publishing. Articles and anecdotes.

Suggestions for Writing (and Printing)

1. Plan and produce a workshop *assemblage.* If you are not in a writing class or workshop group, give friends plenty of advance notice and set a date for an assemblage party. Each contributor makes a set number of copies of his or her page or pages of original work. The contributors meet to assemble their pages into group anthologies. These anthologies or assemblages are stapled or bound in some other way, then divided among the members of the group.

2. A *broadside* is a single page or poster-like presentation of a literary work. Design a broadside of one of your poems, incorporating a visually interesting typeface, hand lettering, linoleum block illustration, collage, or other embellishment.

3. Select four of your poems that seem to make a group, or combine your poems with someone else's, and publish them as a *chapbook*, or pamphlet, with a cover. You can make one copy or several, as you prefer.

GLOSSARY OF KEY TERMS

Abstract - Having to do with ideas, essence, or other intangibles. The opposite of abstract is **concrete,** which has to do with the physical. A poem may have both an abstract subject (such as truth or beauty) and a concrete subject (such as a bare apple tree in snow).

Aleatory - Accidental. Referring to art, aleatory means accidental or random elements, such as dripping paint, picking words at random, or incorporating spontaneous audience remarks as part of a reading or play. Part of the search for freshness and spontaneity in modern art.

Alliteration - The repetition of a sound, usually a consonant, at the beginning of words or stressed syllables, such as "Mary ate mountains of mutton." In poetry, alliteration is used to give a musical, integrated quality to the sound of a poem. In light verse, it is used for comic effect.

Allusion - A reference to something outside the piece of writing itself. Allusions may be drawn from the common culture, from classical mythology, from politics or current events, from history, or any other source. Allusion is a way of adding complexity and layers of meaning to poetry.

Ambiguity - The quality of having two or more possible meanings. In poetry, deliberate ambiguity can enrich the meaning of a work, convey irony, and add a dimension of mystery or playfulness.

Anglo-Saxon - The language of the Anglo-Saxons, also called Old English. As an ancestor of modern English, Anglo-Saxon is the source of many of our short, direct words, in contrast to many polysyllabic words that commonly derive from Latin sources.

Apostrophe - A literary device in which the speaker addresses someone or something other than the true audience or reader of a work for rhetorical effect. Apostrophe may provide a structure or reason for the poem. It can also provide tonal and figurative effects such as giving the poem an intimate or ironic tone.

349

Archetype - The first or original model of a thing, whether that thing is a mythic figure, an abstract concept, or an ideal. The word also describes basic patterns, themes, or images that recur in mythology, dreams, folklore, art, and religion.

Association - The process of connecting or joining words or ideas together. Image-making, basic to poetry, is an associative process.

Automatic writing - A form of free association in which the writer composes without conscious control, often as a device for loosening up the associative process and language flow.

Avante-garde - A French term for "advance guard," meaning those who are ahead of the rest, and thus artists who are extremely inventive or original.

Ballad - Originally an anonymous, traditional form of folk poetry set to music. The ballad usually tells a simple, often tragic, story, commonly of love, death, or betrayal. The typical ballad uses short, rhymed stanzas, often with a refrain. The typical ballad stanza is four lines long with short lines and strongly stressed meter, but the form may be improvised.

Ballade - A French form with twenty-eight lines of no set length, divided into three octaves and a quatrain.

Catalog poem - A poem using the structure of a list, as in Anne Waldman's "Fast Speaking Woman" or Whitman's "Song of Myself." It is flexible in form and length and lends itself to improvisation.

Chapbook - A pamphlet-sized book of poems or other works.

Closure - In a poem is simply its being finished or closed, whether definite and formal or soft and ambiguous.

Collage poem - A poem using words taken or actually cut out from other sources and reassembled in a different way for visual and verbal effect, or a poem written and organized in such a way as to give the impression that it was assembled from unrelated parts (such as fragments of conversation, quotations, statements and so on).

Concrete poem - A poem in which the shape and arrangement of the poem on the page is part of its meaning, such as "Angel Wings" by George Herbert and "Lilac" by Mary Ellen Solt.

Concrete - Dealing with the physical and sensory, rather than abstract ideas and feelings. Concrete or image-making language—such as *blue, rough, fire truck, tiny white shoes, sitting in the dark restaurant smelling fries while outside the Pacific Ocean sloshed against the piling*—is the basic element in most poetry.

Confessional poem - A poem which deals with personal, often shocking material. The confessional poet speaks in the first person and gives the impression that he or she is telling secrets. The personal material often reveals weaknesses or personal problems. However, one should not mistake the *persona* presented by the poet for literal reality. Even the confessional poet is selective and artfully shapes a persona in order to explore particular taboo kinds of experience and to invest the poem with the powerful feelings associated with such experience. Some poets commonly described as confessional are Robert Lowell, Anne Sexton, Sylvia Plath, and Diane Wakoski.

Couplet - Two paired lines of poetry, particularly two rhyming lines of approximately the same length.

Dadaism - An absurdist and nihilistic modern art movement starting in Zurich during World War I. As an expression of disillusionment with modern life, dadaism involved collage, absurd and disruptive performances or readings, art which emphasized nothingness and chaos, humor, surprise, randomness, social affrontery, and satire.

Deep Image - An image produced by intuition, imagination, and associations from the subsconscious, provoking powerful emotional and archetypal responses.

Dialogue - Speech between two or more individuals. Although more commonly associated with fiction or drama, dialogue in poetry can be used for dramatic effect. Compare *Monologue*.

Didactic - Instructive or educational. Didactic poetry is sometimes associated with sentimentally inspirational or school-room verse, but there is a didactic element in any poetry that espouses a moral or ethical viewpoint, such as antiwar poetry.

Dramatic poetry - One of the two genres set forth by Aristotle (the other being *narrative*). Dramatic poetry embodies *mimesis* or imitation of reality. Poetic drama is uncommon today, although a few modern writers such as T. S. Eliot and Federico García Lorca have written plays in verse.

Elegy - A lament or memorial. The elegy has a long tradition in poetry and ranges from meditations on the passing of time or the passing of an era to poems mourning and commemorating specific individuals.

Enjambment - The running of a sentence from one line of poetry to the next without a pause at the end of the line. Enjambment can be used to establish an interesting rhythmic counterpoint in the system of

pauses and stops created by punctuation, rhyme, meaning, and line
breaks.

Epic - A long narrative poem. The epic generally consists of heroic
characters and actions, sometimes telling the story of the origin of a
nation or culture.

Figure of speech - A word or group of words that expresses a thing
or concept in terms that are not to be taken literally. Irony, metaphor,
onomatopoeia, and simile are types of figurative speech used for
rhetorical effect.

Fixed forms - Traditional and recognized forms of poetry in which
some of the formal elements (such as *rhyme* scheme, *meter,* number of
syllables per line, or stanza breaks) are prescribed. Some of the best-
known fixed forms are the haiku, the sestina, the sonnet, and the
villanelle, but there are many more.

Foot - A rhythmical unit in poetry. A foot consists of one or more
stressed (/) or unstressed (u) syllables. Common feet are:

iamb (iambic)	the tréé
trochee (trochaic)	beát-en
anapest (anapestic)	up the roád
dactyl (dactylic)	Bú-da-pest
spondee (spondaic)	buílt-iń

As well as being described by the kind of foot, poetry may be described
by the number of feet in the line, i.e. monometer (one foot), dimeter
(two feet), trimeter (three feet), tetrameter (four feet), pentameter (five
feet), hexameter (six feet), heptameter (seven feet), and so on.

Form - Referring to line length, *rhyme* and other sound structures, spaces,
metrical units and rhythms, *stanzas,* and other elements that constitute
the way a poem is organized and sounds to the ear.

Formal - With reference to poetry, tending to use set *forms* and traditional
or regular patterns of *rhyme, meter,* and *stanza* length. Contrast *Informal.*

Found poem - A text taken from a nonliterary source, such as advertising copy or a newspaper, lifted out of context and broken into lines
to create a poem.

Free verse - Poetry in which form is improvised and irregular. It is a
misconception to say that free verse has no form at all, for the elements
of form do in fact exist in free verse, but they do not occur regularly or
according to a preconceived pattern.

Genre - A type or kind of literature, such as poetry, the novel, or the short story.

Ghazal (or ghasel) - A form loosely adapted in English from Arabic and Persian. Originally the ghazal consisted of a series (5–15) of rhymed couplets. In English poetry, the form usually consists of a series of unrhymed couplets with a full stop and a break after each couplet.

Haiku - A Japanese *form*. A seventeen-syllable poem divided into three lines of five, seven, and five syllables and frequently dealing with nature.

Harlem Renaissance - A literary movement originating in the Harlem area of New York during the 1920s. The poets of the movement frequently developed rhythms and forms based on jazz and colloquial speech and addressed themes of African-American pride and social justice. Prominent poets in the movement include Langston Hughes, Helene Johnson, Countee Cullen, Arna Bontemps, and Jean Toomer.

Hyperbole - A figure of speech which uses exaggeration for extravagant effect, such as "eyes like saucers."

Iambic pentameter - A line consisting of five iambic feet. The traditional measure of the sonnet form. See *Foot* and *Meter.*

Image - In literature, a representation in words of the experiences of the senses, including sight, touch, taste, sound, smell, rhythm, temperature, and muscle tension. The image is basic to poetry because of the way in which emotion and idea are embodied and communicated in physical sensation. Image is also used to refer to a *figure of speech.*

Imagism - An early twentieth-century movement in poetry emphasizing succinct, concrete language and sharp imagery while deemphasizing abstract commentary. Ezra Pound's "In a Station of the Metro" is a famous example. Out of historical context, one can also describe any poem that works mainly by sensory images as imagist.

Informal - Referring to free verse in which structure is irregular and composed according to content rather than prescribed set forms.

Invocation - An introductory appeal to someone or something—such as God, the muses, the season, a city—to support, bless, or inspire what follows and used in poetry to establish a theme or for dramatic or rhetorical effect.

Irony - Figurative speech in which what is said is incongruent with what is actually meant. Also a state of mind or attitude reflecting awareness of incongruous realities. Sarcasm, saying one thing and meaning the opposite, is a form of irony.

Irregular – Describes poetry which is open, less structured, less conventional, more improvisational in form, in contrast to that which is *regular* or composed in traditional forms and consistent patterns. Free verse is irregular whereas the traditional *sonnet* is regular.

Jung, Carl – Swiss psychologist. Because of his emphasis on individual expression, the symbolic quality of the dream life and archetypal imagery, and mythic experience, Jung's work is frequently viewed by artists and writers as complementary to the creative experience. See *Personal mythology*.

Latinate – Refers to language derived from Latin word roots. Latinate words are frequently polysyllabic and indirect, such as "expectorate" instead of "spit." Compare *Anglo-Saxon*.

Light verse – Humorous verse, usually rhymed, and including such types as the limerick, puzzle poems, parody, and occasional verse. Sometimes used to describe any type of playful, humorous poetry.

Line – A row of words that constitutes an element in the form of poetry. In traditional forms, the line is metrically regular and measured or described by the number of feet and type of *foot* contained within the line, such as *iambic pentameter*. Lines may also be described simply according to the number of stressed syllables in the line, regardless of unstressed syllables, or may also be measured and described according to the number of syllables in a line regardless of stress (see *Syllabic verse*). *Prose poems* do not use line breaks at all but look like paragraphs, moving on to the next line after the break required by the margins of the page.

Lyric poetry – One of the *genres* of poetry. (The others are *narrative* and *dramatic*.) The word *lyric* comes from the name of a musical instrument, the lyre. A lyric poem is an expression of emotion communicated by musical qualities such as melodious sounds, *rhyme,* or *rhythm*. Because the lyric expresses emotion, the organization of a lyric is often associative and evocative, rather than chronological or logical, and tends to be short. Lyric poetry is the dominant type of modern poetry.

Meditation – A reflection on something. In poetry, a poet commonly gives the object of meditation close, undistracted attention with an open mind, then moves by association to other levels of meaning and abstraction.

Metaphor – A *figure of speech* that implies a comparison between two different things. (See also *Simile*.) Although metaphor and simile both work by comparison, metaphor is capable of being more complex and more subtle than simile, because of the greater leap of intuition required by implication.

Meter. - The regular rhythmic pattern in the words in a line of poetry created by stressed or drawn out syllables. Meter is described in terms of the *foot*. The process of analyzing or reading the meter of a line is called *scansion*.

Mimesis - Imitation. The mimetic theory of art is that art imitates or gives the illusion of life.

Modern - Anything up-to-date; more specifically referring to the Modernist movement in the arts, sciences, and society in general which occurred in the late-nineteenth and early twentieth centuries, in part as a reaction to nineteenth-century *Romanticism*. In poetry, it is associated with a search for freshness and new ways to use and perceive language. American poets associated with Modernism include T. S. Eliot, Ezra Pound, Marianne Moore, H D, Wallace Stevens, and William Carlos Williams.

Monologue - Speech by one person. The dramatic monologue, such as in Robert Browning's "My Last Duchess," implies actions performed during or in the context of the speech, as if the reader is an onlooker observing a scene played out in a drama.

Motif - Both a theme, or major idea, of a work and a repeated element in a pattern.

Myth - A myth is a story, usually anonymous, expressing cultural values or deep human concerns. Myth is interpreted both as a symbolic framework for interpreting all experience and as a body of traditional literature or stories.

Mythopoeia - The process of myth-making. The relation of mythopoeia to poetry occurs in several ways. A writer may turn the materials of his or her own life into a *personal mythology,* so that the poet's perceptions take on a larger or more universal resonance. Or the writer may employ traditional mythologies in modern reinterpretation, as when Louise Bogan and Robert Creeley use "Medusa" and "Kore" to express their own feelings.

Narrative poem - A poem that tells a story by using chronological organization. (Compare *Lyric poetry* and *Dramatic poetry.*) The *epic* and the *ballad* are principal types of narrative poetry. Although the lyric dominates modern poetry, narrative elements (story, chronology, action) are commonly incorporated into the lyric, as in Robert Creeley's "Kore" and D. H. Lawrence's "Snake."

New Formalism - A late-twentieth-century return to writing poetry
in traditional forms, partly as a reaction to the dominance of free verse.

Objective correlative - T. S. Eliot's term for the way in which poetry
expresses and evokes emotion, not by abstract language denoting the
emotion, but by concrete images which stimulate and re-create that
emotion in the reader.

Onomatopoeia - Figurative speech in which the sound of the words
imitates that which is being expressed. This may be in the case of
words that describe actual sounds (*tippety-tap, boom,* and so on) or
poems that more generally imitate the subject by sound and rhythm,
such as Wallace Stevens's horn, antler, and claw clatter sounds in
"An Earthy Anecdote."

Organic form - The form of a poem that has developed from and in
harmony with its content. Reflecting the principle that form cannot
or should not merely be imposed on a subject, poems of organic form
usually have irregular line length, may or may not rhyme, and are
metrically irregular. Free verse is an example of organic form.

Performance poetry - Poetry that is meant to be performed in front
of an audience. Performance poetry may combine elements of the
happening, *dadaism,* theater, and music, unified with the language of
the poem itself.

Persona - The mask or character adopted by the poet. This persona
may be a specific character, mythological, imaginary, or real, in whose
purported voice or point of view the poet speaks, or it may be a public
and artful version of the poet's personal identity.

Personal mythology - A construct of personal history—the poet's "how
I came to be" story. It differs from the poet's actual life in the way the
poet selects events, figures, and details from his or her past and edits and
interprets them to make a coherent pattern. These events, figures, and
details are depicted as symbolic and meaningful.

Personification - A figure of speech in which the nonhuman—for
example, animals, ideas, and objects—is given human attributes.

Poem of address - A poem that uses the form of speaking to some
person or thing in order to give tone, shape, and motive to the poem.
See also *Apostrophe.*

Poetry reading - A performance or recitation of a poet's work for an
audience. During the 1950s an American reading tour by Welsh poet
Dylan Thomas helped popularize the idea of the poetry reading as
opposed to the attitude that poetry was best encountered as a close

study and interpretation on the page. One of the attitudes behind the poetry reading is that poetry is at heart an oral form and must be recited and heard, especially in the poet's own voice, to be fully realized.

Prose poem - A piece of writing which combines the images and feelings of lyric poetry in the paragraph-like form of prose. A prose poem looks like an ordinary prose paragraph. It does not use the traditional elements of form in poetry: end-rhyme, meter, or line breaks. The prose poem may use other conventions of poetry, however, particularly figures of speech and striking imagery. Some prose poems provoke the question of what really constitutes poetry. The answer seems to be, if it works like a poem it is a poem. That is, if it states things that are difficult to say in any other way and uses language poetically, it may well be a prose poem.

Repetend - The irregular repetition of a word or phrase throughout a poem to give a musical quality by repetition of sound.

Repetition - Repetition in various forms is an important part of the sound and rhetoric of poetry. Repetitive elements in poetry include all types of rhyme, the meterical foot, the refrain, repetend, and alliteration, to name a few of the most common examples.

Rhyme - The repetition of sounds in poetry and one of the characteristics most commonly associated with poetry. Along with rhythm, various kinds of repetition, and other word sounds, rhyme gives poetry its musical quality. Some of the terms used to describe rhyme are as follows: Vowel rhyme is the repetition of only the vowel sound or sounds in words. Slant rhyme is an inexact rhyme (such as food and good), also called off-rhyme or partial rhyme. A feminine rhyme is a rhyme with an unstressed final syllable, as in "better" and "let her." A masculine rhyme is in the final accented syllable. An end rhyme occurs at the end of a line while an internal rhyme occurs within the line. Repetend is an informal repetition of sounds or words. Consonance or consonant rhyme is a type of rhyme in which consonants in stressed syllables are repeated but vowel sounds (as in "train" and "turn") are not. In contrast, assonance, or vowel rhyme, is a repetition of vowel sounds but not consonants, as in "seeking" and "neatness."

Traditional rhyme patterns have specific names, such as *rhyme royal* (stanzas of seven ten-syllable lines rhyming *ababbcc*), the *couplet* (two adjacent rhyming lines), and *terza rima* (three line stanzas rhymed in an interlocking pattern, such as *aba bcb cdc* and so on).

Rhythm – Movement with a beat or accent. In poetry, rhythm is marked by stress on certain syllables. A regular pattern of rhythm in poetry is called *meter,* and poetry with such regular repetitions is called *metrical.* However, rhythm is also an important component of even nonmetrical verse.

Riddle poem – A poem making use of a puzzling statement, perhaps seemingly impossible, which becomes clear after one discovers the answer to the riddle.

Romantic – Showing the characteristics of *Romanticism.* That which is romantic emphasizes feeling, the irrational, the intuitive.

Romanticism – A movement in eighteenth- and nineteenth-century literature that embraces emotion, nature, and sometimes a return to values and images of past times perceived as more innocent or natural. Romanticism is also associated with experimentation, rebellion, and the questioning of authority, thus writers as various as John Keats, Allen Ginsberg, and Helen Adam might be described as "romantic."

SASE – Stands for self-addressed stamped envelope. Publishers usually insist that the writer submitting a manuscript for consideration include a SASE.

Scan – To read and analyze a line of poetry with attention to its metrical and rhythmical patterns or to its overall rhyme scheme and structure. The markings used to note the rhythmic scansion of a line represent stressed and unstressed syllables. Rhyme patterns are commonly scanned with letters, *a* representing the first rhyme and its subsequent occurrence, *b* representing the second rhyme, and so on, as in *abba abba cdcdcd.*

Sestina – A poem consisting of six stanzas, each with six lines, followed by a three-line *envoi.* The six words at the end of the first six lines appear in a different, predetermined order in each of the following stanzas, and in the lines of the envoi, as follows: *abcdef faebdc cfdabe ecbfad deacfb bdfeca.* In the envoi, two of the end words usually occur in each of the three lines, one more or less in the middle and the other at the end, in a pattern of *f/e b/d c/a.* Although the sestina was originally *syllabic,* it has often been written in iambic pentameter in English. Invented around 1200, and a popular form with the French troubadours, the sestina continues to challenge modern poets, probably because of the balance it offers between lyrical form and flexibility and the fascination of its interwoven pattern of repeated words. See Jan Clausen's "Sestina, Winchell's Donut House."

Simile - A figure of speech that compares two different things using "like" or "as."

Small press - Refers to the wide variety of publishers and publications outside large or corporate publication. Small presses are a major outlet for poetry publishing in the United States. The main source for small-press titles is *The International Directory of Little Magazines and Small Presses,* published annually by Dustbooks.

Sonnet - The sonnet (Italian for "little song") is a lyric form consisting of fourteen lines, usually *iambic pentameter* or at least ten syllables, with variations in the rhyme scheme. The main types of the sonnet are:

The Shakespearean (or English) sonnet: three quatrains and a couplet, *abab cdcd efef gg.* The quatrains state a problem and its variations and the couplet resolves the problem or somehow gives a different view of it.

The Italian (or Petrarchan): In this form the problem and resolution are divided into the octave and sestet: *abbaabba cdecde* (or *cdcdcd*).

The Spenserian (a variation on the Shakespearean): abab bcbc cdcd ee. The sonnet has a long history in English language poetry and has been written by many poets, either in its traditional form or in variations. Its ten-syllable line and its iambic pentameter meter lend themselves to the tension between form and natural speech that make form poetry appealing, while the rhyme scheme is flexible enough to be adapted to available rhymes in English.

Sound structures - A general term used to refer to all of the ways in which poetry uses patterns of sound to communicate, rouse emotion, create a musical quality, and give order, emphasis and organization to the poem. Sound structures involve *rhyme, meter,* informal repetition of sound and rhythmical qualities in language, pauses for line and stanza breaks, *alliteration,* punctuation (with its associated pauses and stops), *onomatopoeia,* and repetition of words and images.

Stanza - An organizational unit in poetry similar to the paragraph in prose. In traditional poetic forms, stanzas are usually of regular length, whereas in free verse the breaks between stanzas are introduced to show a pause, a change in mood or topic, or for emphasis.

Stanzas can sometimes be described according to number of lines or according to a recognizable pattern. For example, an *octave* is an eight-line stanza or a group of eight lines in a poem. A *sestet* is a six-line stanza or, in particular, the last six lines of the Italian sonnet.

Stream of consciousness - Writing that simulates the free flow of associative thought.

Stress – Elongated pronunciation of a syllable. The reader pauses slightly more on a stressed syllable than on an unstressed syllable. Also called *accent* or *long* syllable.

Surrealism – A modern art movement and a style of art that attempts to re-create the feeling of dreams and the subconscious. Influenced by Freudian analysis, surrealist poetry is associative and dreamlike, using strange images linked unexpectedly.

Syllabic verse – Poetry in which the lines are measured by syllables rather than metric feet. Although metrical measurement of the line is more common in English poetry, syllabic verse can impart a pleasing and natural sense of regularity in the line without the more emphatic feeling of metered verse.

Symbol – An image that represents both the thing described by the image and some abstract quality.

Symbolism – A *romantic* literary movement using symbols and images to communicate emotion directly rather than in an intellectual or discursive way. As a movement proceeding from nineteenth-century *Romanticism* and leading to *Modernism,* Symbolism prepared the way for much modern art. Writers influenced by Symbolism include William Butler Yeats and T. S. Eliot.

Tone – An aspect of *voice,* tone means the attitude of the speaker (or poet) expressed (often implicitly) by the voice (of the poem). Tone is created and conveyed by word choice, images and figures of speech, language rhythms, sound structures, and occasionally typography.

Traditional forms – Set patterns for poems designated by various names such as the *sonnet,* the *villanelle,* and so on.

Verse – Verse means "to turn" and has several associated meanings with regard to poetry. A verse is a line of poetry because the line turns and goes back to the left margin at the line breaks. A verse may also be a stanza, for the same reason: it "turns" at the end and goes back to begin a new stanza. More generally verse is simply poetry, particularly rhymed, metered poetry, as opposed to prose. An additional meaning when the word *verse* is contrasted to the word *poetry* is that verse is light, rhymed, nonserious work, whereas poetry is more serious and more significant.

Villanelle – A nineteen-line French form of poetry, originally syllabic but usually iambic pentameter in English. It is distinguished by the repetition of two rhyming lines and the use of one other rhyme throughout the poem. The pattern of the villanelle is: *A1bA2 abA1 abA2 abA1 abA2 abA1A2,* where *A1* and *A2* are the two repeating lines. The effect of this repetition and close rhyming is a musical, light feeling, although villanelles have been written on serious subjects. For example, see Dylan Thomas's "Do Not Go Gentle into That Good Night."

Voice – In poetry, the character of the poet or speaker coming through the poem. Sometimes the term is used to describe the distinctive style of the mature poet, as in "Her voice is well-developed." Voice can also be related to the idea of the *persona* or mask, as when a poet speaks as an imagined character.

Copyrights and Acknowledgments

Authors, Titles, and First Lines

Poem titles are italicized.
First lines are in regular Roman type.

371

Subject Index